Avoiding War, Making Peace

Richard Ned Lebow

Avoiding War, Making Peace

palgrave
macmillan

Richard Ned Lebow
Department of War Studies
King's College London
London, UK

ISBN 978-3-319-56092-2   ISBN 978-3-319-56093-9   (eBook)
DOI 10.1007/978-3-319-56093-9

Library of Congress Control Number: 2017937471

Cover image: Cover Design by Henry Petrides

Printed on acid-free paper

This Palgrave Macmillan imprint is published by Springer Nature
The registered company is Springer International Publishing AG
The registered company address is: Gewerbestrasse 11, 6330 Cham, Switzerland

To Janice,
for a collaboration that was grand fun

ACKNOWLEDGEMENTS

This book draws on research and writing that dominated my agenda for the last four decades of the twentieth century. My commitment to conflict management developed when I was a university and then postgraduate student during the two Berlin and Cuban missile crises. The study of these and other crises led me to develop a critique of deterrence and compellence. The Cold War heated up in the 1980s and was a spur to extend my investigations and explore alternative strategies of conflict management. The end of the Cold War and collapse of the Soviet Union in the early 1990s provided an opportunity of a different kind. Soviet archives opened up, and it became possible to document Soviet policy in critical Cold War crises. Janice Gross Stein and I made use of these and newly declassified American documents, as well as numerous interviews with Soviet, American, European, Israeli, and Egyptian officials, to reconstruct the 1962 Cuban missile and October 1973 crises. For the first time, we could examine the origins, course, and resolution of these crises from the perspectives of both sides and try to fathom the consequences, often unexpected by leaders, of their interactions. Janice and I had already reconstructed other crises this way on the well-founded assumption that it was absolutely essential to understanding the uncertain and sometimes counterproductive outcomes of threat-based strategies, the reasons why they succeeded or failed, and their longer-term consequences for adversarial relationships.

The critique of deterrence and compellence that I developed grew initially out of my research for *Between Peace and War: The Nature of International Crisis*, published in 1981. I elaborated it further with Janice and other collaborators in *Psychology and Deterrence*, published in 1984, and then in a series of articles Janice and I coauthored in the late 1980s. Our work culminated in *We All Lost the Cold War*, published in 1994. We also thought about the alternative strategies of conflict management, most notably reassurance, and sought to document its role in resolving Cold War crises. This volume contains only one coauthored piece, but much of the thinking in the other chapters reprinted here reflects my collaboration with Janice. So it is to her I accordingly owe my first vote of thanks.

I happily acknowledge other debts, starting with Bob Jervis. He was a thoughtful and most helpful reviewer of *Between Peace and War* for the Johns Hopkins University Press, and coauthor of *Psychology and Deterrence*. Next is the late Alex George, who pioneered the empirical study of deterrence. He did not agree with my critique of deterrence or that of rational decision-making. He was nevertheless supportive of my research, and of Janice's too, and became a good friend and in many ways our most constructive critic. Irving Janis deserves thanks for much the same reason. I made use of his conflict theory of decision-making, and Irving and I also became fast friends. We had fundamental disagreements about the extent to which better decision-making would lead to better policy. He was a firm believer in this relationship, whereas I stressed the critical role of assumptions. We were in the process of writing a book together on the subject when he was diagnosed with terminal cancer.

In Europe, my research has always been better received than in the US. Colleagues at the Frankfurt Peace Research Institute were particularly receptive. They invited me to spend the summer of 1982 at the Institute, where I authored a study of the dual intelligence failures that led to the Falklands-Malvinas war between Britain and Argentina. E.O. Czempiel, then director, Gert Krell, and Harald Mueller, *Mitarbeiters*, deserve special thanks for this and later collaborations and contributions to my intellectual growth.

I subsequently served as Professor of strategy at the US Naval and National War Colleges, in Newport, R.I. and Washington, D.C. respectively, and, during the Carter administration, was the first scholar-in-residence in the Central Intelligence Agency. These posts taught me much about the military and intelligence communities, their understandings of the Cold War, and the kinds of strategies they thought appropriate to it and how they assessed them. The latter post also provided a window on high-level threat assessment and policymaking.

I returned to then life afterwards, first in Bologna, later to Cornell, and then cut to Dartmouth. I profited greatly from interactions with social science, history, and physics colleagues in Cornell's interdisciplinary Peace Studies Program, of which I was the director. At Ohio State, where I was director of the Mershon Center for six years, I worked closely with Rick Herrmann and the Watson Center at Brown to organize a series of conferences on the end of the Cold War that brought together high-ranking officials and their advisors from the USA, Soviet Union, Germany, and the UK. Dartmouth has a distinguished faculty in international relations, and we met regularly to read and critique each other's work.

Finally, I would like to thank my Editor at Palgrave Macmillan, Sarah Roughley. This is my sixth book with Palgrave Macmillan, and my first with Sarah. She is a creative and responsive editor and I am grateful to her.

CONTENTS

LIST OF FIGURES AND TABLES

CHAPTER 1

Introduction

This book revisits and expands on my critique of threat-based strategies of conflict management and discusses the use of reassurance and diplomacy as alternatives. I also explore the sources of political accommodation and the relationship between conflict management and accommodation. My project is particularly timely because many of the less successful strategies of the past are considered relevant to contemporary security problems by American and British policymakers, the media, and scholars. Deterrence and compellence have made a comeback in the light of widespread fears of an aggressive Russia and more assertive China. Intervention is once again an active American strategy; Washington and its allies have been engaged in Afghanistan and Iraq since 2003, and with American backing Europeans intervened in Libya to remove Gadaffi. The American right is pushing for military action against North Korea and mainstream media are debating it.[1]

There are notable differences between the present and the past. Terrorism is the most immediate security threat to the West, foreign adversaries are increasingly non-state groups and movements, and chaos in North Africa and the Middle East has brought a flood of refugees to Europe. Globalization has significantly increased the mobility of pathogens, and with it the possibility that a newly evolved virus in East Asia or Africa could devastate populations worldwide. Most threatening of all in the longer term is global warming and the economic dislocation, water shortages, and domestic and international conflicts it is likely to provoke. Threat-based strategies are not relevant to these problems.

© The Author(s) 2018
R.N. Lebow, *Avoiding War, Making Peace,*
DOI 10.1007/978-3-319-56093-9_1

But they are pertinent to more traditional kinds of conflicts—or thought to be—by those who make or seek to influence policy—and to combatting terrorism as well. Arguments in favor of them frequently invoke the so-called lessons of the Cold War or other past conflicts. It is worth revisiting these lessons, and all the more so because I think they are wrong. I oppose them with a critique of deterrence and compellence, based on the same cases but better historical evidence.

In the 1980s and 1990s, I published a number of articles and chapters on conflict management and prevention. Several of them were coauthored with Janice Gross Stein.[2] They collectively develop a powerful critique of coercive strategies of bargaining and conflict management. Other publications address alternative strategies, like reassurance and diplomacy and the problem of conflict resolution. This volume provides the opportunity to bring some of this work together and to go beyond individual strategies of conflict management to explore the links among them. How do they affect one another and how might they more effectively be combined or staged? My goal is to offer a more holistic view of conflict management and resolution, and the resolution between them.

Strategies of conflict management need to be assessed from the perspective of all the protagonists but during the Cold War there was a paucity of documentation available from the Soviet side about key East–West crises. Much of my research accordingly focused on earlier deterrence encounters, including the run-up to World War I. The end of the Cold War provided access to new information and another case of accommodation, as did the prior Egyptian–Israeli peace and Sino–American accommodation. In recent years, more information about World War I has become available. There is much more to learn from these conflicts about strategies of conflict management that is relevant to their present-day counterparts.

I reprint some of my key articles on chapters on conflict management and accommodation. They were published between 1989 and 2014. At the core is my critique of immediate and general deterrence, conventional and nuclear. I include work on accommodation and the conditions associated with it. In a lengthy, original conclusion, I explore the ways in which the strategies of conflict management can work together or at cross-purposes, the mechanisms responsible for these effects. I also offer some thoughts about the relationship between them and conflict resolution.

I open this chapter with a brief account of the theory and practice of deterrence. I describe how deterrence and compellence have been adapted to the post-Cold War world and how the lessons of the Cold War can be used to critique these applications. This is a teaser for readers, but also intended to demonstrate the relevance and importance of my enterprise.

The critiques of the theory and practice of threat-based strategies that I developed with Janice Gross Stein were well received by international relations scholars troubled by American national security policy and the seeming foundation provided for it by academic literature. Many realists and rationalists resisted the critique for political, psychological, and institutional reasons. I describe some of their response to illustrate how this kind of research can easily touch raw nerves.

As this book is about learning from the past, I consider the problem of learning. The history of threat-based strategies has generated competing lessons about deterrence and compellence, and discriminating among them is no simple matter. There is a very real danger of learning the wrong lessons, confirming them with circular reasoning and selective use of evidence, and applying them to inappropriate situations or in the counterproductive ways. I offer some thoughts about addressing this problem. I conclude with an overview of the chapters that follow.

Deterrence Theory and Practice

Threat-based strategies have always been central to international relations. Deterrence and compellence represent efforts to conceptualize these strategies to make them more understandable in theory and more effective in practice. These efforts, which have been underway since the end of World War II, remain highly controversial.

Deterrence can be defined as an attempt to influence other actors' assessment of their interests. It seeks to prevent an undesired behavior by convincing the party who may be contemplating such an action that its cost will exceed any possible gain.[3] Deterrence presupposes decisions made in response to a rational cost-benefit calculus, and that this calculus can be successfully manipulated from the outside by increasing the cost of non-compliance. Compellence, a related strategy, employs the same tactics to attempt to convince another party to carry out some action it otherwise would not. Deterrence has always been practiced, but the advent of nuclear weapons made it imperative for policymakers to find ways of preventing catastrophically destructive wars while exploiting any strategic nuclear advantage for political gain.

Theories of deterrence must be distinguished from the strategy of deterrence. The former address the logical postulates of deterrence and the political and psychological assumptions on which they are based, the latter the application of the theory in practice. The theory of deterrence developed as an intended guide for the strategy of deterrence.

Scholars and policymakers became interested in deterrence following the development of the atom bomb. The first wave of theorists wrote from the late 1940s until the mid-1960s. Early publications on the subject recognize that a war between states armed with atomic weapons could be so destructive as to negate Carl von Clausewitz's classic description of war as a continuation of politics by other means.[4] In 1949, the problem of deterrence gained a new urgency as the Cold War was well underway and the Soviet Union, in defiance of all US expectations, detonated its first nuclear device in October of that year. In the 1950s, often referred to as the Golden Age of deterrence, William Kaufmann, Henry Kissinger, and Bernard Brodie, among others, developed a general approach to nuclear deterrence that stressed the necessity but difficulty of imparting credibility to threats likely to constitute national suicide.[5] The 1960s witnessed an impressive theoretical treatment by Thomas Schelling that analyzed deterrence in terms of bargaining theory, based on tacit signals.[6]

The early literature began with the assumption of fully rational actors and was deductive in nature. It stipulated four conditions of successful deterrence: defining commitments, communicating them to adversaries, developing the capability to defend them, and imparting credibility to these commitments. It explored various tactics that leaders could exploit toward this end, concentrating on the problem of credibility. This was recognized as the core problem when deterrence was practiced against another nuclear adversary—and the implementation of the threats in question could entail national suicide.[7] Thomas Schelling argued that it was rational for a leader to develop a reputation for being irrational so his threats might be believed.[8] Richard Nixon took this advice to heart in his dealings with both the Soviet Union and North Vietnam.[9]

The so-called Golden Age literature focuses almost entirely on the tactics of deterrence, as do Kaufmann and Brodie, or, like Kissinger, on the force structures most likely to make deterrence credible. Thomas Schelling fits in the former category, but unlike other students of deterrence in the 1950s and 1960s, he attempts to situate his understanding of tactics in a broader theory of bargaining that draws on economics and psychology. His *Strategy of Deterrence* (1960) and *Arms and Influence* (1966) are the only works on deterrence from this era that continue to be cited regularly.

In *Arms and Influence*, Schelling makes a ritual genuflection to material capabilities on the opening page when he observes that with enough military force, a country may not need to bargain. His narrative soon makes clear that military capability is decisive in only the most asymmetrical relationships, and even then only when the more powerful party has little or nothing to lose from the failure to reach an accommodation. When the power balance is not so lopsided, or when both sides would lose from non-settlement, it is necessary to bargain. Bargaining outcomes do not necessarily reflect a balance of interests or military capabilities. Three other influences are important.

First comes *context*, which for Schelling consists of the stakes, the range of possible outcomes, the salience of those outcomes, and the ability of bargainers to commit to those outcomes. In straightforward commercial bargaining, contextual considerations may not play a decisive role. In bargaining about price, there will be a range of intervals between the opening bids of buyer and seller. If there is no established market price for the commodity, no particular outcome will have special salience. Either side can try to gain an advantage by committing itself to its preferred outcomes. Strategic bargaining between states is frequently characterized by sharp discontinuities in context. There may be a small number of possible outcomes, and the canons of international practice, recognized boundaries, prominent terrain features, or the simplicity of all-or-nothing distinctions can make one solution more salient than others. Salient solutions are easier to communicate and commit to, especially when the bargaining is tacit.[10]

The second consideration is *skill*. Threats to use force lack credibility if they are costly to carry out. To circumvent this difficulty, clever leaders can feign madness, develop a reputation for heartlessness, or put themselves into a position from which they cannot retreat. Other tactics can be used to discredit adversarial commitments or minimize the cost of backing away from one's own.[11]

The third, and arguably most important, determinant of outcome is *willingness to suffer*. Paraphrasing Carl von Clausewitz, Schelling describes war as a contest of wills. Until the mid-twentieth century, force was used to bend or break an adversary's will by defeating his army and holding his population and territory hostage. Air power and nuclear weapons revolutionized warfare by allowing states to treat one another's territory, economic resources, and population as hostages from the outset of any dispute. War is no longer a contest of strength, but a contest of nerve and risk-taking, of pain and endurance. For the purposes of bargaining, the ability to absorb pain counts just as much as the capability to inflict it.[12]

Schelling does not say so, but it follows from his formulation that the capacity to absorb suffering varies just as much as the capacity to deliver it. Clausewitz recognized this variation. Increases in both capabilities, he argued, made possible the nation in arms and the revolutionary character of the Napoleonic Wars.[13] By convincing peoples that they had a stake in the outcome of the wars, first the French and then their adversaries were able to field large armies, extract the resources necessary to arm and maintain them, and elicit the extraordinary level of personal sacrifice necessary to sustain the struggle.

The Clausewitz-Schelling emphasis on pain has wider implications for bargaining. The ability to suffer physical, economic, moral, or any other loss is an important source of bargaining power and can sometimes negate an adversary's power to punish. Realist approaches to bargaining tend to neglect this dimension of power and focus instead on the power to hurt and how it can be transformed into credible threats. Schelling also ignores the pain absorption side of the power–pain equation when analyzing compellence in Vietnam, an oversight that led to his misplaced optimism that Hanoi could be coerced into doing what Washington wanted. The power to punish derives only in part from material capabilities. Leaders must also have the will and freedom to use their power. Schelling observes that Genghis Khan was effective because he was not inhibited by the usual mercies. Modern civilization has generated expectations and norms that severely constrain the power to punish. The US bombing campaign in Vietnam, in many people's judgment the very antithesis of civilized behavior, paradoxically demonstrates this truth.

Deterrence played a central role in the US strategy in Indochina during the Johnson and Nixon administrations. Deployment of forces, the character of the engagements they sought, and the level and choice of targets for bombing were never intended to defeat the National Liberation Front of South Vietnam (Viet Cong) or North Vietnam, but to compel them to end the war and accept the independence of South Vietnam. The Indochina intervention ended in disaster and helped to spawn a series of critiques of the theory and strategy of deterrence in the 1970s.

Vietnam paradoxically demonstrates the truth that modern civilization has generated expectations and norms that severely constrain the power to punish. The air and ground war aroused enormous opposition at home, in large part because of its barbarity, and public opinion ultimately compelled a halt to the bombing and withdrawal of US forces from Indochina. The bombing exceeded World War II in total tonnage, but was also more restricted. The USA refrained from indiscriminate bombing of civilians and made no effort to destroy North Vietnam's elaborate system of dikes. The use of nuclear weapons was not even considered. Restraint was a response to ethical and domestic political imperatives. Similar constraints limited US firepower in Iraq in the Gulf War of (1990–1991), and enabled the Republican Guard and Saddam Hussein to escape destruction.

The ability to absorb punishment derives even less from material capabilities, and may even be inversely related to them. One of the reasons why Vietnam was less vulnerable to bombing than Schelling and Pentagon planners supposed was its underdeveloped economy. There were fewer high-value targets to destroy or hold hostage. With fewer factories, highways, and railroads, the economy was more difficult to disrupt, and the population was less dependent on existing distribution networks for its sustenance and material support. According to North Vietnamese strategic analyst Colonel Quach Hai Luong, 'The more you bombed, the more the people wanted to fight you.'[14] Department of Defense studies confirmed that bombing 'strengthened, rather than weakened, the will of the Hanoi government and its people'.[15] It is apparent in retrospect that the gap between the protagonists in material and military capabilities counted for less than their differential ability to absorb punishment. The USA won every battle, but lost the war because its citizens would not pay the moral, economic, and human cost of victory. Washington withdrew from Indochina after losing 58,000 American lives, a fraction of Viet Cong and North Vietnamese deaths even at conservative estimates.

A comparison between South and North Vietnam is even more revealing. The Army of the Republic of South Vietnam (ARVN) was larger and better equipped and trained than the Viet Cong or the North Vietnamese, and had all the advantages of US air power, communications, and logistics. The Republic of South Vietnam crumbled because its forces had no stomach for a fight. The Viet Cong and North Vietnamese sustained horrendous losses whenever they came up against superior US firepower, but maintained their morale and cohesion throughout the long conflict. Unlike ARVN officers and recruits, who regularly melted away under fire, more Viet Cong and North Vietnamese internalized their cause and gave their lives for it. At the most fundamental level, the Communist victory demonstrated the power of ideas and commitment.

CONTEMPORARY DETERRENCE AND COMPELLENCE

The contemporary debate is more international than it was during the Cold War. There is an additional nuclear power, and there are more targets for deterrence. Deterrence has been extended to non-state actors and to the new domain of cyber warfare.[16] Russia has been modernizing its nuclear forces, and even before he took the oath of office, President Trump insisted that the USA should expand its nuclear capability.[17] For me the big question is not whether deterrence helped to prevent World War III but why so many officials and academics believe it did. Reputable scholars also routinely claim that nuclear weapons keep the peace between India and China and promote more peace generally.[18] As in the Cold War, what theorists and analysts say about deterrence often reveals more about their ideological assumptions and national strategic culture than it does about the efficacy of threat-based strategies.

During the Cold War, the theory and practice of deterrence and compellence focused on making credible threats on the assumption that they were necessary to moderate adversaries. Self-deterrence—the reluctance of actors to assume the risks of war independently of efforts by others to deter them—received little attention or credence when it did. Post-Cold War research suggests that self-deterrence was a more important source of restraint than deterrence practiced by adversaries.[19] Successive leaders of the superpowers were terrified of a conventional war, let alone a nuclear one.

Self-deterrence is equally evident in the post-Cold War era. In Somalia, the USA withdrew its forces after losing 18 US Army Rangers.[20] In Rwanda, genocidal Hutus deterred Western intervention by killing ten Belgian soldiers.[21] In Bosnia, compellence clearly failed against Milosevic, who continued his policy of ethnic cleansing of Bosniaks in Bosnia despite Western threats. Pushed by Western public opinion, NATO finally screwed up its courage to intervene, but then failed to go after known war criminals because of the vulnerability of its lightly armed forces, whose primary mission was the distribution of aid.[22]

Self-deterrence also kept the Western powers from intervening in Syria or taking a harder line against Russia in the Ukraine crisis.

There are important lessons here and they have not been widely examined by theorists of threat-based strategies. Perhaps the most important has to do with Clausewitz's dictum the war is a test of wills and accordingly a contest between the ability to inflict pain and the willingness to absorb it.[23] As noted, Thomas Schelling, considered by many the grand theorist of deterrence and compellence, focuses only on the ability to inflict pain. For this reason, he was confident that the Johnson Administration could compel North Vietnam to restrain the Viet Cong.[24] American policymakers concentrated only on how much damage they could inflict on North Vietnam and the Viet Cong. This limited calculus was equally evident in Afghanistan and Iraq, where the Soviet Union, and the USA, paid a huge price for ignoring the Clausewitzian equation. Emanuel Adler rightly observes that weaker states draw in more powerful states, whose leaders feel the need to demonstrate resolve and carry out military action toward that end.[25] Military intervention and the collateral damage it causes mobilize support for the weaker state while generating opposition to the more powerful one. Frost and Lebow refer to these situations as 'ethical traps', and theorize the conditions under which they are successfully set or self-inflicted.[26]

Western deterrence theorists have begun to consider the implications of deterrence in a complex world where there are more nuclear powers, where the rationality assumption may not always be applicable, where many conflicts are chronic rather than acute, where there are chemical and biological weapons to consider in addition to conventional and nuclear ones, and where deterrence practiced by one state against another has important consequences for deterrence in other conflicts.[27]

In the aftermath of the Cold War, the focus of American deterrence turned away from restraining large state actors with nuclear weapons to smaller, so-called rogue states or non-state actors. Washington and its European allies sought to deter Iraq, Iran, and North Korea from developing or testing nuclear weapons.[28] Deterrence did not achieve its goal. Iraq was invaded, Iran was persuaded to put its program on hold in return for concessions, and North Korea continues to build its nuclear arsenal. In all three countries, there are grounds for arguing that deterrent threats might make these weapons more attractive. There is persuasive research that suggests countries are most likely to give up their nuclear programs when new governments come to power that seem them as inimical to their interests or values.[29] Neither deterrence nor compellence is very relevant to these calculations, but the promise of recognition and acceptance are.

Since September 11, 2001, there has been an ongoing debate about the applicability of deterrence to the problem of terrorism. Libya, North Korea, and Iran have been the major target of US pressure because of their support of terrorism in addition to their pursuit or funding of nuclear weapons programs. Regional actors have attempted to deter non-state actors, notably Palestinians, Kurds, and Islamic fundamentalists.[30] One of the emerging conclusions is that it is impossible to deter groups who are willing to give up their lives, but that it may be possible to reduce overall terrorism by deterrence that promises other kinds of punishment and is coupled with non-coercive efforts to reduce some of the incentives for this kind of violence.[31]

Recently, nuclear strategy has made a comeback in the academic and policy world in response to a more aggressive Russia and China.[32] Its advocates claim it is a demonstrable successful strategy, and some claim that nuclear weapons would be usable if the USA had an effective counter-damage strategy.[33] The Obama administration, criticized by Trump for neglecting the military, spent more on nuclear weapons upgrades than the Reagan administration did during its extraordinary buildup in the early 1980s.[34] The Obama buildup spawned numerous critiques; they challenge the concept of first-use, the feasibility of limited nuclear war, or, more fundamentally, the assumption that nuclear threats, explicit or implicit, have value.[35] Nevertheless, there is an active debate over the prospect of the first use of nuclear weapons against Russia, China, North Korea, or other adversaries.[36]

Three observations are in order with regard to the present and the past. The first grows out of the record of deterrence and compellence during the Cold War and its aftermath. These conflicts suggest that powerful states focus on the punishment term of the Clausewitzian equation and less powerful ones on the absorbing cost side. This has the potential to promote misleading conclusions about relative advantage. To date, the more serious miscalculations have been on the part of the powerful. They tend to assume an equal vulnerability to costs and accordingly consider their side greatly advantaged by its ability to inflict them. This helps to explain why highly developed industrial powers are willing to consider military intervention against weaker, less developed, more traditional countries. And also why they so often fail; they have a much lower tolerance for loss of life than countries in which honor remains strong or nationalism is a more powerful motive and source of solidarity. How many Westerners are willing to volunteer for suicide missions?

The second concerns the general efficacy of deterrence as a strategy. Its political and psychological drawbacks do not mean that it should be discarded. Rather, scholars and statesmen must recognize its limitations and make greater use of other strategies of conflict prevention and management. I will argue that the downside of deterrence can sometimes be minimized when it is combined with reassurance and other diplomatic efforts to reduce fear and resolve or finesse substantive differences.

Finally, there is a failure of strategists to take history seriously. Much of the current debate about conventional and nuclear strategy shows little cognizance of past debates or repeats many of the discredited Cold War claims about the political and military utility of nuclear weapons. A case in point is Paul Bracken's *The Second Nuclear Age*, a book that has attracted considerable attention. He contends that 'nuclear weapons were very useful weapons during the cold war', and the nuclear threats were frequently successful in preventing or stopping 'Soviet expansion, coercion, and tyranny'.[37] He repeats the old canard that preparations for war undertaken by the Truman administration in 1948–1949 prevented the Soviet Union from invading Berlin or interfering with the airlift of food and supplies to the beleaguered city.[38] He cites two studies of the crisis conducted during the Cold War without access to Soviet sources that assume Stalin's motives—incorrectly as it turns out—and infer deterrence success on the basis of his restraint.[39] This kind of circular reasoning was endemic during the Cold War and applied to the Taiwan Straits and Cuban missile crises, among others. It is indefensible in an era when documentary evidence to the contrary is available.[40]

TILTING AT THE CONVENTIONAL WISDOM

I have been going after bad policy lessons and attempting to develop better ones for fifty plus years: from the height of the Cold War to the present. For most of the time I worked within the academy, but also spent several years as professor of strategy at the US Naval and then National War Colleges. I engaged obliquely in policy debates; I opposed the Vietnam War, US support of right-wing dictatorships around the world, war-fighting strategies, the Strategic Defense Initiative, and supported American participation in the International Criminal Court and various initiatives to slow global warming. For the most part, my research focused on the underlying assumptions of American and Western national security policies rather than on these policies themselves. I reasoned that successful critiques of their assumptions would provide the foundation for alternative understandings that might be more effective in serving national interests and reducing the risk, not only of global nuclear war, but of costly regional conflicts.

My first books and articles brought history and psychology to the study of foreign policy and international relations. Writing in the aftermath of the Berlin and Cuban crises, I focused on crisis management. I began by thinking that deterrence was a reasonable strategy because I was impressed by the theoretical work that specified the conditions under which it would be effective and the claims that it had worked in Berlin and Cuba and Taiwan.[41] The case study evidence I gathered from fifteen cases of immediate deterrence could not be made consistent with this literature because all the conditions of deterrence had been met but it had failed to prevent a challenge: commitments were publicly defined, communicated to possible challengers, defenders developed the capability to defend them or otherwise punish an adversary, and seemingly established their resolve to do so. I struggled with this contradiction until I had what can only be described as a light bulb moment on the handball court of all places. I considered the possibility that the problem was not my data, but deterrence theory. This insight led me to motivational psychology and ultimately to my psychological–political critique of deterrence and compellence.

For almost two decades, I documented my critique of deterrence and sought to develop more effective strategies for conflict prevention and management. My principal publications were *Between Peace and War: The Nature of International Crisis* (1981), *Psychology and Deterrence* (1984), coauthored with Robert Jervis and Janice Gross Stein, a series of coauthored articles in the *Journal of Social Issues* and *World Politics* (1987–1990), and, coauthored with Janice Gross Stein, *When Does Deterrence Succeed and How Do We Know?* (1990).[42] *Between Peace and War* used evidence from 26 crises between 1898 and 1967 to develop a conceptual and empirical critique of deterrence as a theory and strategy of conflict management. I found that deterrence failed when leaders contemplated challenges of adversarial commitments as solutions to domestic and foreign problems, and most often, a combination of the two. In this circumstance, they became insensitive to the interests of their adversaries and whatever efforts they made to demonstrate capability and resolve. Leaders contemplating challenges rigged intelligence channels to provide them with supportive information and denied, distorted, explained away, or simply ignored information or advice that their expectations were unrealistic. In the follow-on works noted above, Janice Stein and I documented this phenomenon in a broader range of cases and also how threats encouraged leaders facing them to reframe what was at stake. We explored strategies more effective for coping with 'need-based', as opposed to 'opportunity-based' challenges.

In 1994, we published *We All Lost the Cold War*.[43] It reconstructs two Cold War crises from the perspective of multiple participants. We drew on cognitive and motivational psychology to analyze the information collection, evaluation, and post-conflict learning of political leaders. Capitalizing on the opportunity offered by *glasnost*, Stein and I obtained previously classified documents from Soviet and American archives and conducted extensive interviews with former Soviet and American officials to reconstruct the Cuban missile crisis of 1962 and the superpower confrontation arising out of the 1973 Middle East war. We make a plausible case that the Soviet missile deployment was intended to address Khrushchev's political and strategic problems, and demonstrate that he remained blind to warnings from his advisors and from Fidel Castro that the missiles would be discovered and provoke a serious confrontation with the United States. The crisis was the culmination of provocative behavior by insecure leaders on *both* sides designed to demonstrate resolve. The Cuban and the Middle East crises were resolved primarily by efforts to clarify interests and reassure the other side about one's own peaceful intentions. So too, we argue, was the Cold War.

My theoretical and empirical research had some impact on the discipline of international relations. It received many positive citations but also encountered strong opposition. Scholars committed to conventional and nuclear deterrence for intellectual or ideological reasons did not take kindly to research indicating that the strategy had the potential to provoke the very kinds of conflicts it was intended to prevent. My case study of the origins of World War I—among others—showed that neither the Austrians nor the Germans made any careful assessment of risk, were driven by concerns about status and honor, not by security, and were strongly motivated to deny accumulating evidence that their plan of a localized Balkan War was likely to provoke a European War between the two alliance systems and draw in Britain against them.[44]

This case study in particular aroused opposition. realists who argued that German leaders had not miscalculated but were driven by rational fears of growing Russian power, and that they would have been more restrained if the British had practiced deterrence effectively.[45] Bruce Russett and Paul Huth published two articles in defense of conventional deterrence, offering what they contended were numerous cases of deterrence success. Janice Stein and I had a close look at their data set and discovered that most of the so-called successful cases could not even be considered deterrence encounters.[46]

My emphasis on agency, context, and the psychological dynamics of coercive strategies incurred the wrath of rationalists committed to so-called parsimonious explanations of behavior. It led to a heated but amicable exchange in *World Politics*.[47] Not long after, James Fearon, then an assistant professor at the University of Chicago, wrote in an article that if Stein and my findings about deterrence were true it would be the most important finding of postwar international relations research. Invited to my alma mater to give a lecture, I thanked Fearon for his compliment. He insisted that I misunderstood his argument; his compliment was intended facetiously. If Stein and I were right, he said, 'it would make a mockery of several decades of research on deterrence and that was just too absurd to contemplate'.[48]

My turn to counterfactuals proved equally controversial. It was initially motivated by my desire to evaluate the foundational claim of deterrence: if only the West had stood firm at Munich—or better yet, earlier—Hitler could have been nipped in the bud and World War II averted. Some years later, my accounts of the end of the Cold War, in a coauthored with Janice Gross Stein and another one coedited with Richard K. Herrmann, aroused the ire of realists and triumphalists who claimed that Reagan's military buildup and Star Wars had brought the Russians to their knees.[49]

My work attracted some attention in the policy world. In 1981, I was invited to serve as the Central Intelligence Agency's first Scholar in Residence by then Director Admiral Stansfield Turner. This position offered a fascinating window on to the intelligence community and I learned much about how it functions and its uneasy and subservient relationship with the White House. Part of the reason I was hired was to document my critique of strategic analysis, and nuclear war-gaming in particular. I argued that the worst-case assumptions on which they were based greatly exaggerated the threat posed by the Soviet Union. I further suggested that too much attention was paid to Soviet military strength and not enough to its political weakness; that it was a country on the decline and more likely to implode than to expand. My papers circulated within the government but had no observable impact.[50]

In 2000, I participated in a forecasting exercise that brought together representatives of the CIA, State, Treasury, and NSC to identify the problems and threats that the incoming Bush administration might confront. The exercise was surprisingly simplistic. Five working groups composed of experts were asked to assess the current problems with the goal of determining whether they would become more or less acute in the next 4 years. They predictably made linear projections of current trends with high and low alternatives. Nobody considered other problems or the ways in which existing problems might interact in nonlinear ways. In the aftermath of 9/11—terrorism not having been one of the threats considered by the working groups—I participated in a brainstorming session sponsored by the intelligence community on predicting future attacks. I suggested that in addition to gathering intelligence on likely attacks that we commission people, Americans and foreigners, to plan attacks and do everything but actually carry them out. This might provide useful information about likely targets and what would-be terrorists would have to do in preparation. Then people in a position to see any of these preparations and behavior could be alerted about what to look for—rather than being told to report 'anything suspicious'. My suggestion found little support.

My intellectual frustration with American foreign and national security policy prompted a shift in research. I increasingly engaged classics and political theory with the goal of addressing more fundamental questions about war and peace and the nature of successful political orders. The first product was *The Tragic Vision of Politics: Ethics, Interests, and Orders*. It is unambiguously a work of social science but relies on ancient and modern literature for its insights. It reconstructs the wisdom of classical realism through the texts of Thucydides, Carl von Clausewitz, and Hans Morgenthau. It opens with a short story, 'Nixon in Hell', which introduces the principal normative argument of the book: that leaders of government and institutions should be held accountable for the same ethical standards as private individuals. Like tragedy, and art more generally, the story serves its purpose by arousing the emotions as well as the minds of readers. The Greeks understood that cooperation and conflict alike result from the interplay of emotions and reason, and I use their understanding and my story to critique existing theories of cooperation, offer an alternative, and make the case for the instrumental value of ethical behavior. My most important claim is that foreign policies in accord with existing ethical norms are more likely to succeed than those at odds with them. I also argue that great powers—not foreign adversaries—are their own worst enemies; their security is undermined more by their behavior than by that of adversaries. The USA and the Soviet Union, and now China, sadly confirm this proposition.

Greek tragedy provides the basis for an alternative and more productive ontology for the social sciences. The dominant ontology assumes that the egoistic, autonomous, and ahistorical actor is a proper starting point for analysis. The Greeks recognized that people are rarely found at the poles of any social continuum (e.g., self-versus social identity and interest, honor vs. interest, family loyalties vs. civic obligations). At most times and in most societies, human behavior is found along the continuum between the polar extremes that tragedy problematizes. Most people and their societies make uneasy, often illogical, uncomfortable, and usually unstable compromises rather than unwavering commitments to any set of values or responsibilities. Like tragedy, we must start from the premise that these polarities define the extremes of the human condition and are not themselves good starting points for understanding, let alone predicting, behavior. We must embrace and represent the diversity and inherent instability of human identities, interests and motives, and their complex interactions with the discourses, social practices, and institutions they generate and sustain.

I followed up on this theme in *Tragedy and International Relations*, coedited with Toni Erskine.[51] It elaborates ancient Greek and modern understanding of tragedy and explores its application to international relations. Contributors offer different perspectives on tragedy—ancient and modern—and different views about whether knowledge of tragedy has the potential to reduce its frequency in international affairs.

In 2014, Simon Reich and I coauthored *Good-Bye Hegemony! Power and Influence in the Global System*.[52] We argue that the USA is not a hegemon and certainly not recognized as such by other states. Hegemony is a fiction propagated to support a large defense establishment, justify American claims to world leadership, and buttress the self-esteem of voters. Many policymakers, journalists, and American scholars insist that hegemony is essential to ward off global chaos. We contend that it is contrary to American interests and the global order. Realists and liberals claim hegemony is necessary to allow agenda setting, economic custodianship, and the sponsorship of global initiatives. Today, these functions are diffused through the system, with European countries, China, and lesser powers making important contributions. In contrast, the USA has often been a source of political and economic instability.

Good-Bye Hegemony! Also draws on ancient Greek thought. Rejecting the focus on power common to American realists and liberals, we offer a novel analysis of influence that harks back to Thucydides and Sophocles. We differentiate influence from power and power from material resources. Material resources are only one component of power, and the extent to which they contribute to power depends upon investment in the right kinds of capabilities. Power in turn is only one source of influence. Military power applied in the wrong situation—e.g., the USA in Indochina, Afghanistan, and Iraq, and the Soviet Union in Afghanistan, and arguably, Ukraine—can lead to loss of influence. Influence depends largely on persuasion, and that relies at least as much on knowledge, skill, and friendships, as it does on power. Our analysis reveals why the USA, the greatest power the world has ever seen, is increasingly incapable of translating its power into influence. We use our analysis to formulate a more realistic place for America in world affairs.

Old Wine in New Bottles

In the aftermath of dramatic events, pundits are always prepared to proclaim a new world in which many of yesterday's lessons are now obsolete. This happened after the Bolshevik Revolution, World War II, the first Soviet nuclear test, the Cold War, and the terrorist attacks of 9/11. Such pronouncements are always exaggerations as the previous world and its threats and opportunities rarely disappear. If old problems persist, or return in new form, old lessons remain relevant, but perhaps of more limited utility as new challenges require new thinking.

Lessons of history, while essential to good policymaking, are nevertheless a mixed blessing. Political leaders, generals, and businesspeople frequently fall victim to the well-documented human tendency to view the world in linear terms. In contrast to pundits who proclaim that everything they are more likely to err in the opposite direction: they see the past as the guide to the future and think that the future will be more or less like the present. This phenomenon is well illustrated by military planning after both World Wars.[53]

A related cognitive bias, to which even sophisticated analysts succumb, is to mistake the superficial attributes of a situation for more fundamental ones.[54] It is a source of misleading analogies and inappropriate
policies based on them. As the Soviet Union and China opposed the
capitalist West, many American policymakers and scholars concluded that
any new left-wing regimes would be pro-Soviet and implacably hostile.
This belief prompted American support of nationalist China, and coups
in Iran (1953), Guatemala (1954), and later, support for right-wing
efforts in Latin America and elsewhere to stamp out left-wing political and guerrilla movements. American policy toward China, Vietnam,
and Iran rapidly made this belief at least in part self-fulfilling. This bias
contributed to hold deterrence exercised over the minds of American
policymakers and encouraged them to confirm it in a circular manner. I
elaborate on this claim in subsequent chapters.

We must learn lessons from history, but good ones. This is a tall task
because facile analogies invariably dominate policy deliberations and
public discourse.[55] They frequently have moral overtones or attempt to
frame policy choices in moral terms. Consider the civil war in the former Yugoslavia and the German debate over military participation in
NATO intervention. Those in favor invoked the Holocaust; Germany, of
all countries, could not stand by and do nothing in the face of ethnic
cleansing. Those opposed turned to Sarajevo and argued that intervention in the Balkans could once again have unforeseen and escalatory consequences as it did in 1914. Opponents also appealed to German history,
reminding the public of Hitler's invasion and occupation of Yugoslavia in
World War II and how it was morally unacceptable for German forces to
engage in combat anywhere in another country.[56] Who could say beforehand—or even afterward—which, if any, of these historical lessons was
appropriate?

Policy lessons pertain to ends and means. Most foreign policy lessons
are about means as they are the most difficult choices governments routinely confront. The goals of political security, economic stability, good
relations with neighbors, and peace more generally are rarely challenged,
but the methods of achieving them invariably are. Max Weber addressed
this problem—unsatisfactorily in my view—in his famous essay:
'The Vocation of Politics'. He distinguishes the ethics of conviction
[*Gesinnungsethik*] from that of responsibility [*Verantwortungsethik*].[57]
The former requires people to act in accord with their principles regardless of the likely outcome. Weber derides this ethic as an unaffordable

luxury in a world where force must sometimes be used for survival or important policy ends. 'No ethics in the world', he reasons, 'can get round the fact that the achievement of 'good' ends is in many cases tied to the necessity of employing morally dangerous means, and that one must reckon with the possibility or even likelihood of evil side-effects'.[58] The ethic of responsibility directs attention to the consequences of one's behavior, and, he insists, is more appropriate to politics, and international relations especially. Anybody who fails to recognize this truth 'is indeed a child in political matters'.[59]

Weber's ethic of responsibility is problematic because, as he acknowledges, behavior so often has unforeseen and undesired consequences. This is arguably more likely still when violence is used in volatile domestic or foreign conflicts. Morally justifiable policies can produce horrible outcomes, but so too can policies crafted to produce good ones. Responsible politicians, he suggests, make use of both ethics to some degree and think through carefully the conditions in which either is appropriate and the outcomes—negative and positive—to which they may lead. A wise leader must 'be conscious of these ethical paradoxes and of his responsibility for what may become of *himself* under pressure from them'.[60] Leaders must think with their head, but also listen with their heart, because there are some occasions where ethical considerations should be determining. He concludes that the two ethics 'are complementary and only in combination do they produce the true human being who is *capable* of having a 'vocation for politics''.[61]

Weber makes no attempt to identify the conditions that should govern the choice of ethics on the grounds that they are situation specific. They were not evident beforehand in Yugoslavia, or in Afghanistan, Iraq, and Libya. In the absence of clear criteria, leaders are dangerously free to make choices of convenience, as the Bush administration most certainly did in Iraq, claiming that the goal of denying weapons of mass destruction to Saddam Hussein more than justified the use of force and the uncertainty that would follow it.[62]

Historical lessons are helpful because they suggest policy options and help leaders estimate their likely consequences. They are also dangerous when they encourage false confidence in strategies or policies. By their very nature, they encourage analysts and leaders to draw parallels between the past and present situations on the basis of criteria that may or may not be appropriate ones in the situation. Even if they are, there are rarely, if ever, completely analogous situations in politics. They differ in subtle, and more often, important ways. This is why theories and lessons are never more than starting points for explanatory narratives or forward-looking forecasts. Neither lessons nor theories are determining, but contexts are. There is a real danger that leaders and their advisors overvalue the lessons because they are insensitive to context and overvalue the similarities between the present situation and past ones that generated these lessons. This is a well-known cognitive bias, but it can also be motivated. Leaders may take refuge in comforting analogies and their lessons because the policies they support, if successful, solve important strategic or political problems for them. Or, they may do so because they reduce uncertainty and anxiety and thereby enhance their ability to commit to a policy.[63]

The deterrence debate of the 1980s was motivated on all sides by a commitment to assess the efficacy of deterrence on the basis of historical evidence. Scholars drew on historical examples not only from the Cold War but also from earlier periods of history, where contexts may have been different, but about which there was documentary evidence. These deterrence encounters, immediate and general, could also be assessed in a broader perspective as some of them took place 30–50 years earlier than the Cold War. The crisis cycles leading to World Wars I and II were particularly important for many researchers because of the prominence of these wars and the belief by some that they might have been averted by more effective deterrence. Early studies of deterrence invariably cited Munich as the prototypic, but counterfactual, case in which deterrence would have worked had leaders tried.[64] They assume that Adolf Hitler would have backed down had Britain and France remained unequivocal in their commitment to defend Czechoslovakia. German documents make it apparent that by 1938 Hitler wanted war. Indeed, he was disappointed that Prime Minister Neville Chamberlain was so accommodating at Munich and made new demands at the last moment in the hope of forestalling an agreement. By 1938, resolve, commitment, and a serious attempt to deter by Britain and France would not have succeeded any more than appeasement in preventing World War II as Hitler was intent on war.[65]

Had Britain and France stood firm a few years earlier, the future of Europe might conceivably have been different. In 1936, when Hitler ordered the German army into the demilitarized Rhineland, he and his generals estimated that they could not overcome French military resistance. Together with disaffected senior diplomats, they might have conspired to remove Hitler from power had France, with Britain's support opposed remilitarization. As late as 1938, army and foreign office officials made preparations for a coup but lost confidence when the Western powers capitulated once again.[66]

Britain and France did not practice deterrence credible in large part because of the widespread desire in both capitals to avoid war. Not all British and French leaders at the time believed that Hitler was motivated by opportunity, or that he aspired to do more than a return to the pre-Versailles political and territorial status quo. If Hitler's goals had been so limited, Anglo-French tolerance of his remilitarization of the Rhineland would have been a reasonable policy, while its alternative—French military intervention—could have triggered an unnecessary war.

Without a doubt, the tragedy of the 1930s was the failure of European statesmen to recognize that Hitler sought to exploit the weaknesses of others and had unlimited ambitions. It was not enough for the leaders to have recognized the danger Hitler posed. For states to deter adversaries credibly, they must have the strong and obvious support of their publics. British and French opinion was deeply divided over domestic issues overwhelmingly antiwar; it would have undercut any serious attempt at deterrence against Hitler's Germany in 1935, 1936, or 1937. Not until March 1939, in response to Hitler's occupation of Czechoslovakia, did the British public come to appreciate the threat posed by Nazi Germany and support more determined action.[67] In France, a significant segment of opinion continued to believe well into the war that French socialists constituted a greater danger than did Nazi Germany.[68]

The deterrence counterfactual originated with Chamberlain's political opponents: Winston Churchill, Duff Cooper, and early postwar historians Lewis Namier and John Wheeler-Bennett.[69] It was bought lock, stock, and barrel by American policymakers and foreign policy analysts, although subsequently questioned by historians.[70] Deterrence advocates have consistently misused the Munich counterfactual as the paradigm of deterrence failure. By 1938, deterrence was irrelevant because Hitler was intent on war. When deterrence was finally tried the following year in the form of an Anglo-French military guarantee to Poland, it failed for this reason.[71] Those who criticize the Western powers for not vigorously opposing Hitler's first acts of aggression ignore the political constraints that operated within Britain and France, and that precluded deterrence as a strategy. Indeed, this argument reflects the tendency of deterrence theorists to treat war avoidance as a problem between unitary actors, and to ignore entirely the domestic political, psychological, and economic factors that can reinforce or defeat deterrence, or even entirely preclude serious use of the strategy.

The Cold War also spawned lessons, in this instance about the role of deterrence in conflict resolution. Supporters of former US president Ronald Reagan, and conservatives more generally, credit Reagan's arms buildup and the Strategic Defense Initiative (Star Wars) with ending the Cold War. These policies, they allege, brought the Soviet Union to its senses and provided strong incentives for it to seek an accommodation with the USA.[72] Gorbachev and his advisors became convinced that they could not compete with the USA and ought to negotiate the best deal they could before Soviet power declined even further.[73] Western liberals, former Soviet policymakers, and many scholars attribute the end of the Cold War to 'New Thinking' and the political transformation it brought about within the Soviet leadership. Gorbachev, they contend, considered the Cold War dangerous and a waste of resources and sought to end it to bring the Soviet back into Europe, facilitate political reform at home, and free resources for domestic development.[74]

These competing interpretations make different kinds of arguments. Those who credit Reagan's arms buildup with ending the Cold War build their case entirely on inference. The arms buildup is supposed to have signaled resolve to Moscow, and convinced rational Soviet leaders to make the concessions necessary to end the Cold War. No evidence is offered to indicate that Gorbachev and his advisors were influenced by this logic. Those who attribute Gorbachev's eagerness to end the Cold War, and to make some important one-sided concessions toward that end, offer considerable evidence in support of their contentions based on records of discussions among Soviet leaders, including notes of Politburo meetings, interviews with Gorbachev and his principal advisors from 1986 to 1992, and interviews with former Eastern European officials reporting their discussions with the Soviet leadership. In any court, evidence trumps inference, so for the moment at least, the liberal claim that changing ideas were the catalyst for the Cold War's end is more credible than the conservative assertion that it was a growing differential in power between the superpowers.

Deterrence advocates do not restrict their counterfactual arguments to instances where deterrence was not practiced. All attempts to establish the success of deterrence are based on counterfactuals; their assumption is that war would have occurred had it not been implemented effectively. This proposition is the mirror image of the Munich claim. As we have seen, arguments designed to show why certain outcomes did not occur can easily lend themselves to circular reasoning. This is hardly a secure foundation on which to build a strategy of conflict management.

How then do we determine good historical lessons from bad ones? I have argued elsewhere with reference to counterfactuals that it is rarely, if ever, possible to validate a counterfactual argument. The same, I contend, is true of historical arguments that make causal claims.[75] The best we can do is to evaluate arguments and their putative lessons on the basis of their internal logic and use of empirical evidence. Is their chain of logic consistent? Do they consider the counterfactual of whether the same outcome might or would have occurred in the absence of the proposed explanation? Do they make selective use of evidence? Do they seriously engage the secondary literature, or better yet, primary sources? Do they embrace process tracing, that is attempt to show that the actors in questions were moved by the considerations attributed to them? Do they consider alternate explanations and outcomes? And most importantly, are they based on the record or multiple as opposed to a single case?

With respect to historical lessons, I want to offer four conditions that any proposed lesson should meet. The first, as noted, is that it should rely on credible and respected historical readings of the events from which it is derived. There are frequently multiple compelling explanations for events—as in the case of World War I—that are competing or reinforcing. The former suggest that any lesson must be tentative because it rests on a controversial interpretation of history. The latter also points to the need for caution because the interpretation, even if persuasive, may at best be a necessary but insufficient cause of the event in question.

Second, lessons should not generalize from single cases. There is no way of knowing if these cases are idiosyncratic or representative of the phenomenon under study. International relations theory is largely built on two historical cases: World Wars I and II. Theorists simply assume that they are reasonable events from which to generalize about the causes of war and make no explicit attempt to defend their choices. If they are contingent, or reflect a particular set of transient conditions, they are poor candidates on which to base theories.[76] Lessons derived from the statistical analysis of data sets confront the same problems, despite claims of quantitative researchers to the contrary.[77]

Third, like a good theory, it should stipulate its scope conditions. Proponents must identify their political and military assumptions, the mechanisms on which they rely, and the range of situations to which they might be applicable. This is essential to address the uncertainty arising from generalizations based on single or possibly unrepresentative cases. Even representative cases must be hedged by scope conditions to avoid applying them to unrepresentative cases. The condition of 'representativeness' is a statistical term of limited use when addressing international relations where most events are singular, as Max Weber observed of social developments more generally.[78] This does not negate the utility of historical lessons but puts a premium on not only identifying the kinds of situations to which they apply, but also their limits and risks. How, and under what conditions, might they be self-defeating? What are their contraindications, to borrow a term from pharmacology? In the best of circumstances, historical learning are policy have a recursive relationship. Lessons must be updated on the basis of new experience and evidence.

Fourth, as noted, theories and lessons are merely starting points for explaining past events or forecasting future ones. Context in the form of agency, confluence, path dependence, and accident is generally determining of political outcomes, and especially international ones. So lessons, even when robust and appropriate, cannot be used to predict. At best, they identify an outcome that is likely in response to a particular policy or set of policies. They are not solutions to policy dilemmas but suggestions that may or may not work as expected. When used, they must be carefully monitored for evidence that they are not leading to expected outcomes.

These criteria help us to eliminate bad historical lessons. They do *not* allow us to differentiate valid from invalid ones. All lessons of history are subjective, as are their relevance to novel situations. There is no scientific way of determining their applicability.

Good history is in any case only a starting point for good lessons. It can generate bad ones, and good lessons can be misapplied. To complicate matters further, bad history can generate good lessons. Barbara Tuchman's best-selling book, *The Guns of August*, published in 1962, argued that nobody wanted war in 1914 and that it was an avoidable accident.[79] The contemporary historical consensus rejects this interpretation, holding Germany and Austria responsible on the basis of evidence that both wanted at least a limited war in the Balkans.[80] Tuchman's account was subsequently discredited, but her lesson was an important and timely one. President Kennedy read *Guns of August* on the eve of the missile crisis and later said it sensitized him to the problem of loss of control.[81]

Historical learning may be hit or miss. It is still essential because in its absence policymakers are even more likely to invoke inappropriate analogies in support of inappropriate policies. In some countries, notably Britain, many politicians read and sometimes write history. This is much less common in the United States, where most presidents and their advisors are neither as well read nor as open-minded as John F. Kennedy. In both countries—and everywhere else—media tend to resist historical interpretations and lessons that contradict the conventional wisdom. Following the publication of *We All Lost the Cold War* in 1994 I tried to place a short piece on the editorial page of the *New York Times* about how deterrence had helped to provoke the Cuban missile crisis. The then editor of the Op Ed column rejected it, writing to me that surely I could not expect anybody to believe such an outrageous claim. In 2016, the *Atlantic* accepted, copyedited, and subsequently refused to publish a coauthored article exposing the bad history tendentious arguments and of Graham Allison concerning the near inevitability of wars arising from power transitions.[82] The editors alleged they were uncertain about our facts, although they came from a well-documented data set in contrast to Allison's blatant disregard of historical facts. Readers can draw their own conclusions about what motivated the editors of what claims to be a leading intellectual journal. We subsequently published the piece in the *Washington Monthly*.[83]

Chapter Outline

My research corpus has, I believe, important implications for the theory and practice of international relations and national security policy. In recent publications, I have elaborated them in constructivist theories of international relations and war and new understandings of identity, cases studies, and causation.[84] In this volume, I return to my earlier focus on strategy and different approaches to conflict prevention and management. I reprint articles and a chapter that address these problems and alternatives and offer a conclusion, specifically written for this book, that goes beyond these writings in an attempt to integrate their insights into a broader approach to conflict prevention and management.

Chapter 2 examines how the so-called lessons of the past dominate responses to present day problems. I identify five such lessons about the world that the American national security community learned from the run-up to World War II. They have to do with how the world economic crisis of the 1930s facilitated the emergence of aggressive, authoritarian regimes, an uncoordinated response to the Great Depression made economic suffering far worse, US isolationism undermined deterrence. The economic lessons were apt and helped to structure a more prosperous and secure world order. The foreign policy lessons are more questionable, not because they were wrong, but because they were applied in a different and arguably inappropriate context. I draw on cognitive psychology to explain why this happened. This phenomenon should be a reason for caution in applying Cold War lessons to today's world.

Chapter 3 offers a critique of deterrence. It draws on numerous case studies and motivational psychology to explain why immediate conventional deterrence so often fails. It also critiques the political and behavioral assumptions of deterrence. These strategies place unreasonable informational and analytical requirements on policymakers. They misconstrue the process of risk assessment and exaggerate the ability of leaders to estimate the risks inherent in their threats, let alone shape adversarial estimates of their resolve. They overvalue the balance of power and interests, and mistakenly assume that protagonists share common understandings of them. These problems may help explain why deterrence and compellence often fail when practiced by rational and attentive actors against equally rational and attentive targets. Some of the political and behavioral assumptions of deterrence and compellence are unique, but most are shared with other rational theories of bargaining. I illustrate my argument with examples from American and Soviet decision-making in the Cuban missile crisis.

Chapter 4 explores the lessons of World War I's origins, and to a lesser extent, those of World War II. The origins of both World Wars, but especially the First, have been hotly contested by generations of historians. Some theories of war and its prevention build on particular interpretations of its origins, but there is a growing consensus among historians that there is no single, or even dominant, cause of this war. Rather, it was the result of a suite of interactive and reinforcing causes, although there is no consensus about which of them was the most important. The centenary of the Great War in 2014 encouraged a spate of new studies that build on some new primary documents but mostly represent a rethinking of the origins due to a collective shift away from the question of what country was most responsible for war to how such a catastrophe could happen. The focus of historical research has accordingly drawn closer to questions of interest to international relations scholars, and our field has something to learn from the new research.

The new literature offers evidence and arguments relevant to the claims of balance of power, power transition and deterrence theories. It suggests the importance of immediate causes of war, which can be independent of underlying causes and cannot be taken for granted. It highlights the role of agency and the ways in which policy can be driven by idiosyncratic or seemingly inappropriate goals, based on erroneous understandings of other actors and threat assessments and have consequences not expected, and sometimes, not even unimagined by actors. At a more fundamental level, it raises questions about approaches that assume rational actors or rely on outside understandings of their motives and understanding of context. Most importantly, the new research should make us question the conceit that any parsimonious theory of war can tell us much about any single war, or the phenomenon of war more generally.

Chapter 5 explores the lessons of the Cold War for conflict management. It is one of the concluding chapters of *We All Lost the Cold War*, written with Janice Gross Stein. It draws on evidence from Soviet and American archives and extensive interviews with Soviet and American political and military officials to reconstruct the consequences of general deterrence for Soviet-American relations and immediate deterrence for crisis prevention. It indicates that general deterrence was largely unnecessary because both superpowers were self-deterred. Memories of the costs of World War II convinced leaders on all sides, and most military officials, that even a conventional war between the superpowers would be an unrelieved catastrophe. The advent of atomic, and then thermonuclear, weapons strengthened these beliefs and the fear of war. The problem was that neither side knew of the other's fear of war, in part because both did their best to hide it thinking it would convey weakness. Soviet and American leaders accordingly felt the need to build up their strategic arsenals, deploy weapons in forward, provocative positions, and engage in bellicose and threatening rhetoric. General deterrence practiced this way undermined immediate deterrence by making both superpowers feel more insecure and threatened. It was an underlying cause of the crisis spiral of the late 1950s and early 1960s. This ended in the aftermath of the Cuban missile crisis that taught leaders on both sides the extent to the other also feared war.

Chapter 6 looks beyond crisis management to conflict resolution. I ask what accommodation means and distinguish between a rapprochement that significantly reduces the threat of war, but may do nothing else to improve relations, and an accommodation that relations them on a normal footing. Post-peace agreement Egyptian–Israeli relations are an example of the former, and Anglo-French relations after their Entente a case of the latter. Russian–American relations after the Cold War and Sino–American relations following the thaw inaugurated by Nixon and Mao lie somewhere in between.

How did these rapprochements and accommodations come about? I find three conditions common to the Anglo-French, Egyptian–Israeli, and Soviet–American cases. There was a new leader on one side committed to far-reaching reforms that required a winding down of the country's primary foreign conflict, to free resources but also to undercut hardliners who also opposed domestic changes. Leaders on both sides concluded that it was impossible to achieve their political goals by military force. This belief was promoted by the failure of a recent challenge or confrontation. Leaders committed to reform accepted risks by extending the olive branch, and diplomacy made progress only when their initiatives were encouraged and reciprocated. Threat-based strategies were both a cause of conflict and contributed to its resolution, but not in the ways generally theorized.

Chapter 7, my conclusion, takes hesitant steps toward a holistic approach to conflict management and resolution. It recognizes that deterrence, although a deeply flawed strategy, nevertheless has an important place in international relations. It is appropriately directed against states whose leaders harbor aggressive intentions, although those practicing deterrence must do so with finesse and recognition that the success rate of general and immediate deterrence is low. Threat-based strategies are only one response to international conflict. Of equal importance are reassurance and diplomacy aimed at reducing or finessing substantive differences. I describe these strategies, identify their associated mechanisms and how they are expected to work, and the conditions in which they are most appropriate. Regardless of how international conflicts begin, they are usually characterized over time by hostility, conflicts of interests, and misunderstandings. The critical question is not the choice of a particular strategy—as they are often all relevant—but rather how they are combined, staged, and integrated into a sophisticated approach to conflict management tailored to the conflict in question.

NOTES

1. Suji Kim, "Is it Time to Intervene in North Korea?," *New Republic*, 11 January 2016, https://newrepublic.com/article/127280/time-intervene-north-korea; Pascal-Emanuel Gobry, "The Case for Invading North Korea," *The Week*, 7 January 2015, http://theweek.com/articles/441214/case-invading-north-korea; Mark Thompson, "Is it Time to Attack North Korea?," *Time*, 9 March 2016, http://time.com/4252372/north-korea-nuclear-missile-attack/; Robert E. Kelly, "The Ultimate Nightmare: Why Invading North Korea is a Really Bad Idea," *National Interest*, 30 January 1015, http://nationalinterest.org/blog/the-buzz/the-ultimate-nightmare-why-invading-the-north-korea-really-12157 (all accessed 25 November 2016).
2. See note 57.
3. Richard Ned Lebow, *Between Peace and War: The Nature of International Crisis* (Baltimore: Johns Hopkins University Press, 1981), p. 83.
4. Bernard Brodie, "The Absolute Weapon: Atomic Power and World Order," *Bulletin of the Atomic Scientists*, 3 (1947), pp. 150–155; Carl von Clausewitz, *On War*, trans. M. Howard and P. Paret (Princeton: Princeton University Press, 1976), pp. 75–89.
5. William W. Kaufmann, *The Requirements of Deterrence* (Princeton: Center of International Studies, 1954); Henry Kissinger, *Nuclear Weapons and Foreign Policy* (New York: Harper, 1957); Bernard B. Brodie, "The Anatomy of Deterrence," *World Politics* (1959) 11, no. 1, pp. 173–192; Morton A. Kaplan, "The Calculus of Deterrence," *World Politics*, 11, no. 1 (1958), pp. 20–43.
6. Thomas Schelling, *The Strategy of Conflict* (Cambridge: Harvard University Press, 1960) and *Arms and Influence* (New Haven: Yale University Press, 1966).
7. Ibid.
8. Schelling, *Arms and Influence.*
9. Jeffrey Kimball, *Nixon's Vietnam War* (Lawrence: University Press of Kansas, 1998), pp. 76–86.
10. Schelling, *Arms and Influence*, pp. 6–16.
11. Ibid.
12. Ibid; Clausewitz, *On War*, pp. 479–483.
13. Clausewitz, *On War*, pp. 585–594.

14. Robert S. McNamara, James G. Blight, and Robert K. Brigham, *Argument Without End: In Search of Answers to the Vietnam Tragedy* (New York: Public Affairs, 1999), p. 194.

15. Ibid, pp. 191, 341–345.

16. Emanuel Adler, "Complex Deterrence in the Asymmetric-Warfare Era," in T.V. Paul, Patrick M. Morgan and James Wirtz, eds., *Complex Deterrence: Strategy in the Global Age* (Chicago: University of Chicago Press, 2009), pp. 85–109; Alex Wilner, "Deterring the Undeterrable," *Journal of Strategic Studies*, 3, no. 5 (2010), pp. 597–619; Ivan Arreguin Toft, "Unconventional Deterrence: How the Weak Deter Strong," in Wirtz, *Complex Deterrence*, pp. 222–259, and "Targeted Killings in Afghanistan: Measuring Coercion and Deterrence in Counterterrorism Counterinsurgency," *Studies in Conflict and Terrorism*, 33 (2010), pp. 53–94; Patrick B. Johnston, "Does Decapitation Work? Assessing the Effectiveness of Leadership Targeting in Counterinsurgency Campaigns," *International Security*, 36, no. 4 (2002), pp. 47–79.

17. Michael D. Shear and James Glanz, "Trump Says US Should Expand its Nuclear capability," *New York Times*, 22 December 2016, http://www.nytimes.com/2016/12/22/us/politics/trump-says-us-should-expand-its-nuclear-capability.html?_r=0 (accessed 22 December 1016); Michael D. Shear David E. Sanger, "Trump Says U.S. Would 'Outmatch' Rivals in a New Nuclear Arms Race," *New York Times*, 23 December 2016, http://www.nytimes.com/2016/12/23/us/politics/trump-nuclear-arms-race-russia-united-states.html?hp&action=click&pgtype=Homepage&clickSource=story-heading&module=first-column-region&region=top-news&WT.nav=top-news&_r=0 (accessed 23 December 2016).

18. For this debate, Scott Sagan and Kenneth Waltz, *The Spread of Nuclear Weapons: A Debate* (New York: Norton, 1995).

19. Richard Ned Lebow and Janice Stein *We All Lost the Cold War* (Princeton: University Press, 1994); T.V. Paul, *The Tradition of Non-Use of Nuclear Weapons* (Stanford: Stanford University Press, 2009).

20. Walter Clarke and Jeffrey Herbst, eds., *Learning from Somalia: The Lessons of Armed Humanitarian Intervention* (Boulder: Westview, 1997).

21. Mahmood Mamdani, *When Victims Become Killers: Colonialism, Nativism, and the Genocide in Rwanda* (Princeton: Princeton University Press, 2002); Roméo Dallaire, *Shake Hands with the Devil: The Failure of Humanity in Rwanda* (London: Arrow Books, 2002); Gerard Prunier, *The Rwanda Crisis: A History of a Genocide*, 2nd ed. (London: Hurst, 1998).

22. Daniel L. Byman and Mathew C. Waxman, "Kosovo and the Great Air Power Debate," *International Security*, 24, no. 4 (2000), pp. 5–38; Lawrence A. Freedman, *Deterrence* (Cambridge: Polity, 2004), pp. 124–130.

23. Clausewitz, *On War*, Chap. 1.
24. Thomas Schelling, *Arms and Influence* (New Haven Yale University Press, 1966). For a critique, Richard Ned Lebow, "Thomas Schelling and Strategic Bargaining," in Lebow, *Coercion, Cooperation, and Ethics in International Relations* (New York: Routledge, 2007), Chap. 7.
25. Adler, "Complex Deterrence in the Asymmetric-Warfare Era".
26. Mervyn Frost and Richard Ned Lebow, "Ethical Traps," paper under review.
27. Patrick M. Morgan and T.V. Paul, "Deterrence Among the Great Powers in an Era of Globalization," in Paul, Morgan and Wirtz, *Complex Deterrence*, pp. 259–276; Paul Bracken, *The Second Nuclear Age: Strategy, Danger, and the New Power Politics* (New York: St. Martin's, 2012); Jeffrey A. Larsen and Kerry M. Kartchner, eds., *On Limited Nuclear War in the 21st Century* (Stanford: Stanford University Press, 2014).
28. Frank Harvey and Patrick James, "Deterrence an Compellence in Iraq, 1991–2003: Lessons for a Complex Paradigm," in Paul, Morgan and Wirtz, *Complex Deterrence*, pp. 222–258; Jacquelyn K. Davis and Robert L. Pfaltzgraff, Jr., *Anticipating a Nuclear Iran: Challenges for U.S. Security* (New York: Columbia University Press, 2013); Er-Win Tan, *The US Versus the North Korean Nuclear Threat: Mitigating the Nuclear Security Dilemma* (New York: Routledge, 2013).
29. On renouncing weapons programs, see Jacques E., Hymans, *The Psychology of Nuclear Proliferation: Identity, Emotions, and Foreign Policy* (**Cambridge: Cambridge University Press, 2006**); Etel Solingen, *Nuclear Logics: Contrasting Paths in East Asia and the Middle East* (Cambridge University Press, 2007).
30. Shmuel Barr, "Deterrence of Palestinian Terrorism: The Israeli Experience," in Andreas Wenger and Alex Wilner, eds., *Deterring Terrorism: Theory and Practice* (Stanford: Stanford University Press, 2012), pp. 205–227; Michael D. Cohen, "Mission Impossible? Influencing Iranian and Libyan Sponsorship of Terrorism," in Wenger and Wilner, *Deterring Terrorism*, pp. 251–272; Fred Wehling, "A Toxic Cloud of Mystery: Lessons from Iraq for Deterring CBRN Terrorism," in Wenger and Wilner, *Deterring Terrorism*, pp. 273–300; David Romano, "Turkish and Iranian Efforts to Deter Turkish Attacks," in Wenger, Andreas and Alex Wilner, *Deterring Terrorism*, pp. 228–250.
31. Janice Gross Stein, "Deterring Terrorism, Not Terrorists," in Wenger and Wilner, *Deterring Terrorism*, pp. 46–66.
32. Stephen van Evera, *Causes of War: Power and the Roots of Conflict* (Ithaca: Cornell University Press, 1999), Chap. 8; Daniel Deudney, *Bounding Power: Republican Security Theory from the Polis to the Global*

Village (Princeton: Princeton University Press, 2007) and "Unipolarity and Nuclear Weapons," in G. John Ikenberry, Michael Mastanduno, and William Wohlforth, eds., *International Relations Theory and the Consequences of Unipolarity* (Cambridge: Cambridge University Press, 2011); Avery Goldstein, *Deterrence and Security in the 21st Century: China, Britain, France and the Enduring Legacy of the Nuclear Revolution* (Palo Alto: Stanford University Press, 2000); Randall Schweller, *Unanswered Threats: Political Constraints on the Balance of Power* (Princeton: Princeton University Press, 2006), pp. 2–3; Susan B. Martin, "The Continuing Value of Nuclear Weapons: A Structural Realist Analysis," *Contemporary Security Policy* 34, no. 1 (Spring 2013), pp. 174–194; Casper Sylvest and Rens van Munster, *Nuclear Realism: Global Political Thought During the Thermonuclear Revolution* (London: Routledge, 2016); Charles Glaser and Steve Fetter, "Should the United States Reject MAD? Damage Limitation and U.S. Nuclear Strategy Towards China," *International Security*, 41, no. 1, pp. 49–98; Nuno Monteiro, *Theory of Unipolar Politics* (Cambridge: Cambridge University Press, 2014).

33. Keir Lieber and Daryl Press, "The End of MAD? The Nuclear Dimension of US Primacy," *International Security*, vol. 30, no. 4 (Spring 2006), pp. 7–44; Lieber and Press, "The New Era of Nuclear Weapons, Deterrence and Conflict," *Strategic Studies Quarterly*, vol. 7, no. 1 (Spring 2013), pp. 3–12; Larsen and Kartchner, *On Limited Nuclear War*; Matthew Kroenig, "Nuclear Superiority and the Balance of Resolve: Explaining Nuclear Crisis Outcomes," *International Organization*, vol. 67, no. 1 (Winter 2013), pp. 141–171 and "Facing Reality: Getting NATO Ready for a New Cold War," *Survival: Global Politics and Strategy*, vol. 57, no. 1, (Winter/Spring 2015), pp. 49–70; Brad Roberts, *The Case for U.S. Nuclear Weapons in the Twenty-First Century* (Palo Alto: Stanford University Press, 2015), Chap. 6; Austin Long and Brendan Rittenhouse-Green, "Stalking the Secure Second Strike: Intelligence, Counterforce, and Nuclear Strategy," *Journal of Strategic Studies*, 38, nos. 1–2 (2015), pp. 38–73; Francis Gavin, "Strategies of Inhibition: U.S. Grand Strategy, the Nuclear Revolution, and Nonproliferation," *International Security*, 40, no. 1 (2015), pp. 16–17; ISFF "Policy Rountable 9-4 on U.S. Nuclear Policy," with an introduction by Francis J. Gavin and essays by James M. Acton, Keir A. Lieber, Austin Long, Joshua Rovner, and Nina Tannenwald, *H-Diplo*, 22 December 2016, https://networks.h-net.org/node/28443/discussions/157862/issf-policy-roundtable-9-4-us-nuclear-policy (accessed 22 December 2016).

34. Jon Wolfsthal, Jeffrey Lewis, and Marc Quint, "The Trillion Dollar Nuclear Triad".

35. James Cartwright, Richard Burt, Chuck Hagel, Thomas Pickering, Jack Sheehan, and Bruce Blair, "Global Zero U.S. Nuclear Policy Commission Report: Modernizing U.S. Nuclear Strategy, Force Structure and Posture," www.globalzero.org, 2012; James Cartwright and Bruce Blair, "End the First-Use Policy for Nuclear Weapons," *New York Times*, August 15, 2016, p. A39; Thomas Nichols, *No Use: Nuclear Weapons and U.S. National Security* (Philadelphia: University of Pennsylvania Press, 2014).
36. James Martin Center for Nonproliferation Studies, Monterey, 2014. Scott Sagan, "The Case for No First Use," *Survival*, vol. 51, no. 3 (Summer 2009), pp. 163–182; Morton Halperin, Bruno Tertrais, Keith B. Payne, K. Subrahmanyam, and Scott Sagan, "The Case for No First Use: An Exchange," *Survival*, vol. 51, no. 5 (Autumn 2009), pp. 17–46.
37. Bracken, *Second Nuclear Age*, pp. 33–35.
38. Ibid, pp. 50–57.
39. Ibid, pp. 289–290 for his references. Mihail M. Narinskii, "The Soviet Union and the Berlin Crisis, 1948–1949," in Francesca Gori and Silvio Pons, *The Soviet Union in the Cold War, 1943–1953* (New York: St. Martin's, 1996), pp. 57–75; Victor Gorbarev, "Soviet Military Plans and Actions During the First Berlin Crisis," *Slavic Military Studies*, 10, no. 3 (1997), pp. 1–23. Vladislav Zubok and Constantine Pleshakov, *Inside the Kremlin's Cold War* (Cambridge: Harvard University Press, 1997), pp. 134–137, 194–197.
40. Lebow and Stein, *We All Lost the Cold War*, Chaps. 2–4 for discussion and exposure of these kinds of argument with reference to the Cuban missile crisis.
41. For the theory, Brodie, "Anatomy of Deterrence"; Kaufmann, *Requirements of Deterrence*; Kaplan, "Calculus of Deterrence; Schelling," *Arms and Influence*.
42. Lebow, *Between Peace and War*; Robert Jervis, Richard Ned Lebow and Janice Gross Stein *Psychology and Deterrence*, co-authored with (Baltimore: The Johns Hopkins University Press, 1985); Richard Ned Lebow, *Nuclear Crisis Management: A Dangerous Illusion* (Ithaca: Cornell University Press, January 1987); Richard Ned Lebow, "Deterrence Failure Revisited: A Reply to the Critics," *International Security*, 12 (Summer 1987), pp. 197–213, and "Deterrence: A Political and Psychological Critique," in Robert Axelrod, Robert Jervis, Roy Radner, and Paul Stern, eds., *Perspectives in Deterrence* (New York: Oxford University Press, 1989); Richard Ned Lebow and Janice Gross Stein, "Beyond Deterrence," *Journal of Social Issues*, 43, No. 4 (1987), pp. 5–71, "Beyond Deterrence: Building Better Theory," *Journal of Social Issues*, 43, No. 4 (1987), pp. 155–169, "Conventional and Nuclear

Deterrence: Are the Lessons Transferable?," *Journal of Social Issues*, 43, No. 4 (1987), pp. 171–191, "Rational Deterrence Theory: I Think Therefore I Deter," *World Politics*, 41 (January 1989), pp. 208–224, and *When Does Deterrence Succeed and How Do We Know?* (Ottawa: Canadian Institute for International Peace and Security, 1990).

43. Lebow and Stein, *We All Lost the Cold War*.
44. Lebow, *Between Peace and War*, Chap. 4.
45. For example, John Orme, "Deterrence Failures: A Second Look," *International Security*, 11, no. 4 (1987), pp. 96–124; Jack S. Levy, "Preferences, Constraints, and Choices in July 1914," *International Security*, 15, no. 3 (1990–1991), pp. 151–186; Paul W. Schroeder, "International Politics, Peace, and War, 1815–1914," in T.C. Blanning, ed., *The Nineteenth Century: Europe 1789–1914* (Oxford: Oxford University Press, 2001), pp. 158–209.
46. Paul K. Huth and Bruce Russett, "What Makes Deterrence Work? Cases from 1900 to 1980," *World Politics*, 36 (July 1984), Richard Ned Lebow and Janice Gross Stein, "Deterrence: The Elusive Dependent Variable," *World Politics*, 42 (April 1990), pp. 336–369.
47. Christopher H. Achen and Duncan Snidal, "Rational Deterrence Theory and Comparative Case Studies," *World Politics*, 41, no. 2 (1989), pp. 143–169; Lebow and Stein "Rational Deterrence Theory."
48. Conversation with James Fearon, University of Chicago, PIPES seminar, February 1994.
49. Ibid; Herrmann and Lebow, *Ending the Cold War*.
50. For unclassified versions of these papers, Richard Ned Lebow, "Superpower Management of Security Alliances: The Soviet Union and the Warsaw Pact," in Arlene Idol Broadhurst, ed., *The Future and The Future of European Alliance Systems* (Boulder, Westview Press, 1982), pp. 185–236 and "Misconceptions in American Strategic Assessment," *Political Science Quarterly*, 97 (Summer 1982), pp. 187–206.
51. Toni Erskine and Richard Ned Lebow, eds., *Tragedy and International Relations* (London: Palgrave, 2012).
52. Simon Reich and Richard Ned Lebow, *Good-Bye Hegemony! Power and Influence in the Global System* (Princeton: Princeton University Press, 2012).
53. Robert Jervis, *Perception and Misperception in International Relations* (Princeton: Princeton University Press, 1976), pp. 266–269.
54. I. Blanchette and K. Dunbar, "How Analogies are Generated: The Roles of Structural and Superficial Similarities," *Memory & Cognition* (2000) 28, no. 1, pp. 108–124.
55. Jervis, *Perception and Misperception in International Relations*, pp. 217–286; Yuen Foong Khong, *Analogies at War: Korea, Munich, Dien Bien*

Phu, and the Vietnam Decisions of 1965 (Princeton: Princeton University Press, 1995).

56. Maja Zehfuss, "Constructivism and Identity: A Dangerous Liaison," *European Journal of International Relations* (2001) 7, no. 3, pp. 315–348; Anja Dalgaard-Nielsen, *Germany, Pacifism and Peace Enforcement* (Manchester University Press, 2006).

57. Max Weber, "The Profession and Vocation of Politics," in Peter Lassmann and Ronald Speirs, *Weber: Political Writings* (Cambridge: Cambridge University Press, 1994), pp. 309–369.

58. Ibid.

59. Ibid.

60. Ibid.

61. Ibid.

62. John Prados, *Hoodwinked: How the Bush Administration Sold US a War* (New York: New Press, 2006); Jeffrey Record, *Wanting War: Why the Bush Administration Invaded Iraq* (Lincoln, Neb.: Potomac Books, 2010).

63. Irving L. Janis, and Leon Mann, *Decision-Making: A Psychological Model of Conflict, Choice, and Commitment* (New York: Free Press, 1977).

64. George, Alexander L. and Richard Smoke, *Deterrence in American Foreign Policy: Theory and Practice* (New York: Columbia University Press, 1974), p. 142.

65. Gerhard L. Weinberg, *The Foreign Policy of Hitler's Germany*, 2 vols (Chicago: University of Chicago Press, 1970–1980), I, pp. 462–463.

66. Zara Steiner, *Triumph of the Dark: European and International History 1933–1939* (Oxford: Oxford University Press, 2011), pp. 589–590; Terry M. Parssinen, *The Oster Conspiracy of 1938: The Unknown Story of the Military Plot to Kill Hitler and Avert World War II* (London: Harper Collins, 2001); R.A.C. Parker, *Chamberlain and Appeasement: British Policy and the Coming of the Second World War* (London: Macmillan, 1993); Andrew David Stedman, *Alternatives to Appeasement: Neville Chamberlain and Hitler's Government* (London I. B. Tauris. 2015).

67. Steiner, *Triumph of the Dark*, pp. 765–770, 819–823; Stedman, *Alternatives to Appeasement*, pp. 196–231.

68. Steiner, *Triumph of the Dark*, pp. 765–770, 819–823.

69. Winston Churchill, *The Gathering Storm* (London: Thomas Allen, 1948); Lewis Namier, *Diplomatic Prelude, 1939–1939* (London: Macmillan, 1948); John Wheeler-Bennett, *Munich: Prologue to Tragedy* (London: Macmillan, 1948); Alfred Duff Cooper, *Old Men Forget* (London: Faber & Faber, 1953).

70. Stedman, *Alternatives to Appeasement*, pp. 1–13, 119–160 for an account and thoughtful assessment of this ongoing debate.

71. Steiner, *Triumph of the Dark*, pp. 727–754.
72. Matlock, *Autopsy on an Empire: The American Ambassador's Account of the Collapse of the Soviet Union* (New York: Random House. 1995).
73. James W. Davis and William C. Wohlforth, "German Unification," in Richard K. Herrmann and Richard Ned Lebow, eds., *Ending the Cold War* (New York: Palgrave-Macmillan, 2003), pp. 131–160.
74. Archie Brown, A, 1996. *The Gorbachev Factor* (Oxford University Press, 1996); Robert D. English, *Russia and the Idea of the West: Gorbachev, Intellectuals and the End of the Cold War* (New York: Columbia University Press, 2000); Jacques Lévesque, **The Enigma of 1989: The USSR and the Liberation of Eastern Europe (Berkeley: University of California Press, 1997)**; Richard K. Herrmann, "Learning from the End of the Cold War," in Richard K. Herrmann and Richard Ned Lebow, *Ending the Cold War* (New York: Palgrave-Macmillan, 2004), pp. 219–238.
75. Ned Lebow, *Forbidden Fruit: Counterfactuals and International Relations* (Princeton: Princeton University Press, 2010), Chap. 2.
76. Ibid, Chap. 1.
77. On this point, Lebow, "A Data Set Named Desire: A Reply to William P. Thompson," *International Studies Quarterly*, 47 (2003), pp. 475–458 and *Constructing Cause in International Relations* (Cambridge: Cambridge University Press, 2014).
78. Max Weber, "Conceptual Exposition," *Economy and Society*, ed. Guenther Roth and Claus Wittich (Berkeley: University of California Press, 1978), p. 9; Richard Ned Lebow, *Wissenschaftliche Warheit*: "Max Weber and Knowledge," in Richard Ned Lebow, ed., *Max Weber and International Relations* (Cambridge: Cambridge University Press, 2017).
79. Barbara Tuchman, *The Guns of August* (New York: Macmillan, 1961).
80. Thomas G. Otte, *July Crisis: The World's Descent into War, Summer 1914* (Cambridge: Cambridge University Press, 2014), pp. 518–519.
    Hew Strachan, *The First World War* (London: Penguin, 2005); Holger Afflerbach, *Der Dreibund. Europäische Grossmacht-und-Allianzpolitik vor dem Ersten Weltkrieg* (Vienna: Böhlau Verlag, 2002); Holger Afflerbach and David Stevenson, eds., *An Improbable War: The Outbreak of World War I and European Political Culture Before 1914*. New York: Berghahn Books, 2007); Margaret MacMillan, *The War That Ended Peace: How Europe Abandoned Peace for the First World War* (London: Profile, 2013); John C. Röhl, *The Kaiser and his Court: Wilhelm II and the Government of Germany* (Cambridge: Cambridge University Press, 1994); Annika Mombauer, *Helmuth von Moltke and the Origins of the First World War* (Cambridge: Cambridge University Press, 2001) and "Of War Plans and War Guilt: The Debacle Surrounding the Schlieffen Plan" *Journal*

of Strategic Studies, 28, no. 5 (2005), pp. 857–885. Christopher Clark, *The Sleepwalkers* (London: Allen Lane, 2013) is the principal exception as he argues that the war was unintended. On Austria, Holger H. Herwig, *The First World War: Germany and Austria-Hungary, 1914–1918* (London: Arnold, 1998); Lawrence Sondhaus, *Franz Conrad von Hötzendorf: Architect of the Apocalypse* (Boston: Humanities Press, 2000); Günther Kronenbitter, *Krieg im Frieden: die Führung der k.u.k. Armee und die Grossmachtpolitik Österreich-Ungarns 1906–1914* (Munich: Oldenbourg, 2003); Manfred Rauchensteiner, *Der erste Weltkrieg und das Ende der Habsburger-Monarchie* (Vienna: Böhlau Verlag, 2013); Wolfram Dornik, *Des Kaisers Falke: Wirken and Nach-Wirken von Franz Conrad von Hötzendorf* (Innsbruck: Studien Verlag, 2013); Geoffrey Wawro, *A Mad Catastrophe: The Outbreak of World War I and the Collapse of the Habsburg Empire* (New York: Basic Books, 2014). For a review, Richard Ned Lebow, "What Can International Relations Theory Learn from the Origins of World War I?" *International Relations*, 28, no. 4 (2014), pp. 387–411.

81. Evan Thomas, *Robert Kennedy* (Simon & Schuster, 2002), p. 211.
82. Graham Allison, "The Thucydides Trap: Are the U.S. and China Headed for War?" *Atlantic*, 24 September 2015.
83. Richard Ned Lebow and Daniel Tompkins, "The Thucydides Claptrap," *Washington Monthly*, June 2016, http://washingtonmonthly.com/thucy-dides-claptrap (accessed 7 October 2016).
84. Richard Ned Lebow, *A Cultural Theory of International Relations* (Cambridge: Cambridge University Press, 2008), *Forbidden Fruit, Why Nations Fight: The Past and Future of War* (Cambridge: Cambridge University Press, 2013), *Constructing Cause in International Relations*, and *National Identifications and International Relations* (Cambridge: Cambridge University Press, 2016).

CHAPTER 2

Generational Learning and Foreign Policy

Until March of 1985, one of the themes most frequently touched upon by the students of the Soviet Union was the advanced age of the Soviet leadership. Prior to Brezhnev's death, the average age of the Politburo was 71. Under Andropov and Chernenko, the Soviet Union continued to be run by a gerontocracy wedded to traditional and demonstrably ineffective programs in almost all important policy areas. With the accession to power of Mikhail Gorbachev, aged 54, a much younger generation of Soviet leaders has come to the fore. The passing of the old guard has prompted widespread expectations of major changes in Soviet Union's domestic and foreign policy.

Westerners would do well to consider their own situation. Superficially, Western political leaderships have displayed considerable turnover; fresh blood, sometimes men and women in their 40s and 50s, has regularly penetrated the inner circles of policymaking elites. Only two of the prime ministers and presidents of the states in the North Atlantic Treaty Organization are over 70; the mean age of these fifteen leaders is 60. But while the governing faces have changed, what about the ideas and policies behind them? To a remarkable degree, concepts formulated in the late 1940s and early 1950s continue to dominate

Richard Ned Lebow, 'Generational Learning and Conflict Management', International Journal, 1985, Vol. 40, No. 4, pp. 555-585. Copyright © 1985 SAGE Publications. Reprinted by permission of SAGE Publications.

© The Author(s) 2018
R.N. Lebow, *Avoiding War, Making Peace*,
DOI 10.1007/978-3-319-56093-9_2

Western foreign and security policy even when they have been shown to be severely wanting. What accounts for the tenacious endurance of these ideas and policies? What implications does this have for the future course of East–West relations? What, if anything, could be done to break the hold over policymakers of outmoded notions of conflict management?

Probably the best way to explain the evolution and endurance of the dominant Western concepts of conflict management is by reference to some of the principles of cognitive psychology. The cognitive approach emphasizes the ways in which people distort decision making by gross simplifications in problem representation and information processing. Some psychologists have suggested that human beings may be incapable of carrying out the procedures associated with rational decision making.[1] Whether or not this is actually so, there is growing evidence that people process and interpret information according to a set of mental rules that bear little relationship to those of formal logic. Robert Abelson refers to these as yet poorly understood procedures as 'psycho-logic'.[2]

One principle of psycho-logic that has received some empirical verification is 'cognitive consistency'. Many experiments point to the conclusion that people try to keep their beliefs, feelings, actions, and cognitions mutually consistent. Thus, we tend to believe that people we like act in ways we approve of, have values similar to ours, and oppose people and institutions we dislike. We expect people we dislike to behave in ways repugnant to us, to have values totally dissimilar from ours, and to support people and institutions we scorn.[3] Psychologists theorize that cognitive consistency is an efficient scheme of the mental organization because it facilitates the interpretation, retention, and recall of information.[4] Be this as it may, our apparent need for cognitive order also has some adverse implications for decision making because it appears to be responsible for a systematic bias in favor of information consistent with impressions and expectations that we have already formed.

Cognitive psychologists contend that it is impossible to explain policy decisions without reference to policymakers' beliefs about the world and about the motives of other actors in it. These beliefs, organized as 'images', shape the way in which policymakers respond to external stimuli. Robert Jervis, who has applied cognitive concepts to the study of foreign affairs, suggests that the primary source of images about international relations for policymakers is stereotyped interpretations of dramatic historical events, especially wars and revolutions. These upheavals have a particularly strong impact on the thinking of younger people whose opinions about the world are still highly impressionable. Images formed by adolescents and young adults can still shape their approach to international problems years later when they may occupy important positions of authority. This may explain in the words of Jervis why 'generals are prepared to fight the last war and diplomats prepared to avoid it'.[5]

Lessons learned from history are reinforced or modified by what policymakers learn from the first-hand experience. Jervis finds that events that are personally experienced can be a 'powerful determinant' of images. This too may be a source of perceptual distortion because personal experiences may be unrepresentative or misleading. As with historical lessons, events experienced early in adult life have a disproportional impact on perceptual predispositions.[6]

Jervis makes an important distinction between what he calls 'rational' and 'irrational' consistency. The principle of consistency, he argues, helps us to make sense of new information as it draws upon our accumulated experience, formulated as a set of expectations and beliefs. It also provides continuity in our behavior. But the pursuit of consistency becomes irrational when it closes our minds to new information or different points of view. Even irrational consistency can be useful in the short run because it helps to make a decision when the time comes to act. However, persistent denial of new information diminishes our ability to learn from the environment. Policymakers must strike a balance between persistence and continuity on the one hand and openness and flexibility on the other. Jervis marshals considerable evidence to indicate that they more often err in the direction of being too wedded to established beliefs and of defending images long after they have lost their utility.[7]

Irrational consistency can leave its mark on every stage of the decision-making process. Most importantly, it affects the policymaker's receptivity to information relevant to a decision. Once an expectation or belief has taken hold, new information is assimilated to it. This means that policymakers are more responsive to information that supports their existing beliefs than they are to information that challenges them. When confronted with critical information, they tend to misunderstand it, twist its meaning to make it consistent, explain it away, deny it, or simply ignore it.

To the extent that a policymaker is confident in his expectations, he is also likely to make a decision before sufficient information has been collected or evaluated. Jervis refers to this phenomenon as 'premature cognitive closure' and sees it as a major cause of institutional inertia. As all but the most unambiguous evidence will be interpreted to confirm the wisdom of established policy and the images of reality upon which it is based, policymakers will proceed a long way down a blind alley before realizing that something is wrong.[8]

THE LESSONS OF THE 'THIRTIES

The concept of irrational consistency seems especially germane to postwar Western security policy. Until quite recently, these policies were formulated almost entirely by men who had reached maturity in the years before World War II. The origins of that monumental upheaval provided them with 'lessons' about the nature of the conflict, lessons they applied to postwar problems. Even though the policies derived from these lessons failed in many instances to achieve the ends they sought, they continue to dominate Western, particularly American, thinking about foreign policy. The most vocal criticism of these policies has come from representatives of the younger, postwar generation whose outlook on world affairs reflects a very different set of historical lessons.

Several caveats are in order before elaborating the lessons of the 1930s and their implications for postwar conflict management. From the outset, we must recognize that any portrayal of these lessons represents something of an idealized overly coherent description of what is in fact a more general, diffuse, and often inarticulate generational orientation toward international relations.[9] In practice, policymakers rarely spell out the most fundamental assumptions they make about the world, nor are they necessarily fully conscious of them. These assumptions are nevertheless crucial to understanding the evolution of policy. James Joll writes:

> When political leaders are faced with the necessity of making decisions the outcome of which they cannot foresee, in crises which they do not wholly understand, they fall back on their own instinctive reaction, traditions, and modes of behaviour. Each of them has certain beliefs, rules or objectives which are taken for granted; and one of the limitations of documentary evidence is that few people bother to write down, especially in moments of crisis, things which they take for granted. But if we are to understand their motives, we must somehow try to find out what, as we say, 'goes without saying'.[10]

A second caveat pertains to the extent to which any generational lesson is shared by the members of that particular generation. The lessons about international relations we are about to describe, while they have dominated Western and especially American foreign policy since the beginning of the Cold War, are by no means universally held by everyone who reached maturity in the late 1930s and early 1940s. There are representatives of that generation, today aged 50–75, who hold quite different views about the causes of war, the necessity of military preparedness, and the importance of demonstrating resolve. At the same time, there are many people both older and younger who share that generation's outlook on the world. Older individuals are often particularly important in formulating and articulating lessons for a younger generation. John Foster Dulles, born in 1888, and Dean Acheson, born in 1893, both played such a role for the generation under discussion. E.P. Thompson, born in 1924, has performed a similar service for much younger peace movement activists whose viewpoints, which we shall also briefly examine, clash notably with those of their elders.

Five lessons based on the origins of World War II seem particularly germane to understanding postwar approaches to conflict management. The first of these concerned the genesis of aggressive and expansionist regimes; it was attributed to the severe economic malaise which sapped the strength and undermined the legitimacy of democratic governments. This was seen to have happened in Italy, Germany, Spain, and most of Eastern Europe, where economic turbulence and decline paved the way for fascism or authoritarian regimes.

The second lesson pertains to the root causes of economic collapse, one of which was the breakdown of the international economic order. In the absence of mechanisms for regulating trade, currency exchange rates, and international debt, nations dealt with pressing economic problems in terms of their own narrow self-interests. As a result, all suffered.

The third lesson was that the relative isolation of the United States from Europe had been another fundamental cause of both the economic and political collapse of that continent. Although it was the dominant economic power, the United States provided insufficient economic leadership and remained aloof from European security problems. Washington's handling of the war debt question, its most important intervention in European economic affairs during this period, only aggravated. European economic ills after 1930. The obvious lesson was that the United States should take a more active and responsible role in European affairs in the postwar period.

The fourth lesson was about the nature of foreign policy aggression; it was an expression of a particular domestic political structure. Aggression was the fuel totalitarian dictatorships burned to maintain legitimacy; they could not survive at home without seeking to expand abroad. Their appetites for conquest were insatiable. Totalitarian states could not be appeased; concession only encouraged further demands. Hitler's Germany, Mussolini's Italy, and imperial Japan all appeared to testify to this tragic truth.

The fifth and final lesson pertained to why these dictatorships had been so successful, at least initially, in subjugating their neighbors. They had confronted a divided international community that proved incapable of organizing a united front against them. Each of the major powers sought instead to protect its security by making peace with one or more of the expansionist regimes, often at a rival's expense. The United States, Britain, and France looked the other way throughout the 1930s, allowing Japan to invade Manchuria, then China proper, and, finally, to occupy Indochina before turning on them. Italy, in turn, was given a free hand in Ethiopia and encouraged by the spinelessness of the democracies to plight its troth with Hitler. The German saga is equally well known: renunciation of the Treaty of Versailles, followed by reoccupation of the Rhineland, Anschluss with Austria, Munich and the subsequent dismemberment of Czechoslovakia, and the invasion of Poland. All of these ventures were either unopposed or even abetted by France and Britain or the Soviet Union.

In retrospect, it seems likely that Mussolini would have moderated his foreign policy if Britain and France had opposed him early on. In the beginning, Hitler too only defied the status quo when he thought he could get away with it. In his first military venture, the reoccupation of the Rhineland, he gave his generals strict instructions to beat a hasty retreat at the first sign of French resistance. Later, in May 1938, he backed away from his challenge of Czechoslovakia when it appeared that the Western powers were prepared to go to war in its defense. A.J.P. Taylor has even argued—quite incorrectly in my view—that Hitler really did not want war in 1939 but rather miscalculated. He was allegedly convinced that the British and French would back down once again in Poland as they had at Munich.[11] The policy lesson of the 1930s was painfully obvious: aggressive regimes must be opposed from the outset. Failure to do so only invites further challenge.[12]

As the preceding discussion indicates, each of these historical lessons generated specific policy imperatives. Fear of the political consequences of economic collapse led to the commitment to remake the defeated Axis nations into democracies and to encourage the revitalization of their economies in order to provide a fertile soil for democratic institutions to take root and flower. The Americans in particular feared that in the absence of a rapid reconstruction of Europe's economy, Europeans, somewhat demoralized and lacking in self-confidence, would become vulnerable to communist electoral blandishments or even communist-led coups. Well-known policy initiatives that derived from this concern include the integration of the Western occupation zones of Germany, the European Recovery Act and efforts to link West European economies together in the Coal and Steel Community and, later, the common market. American efforts to revitalize the wartorn economies of Europe and Japan by injecting capital into them were extraordinarily successful.

The second policy lesson, very much related to the first, was the need to bind the economies of all of the developed nations together in some kind of institutional framework. The purpose in doing so was to protect them against the shocks that had upset the equilibrium of Europe in the 1920s and 1930s. The Bretton Woods Agreements of 1944 marked the first step in this direction. Subsequent agreements further facilitated international economic cooperation and, in the case of Europe, have brought about a high degree of economic integration. Clearly, these policies have been remarkably successful, even allowing for the current economic troubles associated with inflation, high interest rates, and the rising value of the United States dollar.

The third policy lesson was that the United States must not withdraw from European affairs the way it had after World War I. Instead, Washington continued to take an active interest in European affairs, sponsoring or supporting numerous programs designed to facilitate European economic and political recovery. The Marshall Plan, which made billions of dollars available to the Europeans, was a significant departure from American policy following World War I, which had been primarily concerned with recovering funds loaned to the Europeans during that conflict. The United States also committed itself to the defense of Western Europe, a commitment that received institutional expression in the creation of NATO in 1949.

The final and ultimately the most controversial policy lesson was the need to oppose aggression at the outset. Putting pressure on the Russians to withdraw from northern Iran in 1947, the Truman Doctrine calling for security assistance to Greece and Turkey, and the Korean intervention in 1950 are cases in point. The influence of the events of the 1930s on the American decision to fight in Korea is particularly well documented. In his memoirs, Harry Truman relates that he was at home in Independence, Missouri, when he received word of the North Korean attack. He immediately returned to Washington:

> I had time to think aboard the plane. In my generation, this was not the first occasion when the strong had attacked the weak. I recalled some earlier instances: Manchuria, Ethiopia, Austria. I remembered how each time that the democracies failed to act it had encouraged the aggressors to keep going ahead. Communism was acting in Korea much as Hitler, Mussolini, and the Japanese had acted ten, fifteen and twenty years earlier ... If this was allowed to go on unchallenged it would mean a third world war, just as similar incidents had brought on the second world war.[13]

The apparent success of early ventures to stop communism encouraged further and more far-reaching initiatives. Korea set the pattern for Vietnam. In July 1964, on the eve of American intervention in Vietnam, Lyndon Johnson described the challenge in southeast Asia as fundamentally similar to the earlier challenges the United States had faced in Greece, Turkey, Berlin, Korea, Lebanon, and Cuba. 'The great lesson of this generation', he told a sympathetic college audience, 'is that wherever we have stood firm, aggression has ultimately been halted'.[14]

The overall record of the foreign policies derived from these five historical lessons is mixed. There were many ways in which the lessons of the 1930s were directly applicable to the postwar world and led to resounding successes. This was most notable in the economic sphere where initiatives based on the lessons we have discussed facilitated the revitalization of Western Europe and Japan. Their prosperity and political stability exceed the greatest expectations that anyone might reasonably have entertained in 1945 or 1950. The political balance sheet is less impressive. Western influence in the world has declined precipitously since 1945 and Western resources, especially American resources, have often been squandered in pursuit of illusory goals. Public opinion polls reveal that Europeans and Americans alike feel less secure today than they did 10 or 15 years ago. While there are many complex reasons why this is so, one of them is certainly the almost reflex way in which the lessons of the 1930s were applied to postwar problems.

When the Cold War began, the Soviet Union replaced Nazi Germany as the enemy and what had been learned about Hitler and his regime was held to apply to Stalin and the Soviet Union. The experience of Germany and Italy seemed to demonstrate that totalitarian regimes were driven to pursue aggressive foreign policies as the domestic atmosphere of tension and sacrifice this created was necessary for them to maintain power. They were also compelled to seek the destruction of democracies because the very existence of open societies posed a potent threat to their survival. National Security Council (NSC) 68, written on the eve of the Korean War in April 1950, and by general agreement the most influential American document of the Cold War, described the Soviet foreign policy in much these terms. 'The persistence of the idea of freedom', NSC 68 declared, 'is a permanent and continuous threat to the foundations of a slave society; and it therefore regards as intolerable the long continued existence of freedom in the world'.[15] Soviet expansion into Eastern Europe during and after World War II and the suppression of any democratic governments in these countries were taken as unambiguous confirmation of this truth.

The Soviet threat was further magnified by the application of a second insight from the 1930s to Moscow's foreign policy: the extent to which totalitarian regimes acted in terms of their avowed ideology. One of the tragic mistakes made by statesmen in the interwar years was not to read *Mein Kampf* or not to take it seriously if they had. In fact, it was a clear statement of Hitler's domestic and foreign policy objectives. Realizing their error in retrospect, Western leaders and foreign policy analysts were not going to make the same mistake a second time around. They accordingly took the writings of Marx, Lenin, and Stalin quite seriously, and many became convinced that these constituted a blueprint for Soviet behavior. The secretary of defense, James Forrestal, wondered whether Stalin kept a diary that would readjust like *Mein Kampf*.[16] John Foster Dulles declared that communist plans were all spelled out in Stalin's *Problems of Communism*: 'The present-day Communist bible ... [that] gives us the same preview that Hitler gave in *Mein Kampf*'.[17] The experience with Hitler led to an unfortunate emphasis in the West on ideology as the principal determinant of Soviet foreign policy. In its most extreme expression, Moscow's foreign policy was portrayed as part of a communist master plan for world domination. As late as 1965, the joint chiefs of staff described Vietnam in these terms to the secretary of defense and the president. In their view, that insurgency was 'part of a major campaign to extend communist control beyond the periphery of the Sino-Soviet bloc and overseas to both the island and continental areas of the Free World ... It is, in fact, a planned phase in the communist timetable for world domination'.[18] Even more moderate versions of the ideological interpretation conveyed a greater sense of threat than perhaps the reality of Soviet policy warranted. Their emphasis on Marxist–Leninist doctrine led these analysts to stress the inevitability of conflict between opposing social systems and the apparent Soviet expectations of the ultimate triumph of socialism over capitalism, probably through war and revolution.

The Soviet Union was accordingly viewed as a revolutionary force out to remake the world in its own image regardless of the price this was certain to entail for the Russian people. Such an image of the adversary made those who shared it blind to the Soviet Union's legitimate security concerns. Everything Moscow did was seen as motivated by aggressive designs. Even conciliatory gestures were viewed in this light. When Stalin's successors tried to ease East–West relations, Dulles was certain that it was a trap. 'Soviet communists', he warned in May 1953, 'have constantly taught and practiced the art of deception, of making concessions merely in order to lure others into a false sense of security, which makes them the easier victims of ultimate aggression'.[19]

As the Nazi threat was principally a military one, so too has the Soviet problem been viewed largely in military terms. Western estimates of Soviet aggressiveness have generally presupposed that it is a function of two conditions: a favorable 'correlation of forces' and an external opportunity to act. The more the conventional and nuclear military balance tilts in Moscow's direction, the greater the expectation of Soviet adventurism. NSC 68, which was based on this kind of analysis, argued that Moscow was likely to start a war when it felt certain of winning it. This might occur as early as 1954 when the Soviet Union was expected to have enough atomic bombs to launch a devastating surprise attack against the United States. NSC 68 called for a crash American effort to build up offensive and defensive military capabilities.

More recently, the same argument has been advanced by members of Reagan's administration who have warned of a 'window of vulnerability', a period during the next few years when the Soviet Union will allegedly have a strategic advantage. Reagan and his advisers (one of whom, Paul Nitze, was the principal author of NSC 68) fear that Soviet leaders will be tempted to exploit their military advantage to act more aggressively or possibly even to launch a surprise attack against the United States. Some foreign policy analysts go so far as to explain the Soviet invasion of Afghanistan as a function of their supposed strategic superiority vis-à-vis the United States.[20]

The correlation of military forces approach to the problem of Soviet aggression seems quite misleading. It naively assumes a constant Soviet desire for adventurism regulated only by external conditions that invite or discourage it. Like water pressing against a dam which will break through if there is a crack, Soviet aggression is expected whenever a political–military 'opening' presents itself. This expectation contradicts most of what we know about the sources of aggression: that it is generally a function of both external and internal conditions and carried out at least as much in response to perceptions of self-weakness as of strength.[21] Soviet policy is probably no exception. It is well to remember that the Cuban missiles crisis, the most serious Soviet challenge of American interests to date occurred at a time when the United States possessed a clear nuclear advantage and overwhelming conventional superiority in the Caribbean. According to most analysts of the crisis, Moscow's decision to put missiles into Cuba was prompted principally by fears arising from its own strategic *weakness*. It may also have appealed to Khrushchev as a means of overcoming his domestic political weakness, the result of previous policy fiascos at home and abroad.[22]

If need is an equal or even more important source of aggression than opportunity, a corresponding shift in the focus of efforts to prevent aggression is required. Too much attention is probably devoted in theory and practice to assessing the military balance and not nearly enough to trying to understand what might prompt an adversary to behave aggressively. A more realistic approach to conflict management would attempt to consider both incentives for confrontation. It would seek to discourage aggression by attempting to limit an adversary's need *and* opportunity to carry it out. It would aim never to allow one's own state to be perceived as so weak or irresolute as to invite a challenge, but at the same time, it would seek to avoid putting an adversary into the position where he felt so weak or threatened that he had the need to do so.

A third failing of Cold War policy also derived from the notion that communists are principally motivated by ideology. This belief encouraged many Western leaders to downplay national interests and differences among communist states. Instead, communist governments were seen as the building blocks of a monolithic structure at whose apex Moscow lay. This thesis was put most forcefully by a Marine colleague of mine at the Naval War College who had a not quite healed shrapnel wound in his leg. He had saved one large piece of the shell and on it was stamped 'S' for Skoda where it had evidently been made. Occasionally, little bits and pieces worked their way out, and he would rush to display them to me as proof of the worldwide nature of the communist threat. 'Look at this piece of steel', he would exclaim. 'It was made in Czechoslovakia. Probably with East German iron and Polish coal. It was then bought by the Russians who made it into a rocket and sold it to the Chinese who in turn passed it on to the North Vietnamese. They gave it to the Vietcong who put it in my leg. Don't tell me communism isn't monolithic!'

Americans who held this view were on the whole insensitive to the development of the Sino-Soviet rift and the emergence of national communism elsewhere within the Soviet bloc. Yugoslavia aside, the United States failed to exploit these differences until the opening to China in the late 1970s. Ronald Reagan still maintains that 'the only argument that caused' the Sino-Soviet split 'was an argument over how best to destroy us'.[23] Fortunately, the reality of intra-communist feuding has nevertheless forced its way into Western consciousness. Today, the continuing overvaluation of ideology has its principal effect with regard to American policy toward Central America.

Washington has been extremely hostile to revolutionary change and the emergence of left-wing regimes, convinced that they will inevitably come under the influence of the Soviet Union. This belief assumes that Marxist ideology rather than self-interest is the force motivating leaders of left-wing movements and that, as a result, they must inevitably be hostile to the West. Their rhetoric aside, the behavior of many so-called Marxist Third-World states belies this assumption. More often than not they have sought to establish amicable economic and political relations with the United States. In the cases where they have turned to the Soviet Union for support, it has often been only after meeting hostility and opposition from the United States and other Western countries. Guinea, Angola, Nicaragua—even Cuba—could be cited as cases in point. To some degree at least, Western policymakers have made their fear of left-wing regimes self-fulfilling.

The fourth policy failure concerns Western policy toward the Third World. For years, the American preoccupation with the Soviet Union made Washington insensitive to other kinds of serious security threats, most notably those arising from within the Third World. The fundamental political and economic instability of so many of these states, which nevertheless possess ever more sophisticated military arsenals and growing control over some very important economic and strategic resources, is a very serious source of conflict. It has taken a number of shocks, among them, the oil embargo, revolution in Iran, and recurrent Middle Eastern wars, to make Western policymakers aware of the extent to which challenges from or upheavals within the Third World can pose threats as grave to their security as any initiatives of Moscow and its allies. The tendency is still pronounced, particularly in Reagan's administration, to view Third-World problems solely within the context of Soviet-American rivalry. This detracts from both the West's understanding of these problems and its ability to respond to them more effectively.

The final policy failing derives from overlearning the lessons of Munich. Anxious not to repeat the British and French failure of the 1930s, American leaders have been positively zealous in their efforts to avoid communicating even the slightest hint of irresolution. They have felt it necessary to attempt to respond to every conceivable 'challenge', lest failure to do so be taken as a sign of weakness by friend and foe alike. 'Should America falter', John F. Kennedy declared, 'the whole world ... would inevitably begin to move toward the Communist bloc'.[24] American concern with credibility led to a policy of indiscriminate globalism. The outcome of regional upheavals and struggles for national liberation) were assessed less in terms of America's concrete interests than they were in terms of how they might affect other countries' perceptions of United States resolve. As the consequences of passivity were usually viewed as graver than the costs of intervention, the United States became the third party to power struggles in every corner of the globe.

The American commitment in Vietnam was the most far-reaching expression of this logic. American policymakers perceived the insurrection in the south as an attempt by world communism to expand its dominion by force. In April 1965, Lyndon Johnson explained to the American public: 'To leave Viet-Nam to its fate would shake ... confidence ... in the value of an American commitment and in the value of America's word'. One month later, he told congressmen: 'There are a hundred other little nations watching what happens ... If South

Viet-Nam can be gobbled up, the same thing can happen to them'.[25] Secretary of State Dean Rusk was particularly concerned with the symbolic value of the American commitment to South Vietnam. His fear, widely shared among Johnson's top foreign policy advisers, was of the impact a communist success would have upon future Soviet and Chinese calculations. In July 1965, he warned the president that if the United States commitment to Vietnam became unreliable, 'the communist world would draw conclusions that would lead to our ruin and almost certainly to a catastrophic war'.[26]

Although the Vietnam War ended in disaster, the logic that led to it has continued to influence American policymakers. In 1974–1975, it led the Ford administration to provide covert aid to two of the contending factions in the Angolan civil war. When Congress compelled the administration to terminate this support, an irate Henry Kissinger predicted that this 'will lead to further Soviet and Cuban pressures on the mistaken assumption that America has lost the will to counter adventurism or even to help others to do so'.[27] Similar arguments were put forward by the Carter administration to explain its commitment to defend the Persian Gulf and more recently by President Reagan to justify the increasingly active role the United States is playing in helping Central American governments combat left-wing military challenges.

There is more than a little irony in the fact that decades of zealous American efforts to safeguard credibility have done more than anything else to undermine it. Public opposition to Vietnam brought an end to the draft and made it all but impossible for any president, at least for the time being, to commit troops to combat in the Third World. It also inspired the first successful congressional efforts to limit the president's war-making powers. Nixon's concern for protecting his prerogatives led him to sanction wiretaps and other illegal acts culminating in the Watergate break-in. The Watergate débâcle further eroded presidential authority, making it difficult for subsequent occupants of the White House to implement 'linkage' or to attain Senate approval of a painstakingly negotiated arms control agreement. Previously high levels of defense spending during the Vietnam War had triggered a nearly worldwide inflation that undercut the willingness and ability of America's NATO allies to meet their defense commitments. All of this did more to encourage than dispel Nixon's and Kissinger's nightmares that friends and adversaries alike would come to see the United States as a 'pitiful helpless giant'.

A Competing Image

The image of the world that has just been described is not the only Western or even American image or set of lessons about foreign affairs. Another image and a set of lessons have emerged with another generation. In recent years, this image finds institutional expression in the European and American peace movements and in the left wing of northern European Social Democratic and Green parties; it generally reflects the views of a much younger generation.[28]

The median age of the American population is 30 and that of Western Europe, with some national variation, is almost the same. The majority of the electorate in these countries, and even some of their leaders, no longer have any personal memories of the events which were so important to those who have guided our destinies for so long. Much of the population of these countries has formulated its images of the world in response to much more recent events. The most dramatic crises and upheavals of the last two decades that have impinged upon the consciousness of young people in the United States and Western Europe are the Cuban missiles crisis, the several wars in the Middle East, and, above all, the war in Vietnam. As these events highlighted the dangers of the contemporary world and, in the case of Vietnam, represented a moral and political disaster, it is not surprising to find that many younger people are more sensitive to the failures of their elders than they are to their successes. Many of the lessons that younger people have drawn about foreign affairs directly contradict those of their parents' generation. Four such contrasts warrant discussion.

The first contrasting assumption concerns the influence of the superpowers. Peace movement activists, especially in Europe, have come to believe that the superpowers constitute equal threats to the peace of the world. If the Soviet Union has invaded Afghanistan, repeatedly used force to maintain its influence in Eastern Europe, and continues to suppress dissent at home, the United States has for its part fought a long and brutal war in Indochina, overthrown left-wing but democratic governments in Latin America, and is currently supporting numerous military dictatorships around the world. The Russians may be a nasty lot but at least they have the virtue of being predictable and on the whole conservative in their behavior. Americans may be a trifle more benign, some are willing to admit, but they may also destroy everyone by reason of their impetuosity and paranoia. For many in the European peace movement uncomfortable with the prospect of their countries becoming a nuclear battleground for the superpowers, the way out is through disengagement. This is the thrust of the Campaign for Nuclear Disarmament in Britain, the Green party in Germany, and similar movements elsewhere in Western Europe. While differences of opinion exist within and among these peace movements, most of the activists oppose any increase in military spending, are against NATO's tactical nuclear modernization program, and generally favor withdrawal of their respective countries from NATO.

Advocates of these positions have for the most part adopted a view of the Soviet Union that is conveniently congruent with their policy recommendations. They describe Moscow's foreign policy as motivated more by defensive than offensive purposes. Soviet domination of Eastern Europe, for example, is portrayed as an understandable reaction to the fear of yet another invasion from the West. The Soviet invasion of Afghanistan is seen in the same light. Peace movement activists also tend to interpret the Soviet arms buildup as a largely defensive measure, as a response to the development of an awesome nuclear arsenal by the West. They maintain that NATO not the Warsaw pact possesses a significant nuclear advantage, an advantage which explains Soviet's efforts to deploy more modern theater and intercontinental weapons. They also hold the United States culpable for pioneering the variety of technological breakthroughs that has fuelled the arms race and led to the present situation where both sides possess the means to destroy much of the human race. E.P. Thompson, for years the leading intellectual in the British campaign for nuclear disarmament, ventures the judgment:

> The United States seems to me to be the more dangerous and provocative in its general military and diplomatic strategies, which press around the Soviet Union with menacing bases. It is in Washington, rather than in Moscow, that scenarios are dreamed up for 'theatre' wars; and it is in America that the 'alchemists' of super-kill, the clever technologists of 'advantage' and ultimate weapons, press forward 'the politics of tomorrow'.[29]

The failure of SALT II, statements by President Reagan and his advisers about the feasibility of limited nuclear war, and, most recently, the administration's commitment to Star Wars have further fuelled anti-American feeling in Europe.

If the older generation has been concerned with the military balance, the younger generation, especially those in the peace movement, is more concerned with weapons themselves. They worry less that war might arise as a calculated act of aggression and more than it could come about as a miscalculated act of defense. In an acute crisis, leaders on either side, convinced that their adversary was preparing to attack, could respond in ways that made their fear of war self-fulfilling.

Some peace movement activists, especially in Europe, hold the United States responsible for the tensions of the Cold War. A more common view interprets the Cold War as an irrational escalating spiral of suspicion and hostility between the superpowers. International theorists have described such a spiral as a 'security dilemma'.[30] According to this formulation, the anarchy of the international environment compels national leaders to expand their power and influence even though this may run counter to their inclinations and interests. The ensuing competition among states, undertaken in the name of security, leads to greater insecurity. The more obvious catalyst of insecurity is military preparations. States arm because they feel threatened. But arms build-ups almost inevitably arouse the fear and suspicion of those they are meant to protect against. As adversaries add to their arsenals, each in the eyes of the other accumulates more weapons than it needs for legitimate defensive purposes, only confirming the other's suspicion of its aggressive intent.

In the end, arms buildups, initially an *effect* of tensions between two states, become a principal *cause* of them. Peace movement spokesmen maintain that this is precisely what has happened with the two superpowers; both are armed to the hilt with the most destructive weapons the world has ever seen but feel ever more threatened as their respective arsenals grow. An open letter to Americans from the German peace movement put it this way:

> The arms race during the past three decades has only made the United States, Europe, and the countries of the Warsaw Pact less secure and more threatened. A further arms buildup raises rather than lowers the chance of war. The strategy of deterrence, pursued in both East and West, has entered a dead-end street. The gigantic armaments programs increasingly affect the social well-being and quality of life of Americans and Europeans as well as impede necessary aid for the Third World. We therefore need a new security policy and a new peace policy.[31]

The peace movement aspires to cut through the escalating spiral of insecurity and armament by halting the deployment of more means of destruction. As the introduction of such weapons in the past significantly exacerbated the fears of both sides, so they expect that restraint would ease those fears in the future. Such an amelioration might pave the way for an actual reduction in arms, leading ultimately to disarmament. It could also be expected to reduce the intensity of superpower competition in other areas, further diminishing mutual perceptions of hostility. For many activists in the peace movement, the 'tragedy' of insecurity, not the 'evil' of the adversary, is responsible for the danger of war. If the insecurity can be assuaged, peace may follow.

A third important difference between the two generations concerns the meaning of affluence. The generation that came to power in the years after 1945 conceived of economic development as the key to stability and did everything in its power to bring it about. Many among the younger generation see affluence as a curse because it destroys the environment, erodes important traditional values, and encourages corruption. In their view, it has led to a Europe of bureaucrats who are insensitive to the needs of the young, the old, and the poor but very solicitous of the interests of those who disfigure the land with expressways and nuclear power plants. 'We're the generation that grew up asking our parents what they did during the Hitler years and the war', explained Anton Whittner, a 38-year- old cabinet maker and Green activist. 'They told us they were innocent and we didn't believe them. When my son grows up and asks "Daddy where were you when they turned Germany into concrete?" I have to have an answer'.[32]

There is truth in this argument. Affluence has often been attained at some cost to the environment and to social values that contribute to the quality of life. Nor has wealth brought happiness or the kind of world young people would like to see. However, no growth, the policy favored by some activists, is not a solution to the problem. Trade-offs must nevertheless be made between development and quality of life even though they are difficult to define with any precision and even more difficult to make in practice.

The fourth lesson that many of the younger generation have drawn from their experience with the world is that their elders erred in giving primacy to East–West questions. For them, the real threat to peace is the widening gap between the rich and the poor and for this reason North–South issues should receive primacy. The West should be more concerned with alleviating the poverty of the Third World than in opposing the spread of Soviet influence. Those in the peace movement, especially in Europe, call for a shift in resources, emotional, human, and economic, in order to address this problem.

Once again, this critique offers an important corrective to the over-emphasis of the older generation of the Cold War.

Economic and political chaos in the Third World may pose a greater threat to the survival of our way of life than do the ambitions of the Soviet Union. Many experts believe that the first nuclear war will not be fought between the Soviet Union and the West but rather between two underdeveloped countries, one of which feels sufficiently threatened to use such weapons against its traditional enemy.[33] This said, the solutions most often put forward to address this problem—more aid and some kind of restructuring of economic relations to free Third-World countries of their continuing dependence on the West—appear simplistic. It is by no means apparent that a trebling or even quadrupling of aid to poorer countries will promote any more development or result in any real improvement in living standards. Much of the aid already given is wasted because the countries in question are structurally unable to absorb it effectively. Even a radical reorganization of North–South economic relations, assuming for the moment that this is possible, would do nothing to affect the political instability or the host of idiosyncratic cultural barriers that often stand in the way of development. Efforts to modernize the countries too rapidly also tend to intensify existing cleavages within them and bring about the kind of anti-modern backlash that we have witnessed in Iran, a phenomenon increasingly apparent in other countries as well.

CONCLUSIONS

The two images of international relations that we have described reflect different generational experiences. They contain foreign policy lessons based on a very different set of events. These images and the lessons associated with them are useful to policymakers in two ways: they provide conceptual tools to understand and order the world, and they offer policy guidelines for dealing with some of the problems so identified. The success of postwar occupation policies in Japan and Germany attests to the prescriptive power of these lessons.

Policy lessons can also be misleading. Lessons appropriate to the context in which they were learned can mistakenly be applied to a new situation because it bears a superficial resemblance to the previous one. While it is certainly true, for example, that the failure to oppose Nazi Germany from the outset helped to bring about World War II, it is by no means obvious that containment was the appropriate response to the problem posed by the Soviet Union. American policy has nevertheless been based on that analogy since the beginning of the Cold War. Tragically, it has also become at least partly self-validating. The American postmortem of the Cuban missiles crisis, itself a major source of foreign policy 'lessons', offers a telling example of how this phenomenon works.[34]

There is not a shred of evidence in support of President Kennedy's belief at the time that Khrushchev acted as he did to demonstrate American weakness and irresolution to the world.[35] As was noted earlier, it seems more likely that the Soviet move was motivated by Moscow's concern for its own strategic weakness and that the missiles were put into Cuba as a 'quick fix' for a questionable Soviet deterrent. Kennedy's view of the matter nevertheless infected the journalists and academics around him who publicized it in their portrayals of the crisis. Confirmed tautologically, the 'courage and commitment' thesis became one of the most entrenched shibboleths of the Cold War. It reconfirmed in the minds of American policymakers the most enduring policy lesson of the 1930s: the axiom that questionable resolve invites challenges and its corollary that unquestioned resolve deters them.

Our critique of historical learning is equally applicable to the competing image of international affairs. It too is based on superficial historical learning and its policy prescriptions are just as unidimensional. Once again, East–West relations provide a useful illustration of this point.

Whereas the Cold War image emphasized the aggressive nature of Soviet foreign policy and totally ignored legitimate defensive motivations, the competing image is extremely sensitive to these defensive needs but denies or seeks to explain away any offensive objectives on the part of Moscow. Both interpretations represent one-sided and simplistic views of both the Soviet Union and the nature of superpower conflict. For this reason, their policy prescriptions also tend to be unrealistic.

The principal policy recommendation of the competing image with regard to East–West relations is to substitute a policy of what might be called reassurance for one of deterrence. Adherents of this image advocate renewal of détente and revival of SALT II, together with new arms control measures. They also call for a declaration of 'no first use' of nuclear weapons and a nuclear moratorium, even a unilateral one, including withdrawal of the recently deployed Pershing IIs and ground-launched cruise missiles in Europe. These recommendations are based on the hope and expectation that Western initiatives to defuse Cold War tensions will elicit a reciprocal Soviet response.

Those who subscribe to the competing image maintain with some justification that the West has more often than not misinterpreted Soviet motives in the past. Western leaders have consistently sought to explain Soviet behavior in terms of their allegedly aggressive design even when such an interpretation was unwarranted by the facts of the situation. John Foster Dulles' belief that the post-Stalin thaw in Soviet policy was a trap, cited earlier, is just one example. Surely, however, there is every reason to suppose that Soviet leaders are just as myopic as their Western counterparts. Their reaction to the Marshall Plan might be cited as evidence. According to John Gaddis, Stalin and Molotov interpreted American offers to postwar reconstruction aid as motivated by America's need to find markets to absorb its expected peacetime over-production. Moscow was accordingly convinced that it would be doing Washington a favor by accepting loans or grants and thus demanded political concessions in return. Needless to say, the Americans, who perceived their offers of assistance as altruistic, took the Russian response as an expression of hostility.[36]

As 30 years of Cold War tensions have done much to reinforce negative expectations on both sides, it is unrealistic to suppose that Moscow would react to unilateral measures of restraint with reciprocal gestures of its own. It seems possible that initiatives of this kind would be interpreted as signs of weakness instead of good will, as concessions to the increasingly powerful peace movements on both sides of the Atlantic. If so, restraint or concessions might elicit the very opposite response of that intended. This is, of course, what Western 'hardliners' contend and the reason they oppose such initiatives. The tragedy here is that if the hardliners are right, they are also responsible to a great extent for bringing this state of affairs about. The confrontational policies they and their predecessors have for so many years pursued toward the Soviet Union have helped to create an image of the United States in Moscow inconsistent with any notion of American self-restraint or freely granted concessions.

Mutual cognitive rigidity may be the most serious impediment to the amelioration of superpower conflict. Like armaments, the expectation of hostile intent was initially an effect of Cold War tensions but today has become a principal cause of them. Leaders on either side of the super-power divide who want to improve relations with the adversary must recognize the gravity of this problem and devise a strategy for overcoming it. For any measure, no matter how well conceived, will do little to defuse tensions unless it is somehow perceived as sincerely motivated by the other side.

It is apparent that these two images of international affairs represent different swings of the generational pendulum. The competing image is primarily a reaction to the policy failures, so apparent in the 1960s and 1970s, of the Cold War image of international relations. Its policy prescriptions are in every case the reverse of those derived from the Cold War image. The Cold War image in turn was formulated in response to the foreign policy failures of the 1930s. It too called for strategies of managing conflict that were just about diametrically opposed to the policies that had preceded it. Appeasement and some of the other unsuccessful policies of the 1930s were for their part a reaction to more confrontational policies that were seen in retrospect to have been responsible for the First World War.

This chain of reaction and response is ominous in its implications. In each instance, strategies of conflict management that sought to avoid repeating the mistakes of the recent past succeeded in doing so but failed for an entirely different set of reasons. One explanation for this we have already noted: the tendency to apply policy lessons learned in one context to another in which they are inappropriate and possibly disastrous. Another explanation probably arises directly from the concern to avoid past mistakes.

Policymakers can become so sensitive to particular problems that they become correspondingly insensitive, perhaps even blind, to other issues or causes of conflict. The policies they implement to address the problems or causes of conflict that concern them, whether successful or not, can have the effect of aggravating those which they have ignored. Deterrence, for example, is a strategy designed to discourage aggression by raising its cost. Proponents of deterrence are often insensitive to the ways in which armaments and threats—the currency of deterrence—can intensify hostility between rival powers by reason of the aggressive intentions they convey. Conversely, those who focus on the detrimental effects of the arms race often ignore the range of problems independent of weaponry that cast the superpowers in adversarial roles. Unilateral restraint with respect to weapons would not address any of these problems and conceivably could make some of them worse.

The preceding discussion is not meant to detract from the fact that both images of international affairs are based on important truths about the nature of conflict and the possible ways of coping with or even preventing it. However, it is equally clear that the flashes of insight permitted to any generation illuminate only a small corner of the truth about the complexities of interstate relations. Policymakers, East and West, nevertheless seem prone to mistake their generation's insights for the total sum of wisdom. Until such time, as scholars and leaders alike can free themselves of this illusion they seem doomed to write yet another act in the continuing tragedy of generational over-reaction and inappropriate response.

NOTES

1. The experimental literature is reviewed by Paul Stone, Baruch Fischoff, and Sara Lichtenstein in 'Behavioral decision theory,' in Mark R. Rosenzweig and Lyman W. Porter, eds, *Annual Review of Psychology* 28 (Palo Alto: Annual Reviews 1977), 1–34; Robert P. Abelson, 'Social psychology's rational man,' in S.I. Benn and G.W. Mortimore, eds, *Rationality and the Social Sciences: Contributions to the Philosophy and Methodology of the Social Sciences* (Boston: Routledge & Kegan Paul 1976), 59–89; Melvin Manis, 'Cognitive social psychology and attitude change,' *American Behavioral Scientist* 21 (May–June 1978), 675–690.

2. Robert P. Abelson and Milton Rosenberg, 'Symbolic psycho-logic,' *Behavioral Science* 3 (January 1958), 1–13; Robert P. Abelson, 'Psychological implication,' in Abelson et al., *Theories of Cognitive Consistency: A Sourcebook* (Chicago: Rand- McNally 1968), 112–139, and Abelson, 'Social psychology's rational man,' 59–89.

3. The literature on cognitive consistency is considerable. For discussion of it, see, Robert Zajonc, 'Cognitive theories in social psychology,' in Gardner Lindzey and Elliot Aronson, eds, *The Handbook of Social Psychology* (2nd ed; Reading MA: Addison-Wesley 1968), 1, 345–353; Abelson et al., *Theories of Cognitive Consistency*, Stevan Sherman and Robert Wolosin, 'Cognitive biases in a recognition task,' *Journal of Personality* 41 (September 1973), 395–411; Jesse Delia and Walter Crockett, 'Social schemas, cognitive complexity, and the learning of social structures,' *Journal of Personality* 41 (September 1973), 412–429.

4. The various explanations for cognitive consistency are discussed by Norman Feather, 'A structural balance approach to the analysis of

communication effects,' in Leonard Berkowitz, ed, *Advances in Experimental Social Psychology* (New York: Academic Press 1967), 111, 99–165.

5. Robert Jervis, 'Hypotheses on misperception,' *World Politics* 20 (April 1968), 454–479, and *Perception and Misperception in International Politics* (Princeton: Princeton University Press 1976), 117–124, 187, 262–270. For another analysis by political scientists of the implications of cognitive processes for decision making, see Robert Axelrod, *Framework for a General Theory of Cognition and Choice* (Berkeley: Institute of International Studies 1972); Robert Axelrod, ed, *Structure of Decision: The Cognitive Maps of Political Elites* (Princeton: Princeton University Press 1976); Richard Ned Lebow, *Between Peace and War: The Nature of International Crisis* (Baltimore: Johns Hopkins University Press 1981).

6. Jervis, *Perception and Misperception*, 239–248.

7. Ibid., 17–42, et passim.

8. Ibid., 187–191.

9. On the concept of the generation and its political significance, the two classical works remain a series of short essays by José Ortega y Gosset first published in book form as *El tema de nuestro tempo* (Madrid 1923) and Karl Mannheim's two- part article, 'Das Problem der Generationen,' *Vierteljahrshefte fur Soziologie* 8 (1928), 157–185, 309–329, reprinted in Paul Kecskemeti, ed, *Essays on the Sociology of Knowledge* (New York: Oxford University Press 1952). For a critical review of more recent literature on the concept, see A. Esler, *Generations in History* (1982).

10. James Joll, *The Unspoken Assumptions: An Inaugural Lecture Delivered 25 April 1968* (London: Weidenfeld & Nicolson 1968) 6.

11. A.J.P. Taylor, *The Origins of the Second World War (2nd ed; New York: Athe-neum 1961).*

12. Ernest R. May, *"Lessons" of the Past: The Use and Misuse of History in American Foreign Policy* (New York: Oxford University Press 1973), attempts to explain the American intervention in Vietnam as at least in part the result of the lessons American policymakers had learned from the 1930s. Although written to influence thinking during the Vietnam debate, it remains a provocative work by reason of its broader implications about the ways in which policy is influenced by history.

13. Harry S. Truman, *Memoirs* (2 vols; Garden City NY: Doubleday 1955–1956), 11, 332–333.

14. Lyndon B. Johnson, press conference statement, 28 July 1965, *Public Papers of the Presidents: Lyndon B. Johnson* (6 vols; Washington DC: Government Printing Office 1965–1969), *1965, 794–795*.

15. NSC 68, in *Foreign Relations of the United States, 1950* (Washington DC: Government Printing Office 1977), 1, 245.

16. Gregg Herken, *The Winning Weapon: The Atomic Bomb in the Cold War, 1945–1950* (New York: Alfred Knopf 1980), 202, citing from Forrestal's papers.

17. John Foster Dulles speech at the National War College, 10 June 1953, *Department of State Bulletin*, 28 (29 June 1953), 895.

18. Joint Chiefs of Staff, memorandum for the Secretary of Defense, 13 January 1962, *The Pentagon Papers: The Defense Department History of the United States Decisionmaking on Vietnam* (4 vols; The Senator Gravel edition; Boston: Beacon Press 1971), 11, 664.

19. John Foster Dulles' speech to New York State Republican Dinner, 7 May 1953. *Department of State Bulletin*, 28 (18 May 1953), 707. For Eisenhower's fixation on the monolithic and uncompromising nature of 'world communism,' see John Lewis Gaddis, *Strategies of Containment: A Critical Appraisal of Postwar American National Security Policy* (New York: Oxford University Press 1982), 140–142.

20. Edward N. Luttwak, 'After Afghanistan, what?' *Commentary* (April 1980), 40–49 Norman Podhoretz, 'The present danger,' *Commentary* (March 1980), 27–40.

21. See Richard Ned Lebow, *Between Peace and War*, *passim*, and 'Windows of opportunity: do states jump through them?' *International Security* 9 (summer 1984), 147–186.

22. This literature is reviewed in Richard Ned Lebow, 'The Cuban missile crisis: reading the lessons correctly,' *Political Science Quarterly* 98 (fall 1983), 431–458.

23. Interview with Robert Scheer, *With Enough Shovels: Reagan, Bush and Nuclear War* (New York: Random House 1982), 242.

24. Remarks at the High School Memorial Stadium in Great Falls, Montana, 26 September 1963, *Public Papers of the Presidents of the United States: John F. Kennedy: 1963* (Washington DC: Government Printing Office 1964.

25. Lyndon Johnson's Johns Hopkins address, 7 April 1965, and Johnson remarks to members of congressional committees, 4 May 1965, *Public Papers of the Presidents: Lyndon B. Johnson: 1965,* 395 and 491.

26. Rusk memorandum, 1 July 1965, *The Pentagon Papers*, iv, 23.

27. Kissinger speech at Dallas, Texas, 22 March 1976, in Henry A. Kissinger, *American Foreign Policy* (3rd ed; New York: W.W. Norton 1977), 360.

28. There is considerable disagreement about the extent to which generational experience has led to significant differences in foreign policy attitudes. Ole R. Holsti and James N. Rosenau, *American Leadership in World Affairs: Vietnam and the Breakdown of Consensus* (Boston: Allen and Unwin 1984), deny that there is any such effect in the case of the United States. Studies that stress the important role of generational

differences in European politics include Harold Muller and Thomas Risse-Kappen, 'Social generational change: the German peace movement and the Western alliance,' and Heinz-Ulrich Kohr and Hans Georg Rader', West German youth and NATO', papers presented at the conference on Generational Learning and Foreign Policy: The Future of the Atlantic Alliance, 16–17 May 1983, at the Bologna Center of The Johns Hopkins University, and Ronald Inglehart, 'Generational change and the future of the Atlantic alliance', *PS* 17 (summer 1984), 525–535.

29. E.P. Thompson, *Protest and Survive* (2nd ed; London: Campaign for Nuclear Disarmament 1980), 25.
30. The security dilemma was first described by Herbert Butterfield, *History and Human Relations* (London: Collins 1951), 19–20, and later by John Herz, *Political Realism and Political Idealism* (Chicago: University of Chicago Press 1959), 4. For a more recent treatment, see Jervis, *Perception and Misperception*, 58–116.
31. 'An open letter to Americans from the West German peace movement,' *The Nation*, 12 January 1982, 721.
32. Cited in Roger Thurow and Diane Coutu, 'Greening of Germany? Young leftist party shakes Bonn establishment by urging disarmament and leaning eastward,' *Wall Street Journal*, 22 December 1982, 36.
33. See the 'Adelphi Poll' conducted by Warren Boroson with David P. Snyder, 'The first nuclear war,' *NEXT* magazine, 1 (September–October 1980), 29–37.
34. For a critical analysis of the policy 'lessons' of the Cuban crisis see James A. Nathan, 'The missile crisis: his finest hour now,' *World Politics* 27 (January 1975), 265–281.
35. Lebow, 'The Cuban missile crisis: reading the lessons correctly,' addresses this question and the roots of Kennedy's concern.
36. John Lewis Gaddis, *The United States and the Origins of the Cold War*, 1942–1947 (New York: Columbia University Press 1972), 174–198.

CHAPTER 3

Deterrence: A Political and Psychological Critique

Postwar American security policy was built on a foundation of deterrence. In the early Cold War period, American leaders relied on nuclear deterrence to discourage Soviet or Chinese attacks against American allies in Western Europe and the Far East. When these countries developed the means to launch intercontinental nuclear attacks of their own, the USA counted on deterrence to prevent an attack against itself. Over the years, successive American administrations have also attempted to use deterrence to moderate the policies of Third-World states with which the USA or its allies have come into conflict. Partisans of deterrence assert that it has kept the peace between the superpowers and has been useful in managing lesser conflicts. This chapter disputes both claims.[1]

When discussing deterrence, it is important to distinguish between the theory of deterrence and the strategy of deterrence. The former pertains to the logical postulates of deterrence and the assumptions on which they are based. Put succinctly, deterrence is an attempt to influence another actor's assessment of its interests. It seeks to prevent an undesired behavior by convincing the party who may be contemplating it that the cost will exceed any possible gain. Deterrence presupposes that

Richard Ned Lebow, 'Deterrence: A Political and Psychological Critique', Perspectives on Deterrence, 1989, pp. 26-51. Copyright © 1989 Oxford University Press. Reprinted by permission of Oxford University Press.

© The Author(s) 2018
R.N. Lebow, *Avoiding War, Making Peace*,
DOI 10.1007/978-3-319-56093-9_3

decisions are made in response to some kind of rational cost-benefit calculus, that this calculus can be successfully manipulated from the outside, and that the best way to do this is to increase the cost side of the ledger. Different scholars have developed their own variants of deterrence theory. All of them, however, are based on these assumptions.

Deterrence strategy is concerned with applying the theory of deterrence to real world conflicts. It has given rise to its own body of theory about how this is best accomplished. The first wave of this theory, almost entirely deductive in nature, was developed in the 1950s and 1960s by scholars such as Bernard Brodie (1959), William Kaufmann (1954), and Thomas Schelling (1966). Most of these works stressed the importance of imparting credibility to commitments and explored various mechanisms leaders could exploit toward this end. The literature of this period is often referred to as classical deterrence theory (Jervis 1979).

Classical deterrence spawned a number of critiques. For our purposes, the most interesting were those that attempted to evaluate deterrence strategy in light of empirical evidence from historical cases. The works of Milburn (1959), Russett (1967), Snyder and Diesing (1977), and George and Smoke (1974) are representative of this wave of theorizing. These scholars sought to refine the strategy of deterrence in order to make it more useful to statesmen. Milburn, Russett, and George and Smoke argued that deterrence might be made more efficacious if threats of punishment were accompanied by promises of reward for acceptable behavior. George and Smoke and Snyder and Diesing sought to divorce deterrence from its Cold War context and root it in a less politically specific theory of initiation.

Empirical analyses of deterrence had implications for the postulates of deterrence theory. On the basis of their case studies, George and Smoke (1974) argued for a broader formulation of rational choice. They hoped that this would enable the theory to incorporate domestic political concerns and other factors affecting foreign policy behavior that deterrence theory had not previously taken into account.

This essay incorporates and expands upon elements of previous critiques to develop a more far-reaching critique of deterrence. The scholars I have cited argue that deterrence sometimes fails because it is implemented poorly or applied in circumstances in which it is inappropriate. Their criticisms, and those of George Quester in Chap. 3, are directed primarily at the strategy of deterrence. I argue that deterrence is by its very nature a seriously flawed strategy *and* theory of conflict management. I do not believe that attempts to improve and reformulate the theory will produce a better fit between its expectations and observable behavior across cases.

The critique of deterrence that Janice Gross Stein and I have developed (Lebow and Stein 1987a) has three interlocking components: the political, psychological, and practical. Each exposes a different set of problems with the theory and strategy of deterrence. In practice, these problems are often linked; political and practical factors interact with psychological processes to multiply the obstacles to successful prediction of state behavior and successful conflict management.

The political component examines the motivations behind foreign policy challenges. Deterrence is unabashedly a theory of 'opportunity'. It asserts that adversaries seek opportunities to make gains and pounce when they find them. Case studies of actual conflicts point to an alternative explanation for resorts to force, which we term a theory of 'need'. The evidence indicates that strategic vulnerabilities and domestic political needs often constitute incentives to use force. When leaders become desperate, they may resort to force even when the military balance is unfavorable and there are no grounds for doubting adversarial resolve. Deterrence may be an inappropriate and even dangerous strategy in these circumstances. For if leaders are driven less by the prospect of gain than they are by the fear of loss, deterrent policies can provoke the very behavior they are designed to forestall by intensifying the pressures on the challenger to act.

The psychological component is also related to the motivation behind deterrence challenges. To the extent that policymakers believe in the necessity of challenging commitments of their adversaries, they become predisposed to see their objectives as attainable. When this happens, motivated errors can be pronounced and identifiable. They can take the form of distorted threat assessments and insensitivity to warnings that the policies to which our leaders are committed are likely to end in disaster. Policymakers can convince themselves, despite evidence to the contrary, that they can challenge an important adversarial commitment without provoking war. Because they know the extent to which they are powerless to back down, they expect their adversaries to accommodate them by doing so. Policymakers may also seek comfort in the illusion that their country will emerge victorious at little cost to itself if the crisis gets out of hand and leads to war. Deterrence can thus be defeated by wishful thinking.

The practical component of the critique describes some of the most important obstacles to implementing deterrence. These derive from the distorting effects of cognitive biases and heuristics, political and cultural barriers to empathy, and the differing cognitive contexts the deterrer and would-be challengers are apt to use to frame and interpret signals. Problems of this kind are not unique to deterrence; they are embedded in the very structure of international relations. They nevertheless constitute particularly severe impediments to deterrence because of the deterrer's need to understand the world as it appears to the leaders of a would-be challenger in order to manipulate effectively their cost-benefit calculus. Failure to do this in the right way can result in deterrent policies that actually succeed in making the proscribed behavior more attractive to a challenger.

The first two components of this critique challenge core assumptions of deterrence theory. The third component is directed at the strategy of deterrence. But it also has implications for deterrence theory. If the strategy of deterrence is so often unsuccessful because of all of the practical difficulties associated with its implementation, then the theory of deterrence must be judged a poor guide to action.

In assessing deterrence theory it is imperative to distinguish between the motives and opportunity to carry out a military challenge. Classical deterrence theory takes as a given a high level of hostility on the part of the adversary and assumes that a challenge will be made if the opportunity exists. In the absence of opportunity, no challenge will occur even though hostility remains high. Because it sees aggression as opportunity driven, deterrence theory prescribes defensible, credible commitments as the best way to prevent military challenges.

Our case material points to the importance of motive; hostility cannot be treated as a constant. In practice, it waxes and wanes as a function of specific foreign and domestic circumstances. There are, moreover, few states or leaders who are driven by pure hostility toward their adversaries. Hitler is the exception, not the rule. This is not to deny the existence of opportunity-based challenges. Postwar examples include India's invasion of Pakistan in 1971, Iraq's invasion of Iran in 1980, and Israel's invasion of Lebanon in 1982.

In most adversarial relationships, leaders resort to military challenges only in extraordinary circumstances. Our cases suggest that this is most likely to occur when leaders confront acute political and strategic vulnerabilities. In these circumstances, military challenges may be carried out even when there is no apparent opportunity to do so. Leaders may convince themselves, quite without objective reason, that such opportunity

Table 3.1 Deterrence matrix

	Opportunity (in the form of an adversary's vulnerable commitment)	
	No	Yes
Motive (hostility assumed constant)	No challenge	Challenge

Table 3.2 Lebow-Stein matrix

		Opportunity (in the form of an adversary's vulnerable commitment)	
Motive (needs in the form strategic and domestic value)	Low need	No challenge	No challenge
	High need	Possible to likely	Very likely

exists. When leaders do not feel impelled by political and strategic needs, they are unlikely to carry out challenges even when they perceive the opportunity to do so.

The matrices in Tables 3.1 and 3.2 summarize some of the most important differences between the classical theory of deterrence and our findings about military challenges. These differences are explained by the political and psychological components of our critique of deterrence. The third component of that critique, the practical difficulties of implementing deterrence, pertains primarily to deterrence as a strategy. However, to the extent that it indicates the pervasive presence of serious obstacles in the way of applying deterrence, it suggests that deterrence theory is not a good guide for formulating strategy.

In the real world, there can be no truly dichotomous distinction between opportunity and need as motives for military challenges. Many, if not most challenges, contain elements of both motives. In the case of Iran–Iraq, many analysts (Heller 1984; Tripp 1986) argue that Iraq attacked because of a complex mixture of motives. It saw the opportunity to take advantage of Iran's internal disarray—clearly a motive of opportunity—but also acted out of fear that the Ayatollah Ruhollah Khomeini would attempt to export Iran's revolution in order to overthrow Iraq's regime. Most of the cases we examined were nevertheless skewed toward one or the other of the extremes. For the purposes of analysis we have classified these cases accordingly.

DATA AND METHOD

Most of the evidence on which this analysis is based comes from historical case studies Janice Stein and I have published in *Between Peace and
War* (Lebow 1981), *Psychology and Deterrence* (Jervis et al. 1985) and
various articles. Both books analyzed deterrence encounters from the
perspective of both sides; they examined the calculations, expectations,
and actions of the challenger as well as those of the would-be deterrer.
As the key to understanding deterrence successes and failures lies in the
nature of the interactions between the adversaries, case studies of this
kind shed more light on these phenomena than analyses of the deliberations and policies of only one of the involved parties.

Most of these cases are deterrence failures. Janice Stein and I have
chosen to work with failures because they are more readily identifiable,
thereby facilitating the construction of a valid universe of cases. Deterrence
successes can result in inaction. Failures, by contrast, lead to serious crises and often to wars. Events of this kind are not only highly visible but
almost always prompt memoirs, official inquiries, and other investigations
that provide the data essential for scholarly analyses. Deterrence failures are
also more revealing than deterrence successes of the complexities of international relations. Understanding why deterrence fails may lead to insights
into the nature of conflict as well as to a more general understanding of
the circumstances in which deterrence is likely to succeed or fail and the
reasons why this is so. Nevertheless, restricting the analysis to deterrence
failures imposes costs. Explanations of the causes of failure can only be tentative, because some of the factors that appear to account for failure may
also be at work when deterrence succeeds. Hypotheses derived from a controlled comparison of cases of deterrence failure will ultimately have to be
validated against identified instances of deterrence success.

What is a deterrence failure? The goal of deterrence is to dissuade
another actor from carrying out a proscribed behavior. In the context of
international relations, the most important objective of deterrence is prevention of a use of force. To do this, the theory stipulates that the deterrer must carefully define the unacceptable behavior, make a reasonable
attempt to communicate a commitment to punish transgressors (or deny
them their objectives), possess the means to do this, and demonstrate the
resolve to carry through on its threat (Kaufmann 1954; Kissinger 1960;
Brodie 1959; Kaplan 1958; Milburn 1959; Quester 1966; Schelling
1966: 374).[2] When these conditions are met and the behavior still
occurs, we can speak of a deterrence failure.[3]

Researchers can and do disagree among themselves about the extent to which any or all of these conditions were met in a specific instance. These disagreements usually concern the credibility of the threat, something deterrence theorists consider to be the quintessential condition of the strategy's success. Unfortunately, it is also the most difficult to assess. This can be a serious problem, as it hinders a determination of whether a deterrence failure was due to the inadequacy of the strategy or merely to the failure of the country in question to implement it adequately. Deterrence supporters invariably argue the latter when critics make the case for the former (Orme 1987; Lebow 1987b).

The ongoing debate about the efficacy of deterrence is fueled by the inherent subjectivity of all interpretations of historical events. One way to cope with this problem is to use a sample large enough to minimize the significance of disagreements about individual cases. My arguments are therefore based on 10 examples of deterrence failure.[4] These cases are interesting not only because they document a pattern of deterrence failure, but because they illustrate diverse reasons why failures occur. Evidence from conflicts in which leaders used other kinds of strategies of conflict management will also be introduced where it is relevant.

There is a further difficulty that arises from presenting arguments based on case studies. In contrast to experimental or survey research, it is impossible to summarize data of this kind in a succinct manner. Nor would such a summary establish the validity of the findings even if it can be demonstrated that the nature of the database and the data analysis conformed to accepted research practice. As I have already observed, the reader must be convinced of the correctness of our interpretation of individual cases. Consequently, it is important to convey something of the flavor of the cases and the basis for our interpretation of the evidence. For this reason, I have chosen to incorporate as much case material as space permits. Readers who are interested in the data are referred to *Psychology and Deterrence, Between Peace and War*, and the several journal articles cited for a fuller exposition of the cases.

POLITICAL FAILINGS

Deterrence theory assumes that utility, defined in terms of the political and material well-being of leaders and their states, can readily be measured. But political and national interests are subjective concepts. They are perceived different by different leaders, making it extremely difficult for outsiders to determine, let alone measure. It is even more difficult, if not impossible, to weigh the relative importance of emotional, intangible, unquantifiable concerns that history reveals to be at least as important for most peoples, Americans included, as narrow calculations of political interest. Why, for example, did the South challenge the North, which was clearly superior in military power and potential? Why did the Confederacy continue the struggle at tremendous human and economic cost long after leaders and soldiers alike recognized it to be a lost cause? Other examples can be cited where people wittingly began or continued a struggle against great or even impossible odds in the face of prior and even convincing efforts by the superior military power to portray the certain and disastrous consequences of a military challenge or continued resistance. From the Jewish revolts against the Romans to the Irish Easter Rising and the resistance of the beleaguered Finns in 1940, history records countless stories of peoples who began or continued costly struggles with little or no expectation of success. Honor, anger, or national self-respect proved more compelling motives for action than pragmatic calculations of material loss and gain were reasons for acquiescence or passivity.

Both the theory and strategy of deterrence mistake the symptoms of aggressive behavior for its causes. Specifically, it ignores the political and strategic vulnerabilities that can interact with cognitive and motivational processes to compel leaders to choose force.

In a previous study, I analyzed a class of acute international crisis, brinkmanship, whose defining characteristic was the challenger's expectation that its adversary would back away from its commitment in preference to war (Lebow 1981). I found that, much more often than not, brinkmanship challenges were initiated without good evidence that the adversary lacked either the capability or resolve to defend its commitment; on the contrary, in most instances the evidence available at the time pointed to the opposite conclusion. The commitments in question appeared to meet the four necessary conditions of deterrence: they were clearly defined, repeatedly publicized, and defensible, and the defending states gave every indication of their resolve to use force in defense of them. Not surprisingly, most of these challenges resulted in setbacks for the initiators, who were themselves compelled to back down or go to war.

Faulty judgment by challengers could most often be attributed to their perceived need to carry out a brinkmanship challenge in response to pressing foreign and domestic threats. The policymakers involved believed that these threats could be overcome only by means of a successful challenge of an adversary's commitment. Brinkmanship was conceived of as a necessary and forceful response to danger, as a means of protecting national strategic or domestic political interests before time ran out. Whether or not their assessment of international and domestic constraints was correct is a separate question for research. What is relevant is that leaders perceived acute domestic pressure, international danger, or both.

The extent to which policymakers contemplating challenges of their adversaries are inner-directed and inwardly focused is also a central theme of Janice Gross Stein's two contributions to *Psychology* and *Deterrence* (1985a, b). In her analysis of the five occasions between 1969 and 1973 when Egyptian leaders seriously contemplated the use of force against Israel, Stein argues that decision making in all of these instances departed significantly from the core postulates of deterrence theory. All five decisions revealed a consistent and almost exclusive concentration by Egyptian leaders on their own purposes, political needs, and constraints. They spoke in almost apocalyptic terms of Egypt's need to liberate the Sinai before the superpower detente progressed to the stage where Egyptian military action became impossible. They alluded again and again to the escalating domestic crisis that could be arrested only if the humiliation of 1967 were erased by a successful military campaign. By contrast, Israel's interests, and the imperatives for action that could be expected to flow from these interests, were not at all salient for Egyptian leaders. They thought instead of the growing domestic and international constraints and of the intolerable costs of inaction.

In 1969, in the War of Attrition, the Egyptian failure to consider the relative interests of both sides resulted in a serious error. Egyptian leaders did not miscalculate Israel's credibility but rather the scope of Israel's military response. They attached a very low probability to the possibility that Israel would extend the war and carry out deep penetration bombing attacks against Egypt and escalate its war objective to the overthrow of Nasser. This was a miscalculation of major proportions given the magnitude of the punishment Israel in fact inflicted upon Egypt.

Egypt's inability to understand that Israel's leaders believed that defense of the Sinai was important not only for the strategic depth and warning time it provided but also as an indicator of resolve was merely one cause of its miscalculation in 1969. Egyptian leaders overestimated their own capacity to lay down favorable ground rules for a war of attrition and underestimated that of Israel. They also developed a strategy to fight the war, to culminate in a crossing of the canal, that was predicated on a fatal inconsistency: the belief that Egypt could inflict numerous casualties on Israel in the course of a war of attrition, but that Israel would refrain from escalating that conflict in order to reduce its casualties.

These faulty assessments and strategic contradictions are best explained as a motivated response to the strategic dilemma faced by Egyptian planners in 1969. Egypt could neither accept the status quo nor sustain the kind of military effort that would have been necessary to recapture the Sinai. Instead, Egypt embarked upon a poorly conceived limited military action. The wishful thinking and biased estimates were a form of bolstering; this was the way Egyptian leaders convinced themselves that their strategy would succeed. Israel's deterrent failed, not because of any lack of capability or resolve, but because Egypt's calculations were so flawed that they defeated deterrence.

Egyptian decision making in 1969 provides an example of what may be the most frequent cause of serious miscalculation in international crisis: the inability of leaders to find a satisfactory way to reconcile two competing kinds of threats. Our cases indicated that the psychological stress that arises from this decisional dilemma is usually resolved by the adoption of defensive avoidance as a coping strategy. Leaders commit themselves to a course of action and deny information that indicates that their policy might not succeed (Janis and Mann 1977). In the Egyptian case, the decisional dilemma that prompted defensive avoidance was the result of incompatibility between domestic imperatives and foreign realities. The domestic threat, the political and economic losses, was the overriding consideration for Egyptian policymakers. Their estimates of their vulnerability motivated error and miscalculation and culminated in the failure of deterrence.

The Egyptian decision to use force in 1973 was even more damaging to the logic of deterrence than the motivated miscalculation in 1969. Egyptian leaders chose to use force in 1973 not because they miscalculated Israel's resolve or response but because they felt so intolerably vulnerable and constrained. If Egyptian leaders had miscalculated, proponents of deterrence might argue that human error accounted for its failure. Economists advance similar kinds of arguments: The strategy is not flawed, only the people who use it. Egypt's leaders decided to challenge deterrence not because they erred but because they considered the domestic and foreign costs of inaction unbearably high. They anticipated correctly a major military response by Israel and expected to suffer significant casualties and losses. Nevertheless, they planned a limited military action to disrupt the status quo and hoped for an internationally imposed cease-fire before their limited gains could be reversed. In 1973, Egyptian leaders considered their military capabilities inferior to those of Israel but chose to use force because they anticipated grave domestic and strategic consequences from continuing inaction.

The same domestic considerations that compelled Egyptian leaders to challenge Israel also provided the incentives for Egyptian military planners to devise a strategy that compensated for their military weakness. Human ingenuity and careful organization succeeded in exploiting the flexibility of multipurpose conventional weaponry to circumvent many of the constraints of military inferiority. Egyptian officers strove to achieve defensive superiority in what they planned to keep a limited battle zone (Stein 1985a).

The Japanese decision to attack the USA in December 1941 seems analogous to the Egyptian decision of 1973. Like the Egyptians, the Japanese fully recognized the military superiority of their adversary, particularly the greater naval power and vastly superior economic base of the USA. The Japanese, nevertheless, felt compelled to attack the USA in the illusory hope that a limited victory would facilitate a favorable settlement of their festering and costly conflict with China.

As the Egyptians were to do more than 30 years later, the Japanese military devised an ingenious and daring strategy to compensate for their adversary's advantages; they relied on air power and surprise to neutralize US naval power in the Pacific. They too deluded themselves that their foe would accept the political consequences of a disastrous initial defeat instead of fighting to regain the initiative. The Japanese strategy was an act of desperation. Japan's leaders opted for war only after they were persuaded that the military balance between themselves and their adversaries would never again be as favorable as it was in 1941; time was working against them. They were also convinced that they could not attain their objectives by diplomacy (Butow 1961; Borg and Okamoto 1973; Ienaga 1978; Ike 1967; Russett 1967; Hosoya 1968).

The Japanese case highlights the importance of an uncongenial strategic environment as an incentive for a challenge. Leaders who anticipate an unfavorable decline in the relative balance of power may see no alternative to military action. President Sadat, for example, estimated that the longer he postponed war, the stronger Israel would become. This assumption helped to create a mood of desperation in Cairo, so much so that Sadat repeatedly purged the Egyptian military command until he found generals who were confident that they could design around Israel's air and armored capability.

The Egyptian and Japanese cases indicate that a defender's capability and resolve are only some of the factors challengers consider when they contemplate war. They are also influenced by domestic political pressures that push them toward action and their judgments about future trends in the military balance. A pessimistic estimate of the probability of achieving important goals by peaceful means can also create frustration and constitute an incentive to act. This was very much so in Egypt in 1973 and in Japan in 1941. Both these cases illustrate how frustration, pessimism, and a sense of weakness in response to an unfavorable domestic and strategic environment can outweigh considerations of military inferiority.

How Deterrence Can Backfire

When challengers are vulnerable or feel themselves vulnerable, a deterrer's effort to make important commitments more defensible and credible will have uncertain and unpredictable effects. At best, deterrence will be benign; it will simply have no effect. But it can also be malignant by intensifying precisely those pressures that are pushing leaders toward a choice of force. Japan offers an example.

The USA and other Western powers imposed first an asset freeze and then an oil embargo upon Japan in July–August 1941 in the hope of moderating Tokyo's policies. These actions were in fact the catalysts for Japan's decision to go to war. Her leaders feared that the embargo would deprive them of the means of continuing their struggle against China and would ultimately put them at the mercy of their adversaries. It accordingly fostered a mood of desperation in Tokyo, an essential precondition for the attack on Pearl Harbor that followed.

In his contribution to *Psychology and Deterrence*, Jack Snyder (1985: 153–179) explores security dilemmas and their role in the outbreak of war in 1914. The distinguishing characteristic of a security dilemma is that behavior perceived by adversaries as threatening and aggressive is actually a defensive response to an inhospitable strategic environment. A perceptual security dilemma develops, Snyder argues, when strategic and psychological factors interact and strategic assessments are exaggerated or distorted by perceptual biases. In effect, leaders overrate the advantages of the offensive, the magnitude of power shifts, and the hostility of their adversaries.

In 1914, the major continental powers confronted elements of a security dilemma. As French fortifications improved in the 1880s, German security required the vulnerability of Russian forces in Poland; without this vulnerability, the German general staff feared that Russia and France could mobilize to full strength and then attack jointly. Russian security, however, excluded precisely such a weakness: Russia could not tolerate a decisive German advantage in a short war and so planned to increase her standing forces 40% by 1917. With French financial assistance, Russia also constructed new railways to transport these forces more rapidly to her western borders. Defensive preparations by Russia constituted an offensive threat to Germany, and conversely, a defensive strategy by Germany seemed to require offensives directed against France and Russia. Offense and defense thus became virtually indistinguishable.

Although the strategic environment was inhospitable and dangerous, Germany's military leaders greatly exaggerated the dangers and, as Snyder (1985: 170) demonstrates, reasoned inside out. They overrated the hostility of their adversaries and consequently assumed the inevitability of a two-front war. Once they did, the attractiveness of a preventive war-fighting strategy became overwhelming; German military leaders saw preventive war as the only alternative to their vulnerability. Indeed, the general staff gave no serious consideration after 1890 to the possibility of a defensive strategy against Russia and France. From then until 1914, the German military did not overestimate their offensive capabilities and then choose force; on the contrary, they exaggerated the hostility of their adversaries in ways that psychological theories expect and then argued that an offensive capability was the least unsatisfactory option. Because of this choice, Germany's neighbors confronted a real security dilemma.

In this kind of strategic environment, the attempt to deter Germany was counterproductive. Threats of retaliation and shows of force by Russia and France only fueled German fears and, in so doing, further destabilized an already unstable environment. The Russian mobilization designed to deter, for example, could not help but alarm German military leaders committed to an offensive preemptive strategy. In 1914, when Germany's leaders chose to use force, they did so not because they saw an 'opportunity' for gain but because they believed the strategic consequences of inaction would be catastrophic. In an environment where already unfavorable strategic assessments were overlain by exaggerated fear and a sense of vulnerability, deterrence could only provoke the use of force it was designed to prevent.

PSYCHOLOGICAL PROBLEMS

The psychological component of this critique is also related to the motivation behind deterrence challenges. To the extent that policymakers believe in the necessity of challenging commitments of their adversaries, they become predisposed to see their objectives as attainable. Motivated error in the form of distorted threat assessments can result in the unrealistic expectation that an adversary will back down when challenged or, alternatively, that it will fight precisely the kind of war the challenger plans for. Once committed to a challenge, policymakers may also become insensitive to warnings that their chosen course of action is likely to result in disaster. In these circumstances, deterrence, no matter how well it is practiced, can be defeated by a challenger's wishful thinking.

Flawed Assessments

I have already described Egypt's flawed assessments in 1969 and 1973. In 1969, the Egyptians convinced themselves that Israel would engage in a costly war of attrition along the canal, despite the well-known fact that Israeli strategy had always been premised on the need to avoid this kind of conflict. In 1973, the Egyptians assumed that Israel would accept the loss of her positions along the east bank of the Suez Canal as a fait accompli despite Egypt's own inability to do this for much the same reasons. Both expectations flew in the face of obvious political realities. They led to costly wars that very nearly ended in political disaster. Both resorts to force were a response to Egypt's leaders' need to reassert their strength at home and abroad, a need that prompted grossly distorted estimates of Israel's likely responses to a challenge.

The Japanese decision to attack Pearl Harbor is another example of a strategic decision based on wishful thinking. The Japanese military settled on a limited war strategy because they knew that it was the only kind of war they could hope to win against the USA, given the latter's superior economic and military power. They convinced themselves that a successful counterforce strike against US naval units in the Pacific would convince Washington to withdraw from the Western Pacific and give Japan a free hand in the region. The American reaction was, of course, nothing of the kind. Public opinion in the USA was enraged by Japan's 'sneak attack' and intent on waging war against her a *Voutrance*. President Roosevelt and Chairman of the Joint Chiefs of Staff George C. Marshall had a difficult time throughout the war in directing America's principal military effort against Germany, which they rightly concluded constituted the more serious threat, because public opinion was more interested in punishing Japan.

The origins of World War I offer a third example of how wishful thinking can defeat deterrence. German policy in the July crisis was based on a series of erroneous assumptions on the probable Russian, French, and British reaction to the destruction of Serbia by Austria-Hungary. German leaders were on the whole confident of their ability to localize an Austro-Serbian war despite all the indications to the contrary and, one fleeting moment of hesitation by the German chancellor aside, urged Vienna throughout the crisis to ignore all pleas for moderation.

Germany's strategy was remarkably shortsighted. Even if the unrealistic assumptions on which it was based had proved correct, it still would have been self-defeating. Serbia's destruction would only have aggravated Russo-German hostility, making Russia even more dependent on France and Britain and setting the stage for a renewed and more intense clash between the two blocs. This outcome aside, all of the assumptions on which German policy was based proved ill-founded; Austria's declaration of war on Serbia triggered a series of responses that embroiled Germany in a war with Russia, France, Belgium, and Great Britain.

The German strategy only makes sense when it is understood as a response to the contradictions between the country's perceived strategic needs and perceived strategic realities. The former dictated support of Austria, Germany's principal ally, as a means of shoring up her self-confidence and maintaining the all-important alliance. The latter dictated caution because Germany's politicians shied away from responsibility for a European war while her generals were uncertain of their ability to win one. These contradictions were reconciled in a strategy premised on the illusion that Austria, with German support, could wage a limited war in the Balkans without provoking the intervention of the other great powers. German leaders were only disabused of their illusion after it was *too* late to alter the course of events (Lebow 1981: 26–29, 119–124; 1984).

Challenger's Insensitivity to Warnings

Motivated errors can play a major role in blocking receptivity to signals. Once leaders have committed themselves to a challenge, efforts by defenders to impart credibility to their commitments will at best have a marginal impact on their adversaries' behavior. Even the most elaborate efforts to demonstrate prowess and resolve may prove insufficient to discourage a challenger who is convinced that a use of force is necessary to preserve vital strategic and political interests.

Irving Janis and Leon Mann (1977), in their analysis of decision making, argue that policymakers who contemplate a course of action, but recognize that their initiative entails serious risk, will experience psychological stress. They will become emotionally upset and preoccupied with finding a less-risky alternative. If, after further investigation, they conclude that it is unrealistic to hope for a better strategy, they will terminate their search despite their continuing dissatisfaction with available options. The result is a pattern of 'defensive avoidance', characterized by efforts to avoid, dismiss, and deny warnings that increase anxiety and fear.

One of the three forms of defensive avoidance identified by Janis and Mann (1977: 57–58, 107–133) is bolstering. It refers to a set of psychological tactics that policymakers may resort to make a decision they are about to make, or have already made, more acceptable to themselves. Bolstering occurs when policymakers have lost hope of finding an altogether satisfactory policy option and are unable to postpone a decision or shift responsibility to others. Instead, they commit themselves to the least objectionable alternative and proceed to 'spread the alternatives', that is, to exaggerate its positive consequences or minimize its costs. They may also deny the existence of aversive feelings, emphasize the remoteness of the consequence, or attempt to minimize personal responsibility for the decision once it is made. Policymakers continue to think about the problem but ward off anxiety by practicing selective attention and other forms of distorted information processing.

Bolstering can serve a useful purpose. It helps a policymaker forced to settle for a less than the optimal course of action to overcome residual conflict second move more confidently toward decision and action. Bolstering can occur before and after a decision is made. When it takes place before, it discourages leaders from making a careful search of the alternatives. It subsequently lulls them into believing that they have made a good decision, when in fact they have avoided making a vigilant appraisal of the possible alternatives in order to escape from the conflict that would ensue. When leaders resort to bolstering after a decision, it tends to blind to warnings that the course of action to which they are committed may prove unsatisfactory or even disastrous.

Janis and Mann (1977: 74–79) consider insensitivity to warnings a hallmark of defensive avoidance. When this becomes the dominant pattern of coping, 'the person tries to keep himself from being exposed to communications that might reveal the shortcomings of the course of action he has chosen'. When actually confronted with disturbing information, leaders will alter its implications through a process of wishful thinking; they rationalize and deny the prospect of serious loss. Extraordinary circumstances with irrefutable negative feedback may be required to overcome such defenses.

Selective attention, denial, or almost any other psychological tactic used by policymakers to cope with critical information can be institutionalized. Merely by making their expectations or preferences known, policymakers encourage their subordinates to report or emphasize information supportive of those expectations and preferences. Policymakers can also purposely rig their intelligence networks and bureaucracies to achieve the same effect. Perspectives thus confirmed and reconfirmed over time become more and more resistant to discrepant information and more difficult to refute.

In an earlier study, I (1981: 101–228) described in detail how this process occurred in Germany in 1914, in the USA in 1950 with regard to the possibility of Chinese entry into the Korean War, and in India in 1962 during its border dispute with China. In all three instances, policymakers, responding to perceived domestic and strategic imperatives, became committed to risky military policies in the face of efforts by others to deter them. They resorted to defensive avoidance to insulate themselves from the stress triggered by these warnings. They subsequently allowed or encouraged their respective political-military bureaucracies to submit reports supportive of the policies to which the leadership was committed. Institutionalized in this manner, defensive avoidance succeeded in blinding the policymakers to repeated warnings of impending disaster.

Motivated bias is a response to personal needs or external pressures. Evidence drawn from these cases suggests that at least one mediating condition of motivated bias is a choice by policymakers of a course of action that they recognize could result in substantial loss. Once challengers become committed to such an action, even the most strenuous efforts by a deterrer to define a commitment and give it credibility may have little impact. Motivated bias, in the form of faulty assessment of an adversary s resolve, overconfidence, and insensitivity to warnings, can defeat even well-articulated and well-executed deterrence.

PROBLEMS IN APPLYING DETERRENCE

Deterrence is beset by a host of practical problems. One of these is the difficulty of communicating capability and resolve to would-be challengers. Strategies of deterrence generally assume that everyone understands, so to speak, the meaning of barking guard dogs, barbed wire, and 'No Trespassing' signs. This is not so. Signals only take on meaning in terms of the context in which they are interpreted. When sender and recipient use quite different contexts to frame, communicate, or interpret signals, the opportunities for miscalculation and misjudgment multiply. This problem is endemic to international relations and is not limited to deterrence (Jervis 1979: 305–310; Lebow 1985: 204–211).

A second problem, and one that is more specific to deterrence, concerns the difficulty of reconstructing the cost-benefit calculus of another actor. Deterrence requires *the* party intent on forestalling a challenge to manipulate the cost-benefit calculus of a would-be challenger so that the expected costs of a challenge are judged to outweigh its expected benefits. If credible threats of punishment always increased the cost side of the ledger—something deterrence theory takes for granted—then it would be unnecessary for deterrers to understand the value hierarchy and outcome preferences of target states. This convenient assumption is not borne out in practice. Leaders may be driven not primarily by 'opportunity' but rather by 'vulnerability'. When they are, increasing the costs of military action may have no effect on their unwillingness to tolerate the high costs of inaction.

Deterrent threats in these circumstances can also provoke the very behavior they are designed to prevent. This happens when, contrary to the deterrer's expectations, they intensify the pressures on the challenger to act. Unfortunately, the kinds of considerations that determine how a threat will influence an adversary's cost-benefit calculus are often invisible or not easily understood from the outside.

The Cuban Missile Crisis offers a striking example of this phenomenon. Scholars have advanced several hypotheses to explain why the Soviets placed missiles in Cuba in September and October of 1962. By far the most widely accepted is the perceived Soviet need to redress the strategic balance. The deployment was a reaction to American pronouncements of strategic superiority in the fall of 1961 (Horelick and Rush 1966: 141; Hilsman 1967: 200–202; Tatu 1968; Abel 1966; Allison 1971: 52–56). At that time the Soviets possessed a very small fleet of long-range bombers, a sizable number of medium-range ballistic missiles (MRBMs) and intermediate-range ballistic missiles (IRBMs) and a small number of intercontinental ballistic missiles (ICBMs). All of these weapons were based in the Soviet Union and were of limited use in any retaliatory strike against the USA. The bombers were slow and easy to detect; they could not be expected to penetrate American air defenses. The medium- and intermediate-range ballistic missiles were excellent weapons but incapable of reaching the continental USA, and the first-generation ICBMs, for which the Soviets had great hopes, proved too unreliable and vulnerable to serve as a practical weapon. Only a few of them were actually deployed.

American estimates of the size and effectiveness of the Soviet missile force had been highly speculative after May 1960 when U-2 overflights of the Soviet Union had been discontinued. This situation was rectified in the late summer of 1961 by the introduction of satellite reconnaissance, which gave American intelligence a more accurate assessment of the number of Soviet missiles. At that time, a far-reaching political decision was made to tell Moscow that Washington knew of its vulnerability.

The risk inherent in such a course of action was not fully appreciated by President Kennedy, who feared only that the Soviets would now speed up their ICBM program. The president and his advisers were more sensitive to the need to moderate Khrushchev's bellicosity, alarmingly manifest in his several Berlin ultimatums, and thought this could be accomplished by communicating their awareness of American strategic superiority. The message was first conveyed by Roswell Gilpatric, deputy secretary of defense, in a speech delivered in October 1961, and was subsequently reinforced through other channels.

For Soviet leaders, the political implications of this message must have been staggering. Almost overnight, the Kremlin was confronted with the realization that its nuclear arsenal was not an effective deterrent. In words of Roger Hilsman (1967: 164):

It was not so much the fact that the Americans had military superiority—that was not news to the Soviets. What was bound to frighten them most was that the Americans knew that they had military superiority. For the Soviets quickly realized that to have reached this conclusion, the Americans must have made intelligence breakthrough and found a way to pinpoint the location of the Soviet missiles that had been deployed as well as to calculate their total numbers. A soft ICBM system with somewhat cumbersome launching techniques is an effective weapon for both a first strike... and a second, retaliatory strike so long as the location of the launching pads can be kept secret. However, if the enemy has a map with all the pads plotted, the system will retain some of its utility as a first-strike weapon, but almost none at all as a second-strike weapon. The whole Soviet ICBM system was suddenly obsolescent.

The Soviets were in a quandary. The missile gap could be closed by a crash program to develop more effective second-generation ICBMs and perhaps a submersible delivery system. Such an effort was extremely costly and likely to meet strong opposition within the Soviet hierarchy. More importantly, a crash program did nothing to solve the short-term but paralyzing Soviet strategic inferiority that could be exploited by American leaders. The deployment of missiles in Cuba can be viewed as a bold attempt to resolve this dilemma. If this interpretation is correct, the American warning had the paradoxical impact of provoking the action it was designed to deter.

For 25 years, all interpretations of Soviet motives and policies in the missile crisis were speculative. Existing Soviet commentaries, among them Khrushchev's memoirs (1970, 1974) and Anatoly Gromyko's study of the crisis (1971), contained enough obvious falsehoods to make them highly suspect sources. In October 1987, an extraordinary meeting took place in Cambridge, Massachusetts. A small group of scholars—myself among them—and former Kennedy administration officials met with three Soviet officials to talk about the origins and politics of the missile crisis. The Soviet representatives were Georgi Shaknazarov, a member of the Central Committee, Fedor Burlatsky, a former Khrushchev speech writer, and Sergei Mikoyan, a foreign ministry official and son of former deputy prime minister, Anastas I. Mikoyan.

All three Soviets were remarkably forthcoming; they shared with us their personal memories and feelings about the crisis and also what they had learned from talking to other officials at the time and subsequently. They did not always agree among themselves about important aspects of the crisis and were careful to distinguish between fact and opinion and between what they had witnessed or learned about only secondhand. The American participants, some of whom, like Raymond L. Garthoff and Robert McNamara, had extensive prior experience with Soviet officials, came away convinced that the Soviets were telling us the truth as they understood it.

The Russians advanced three explanations for the Cuban missile deployment: the perceived need to deter an expected American invasion of Cuba, to overcome Soviet strategic inferiority, and to attain political-psychological equality with the USA. They disagreed among themselves about the relative importance of these objectives for Khrushchev and other top leaders.

Sergei Mikoyan (1987: 20, 40, 45–47) maintained that 'there were only two thoughts: defend Cuba and repair the [strategic nuclear] imbalance'. 'Our "pentagon"', he reported, 'thought the strategic balance was dangerous, and sought parity'. Marshall Rodion Malinovsky, Soviet defense minister, was adamant about the need to secure a more credible second-strike capability. 'Khrushchev', too, Mikoyan continued, 'was very concerned about a possible American attack. He worried... that somebody in the United States might think that a 17-to ~ 1 superiority would mean that a first strike was possible'. Mikoyan insisted, however, that Khrushchev's primary objective was to prevent an American assault on Cuba, something the Soviet leadership believed to be imminent.

Fedor Burlatsky and Georgi Shaknazarov agreed that Khrushchev wanted to protect Castro but maintained that he was even more concerned to do something to redress the strategic imbalance. They gave somewhat different reasons for why Khrushchev sought to do this.

Georgi Shaknazarov (1987: 17–18, 58, 75–76) emphasized the military consequences of American superiority. 'The main idea', as he saw it, 'was to publicly attain parity'. This was critical 'because there were circles in the United States who believed that war with the Soviet Union was possible and could be won'. The Cuban missile deployment was accordingly attractive to Khrushchev because it offered an immediate solution to the strategic vulnerability problem at very little cost. 'It was an attempt by Khrushchev to get parity without spending resources we did not have.'

Burlatsky (1987a: 17–18, 30–31, 115–116; b: 22) agreed that Soviet leaders had a long sense of nuclear inferiority, especially at this time. Many Soviet officials, he reported, really feared an American first strike.

But Khrushchev did not. He worried instead about American efforts to exploit its superiority politically. Khrushchev was particularly aggrieved by the Kennedy administration's deployment of missiles in Turkey, missiles that, because of their vulnerability to air attack, could only be used a first strike or political intimidation. 'Why do the Americans have the right to encircle us with nuclear missile bases on all sides', he complain to Burlatsky, 'yet we do not have that right?' Burlatsky believed that the Jupiter deployment in Turkey had been the catalyst for Khrushchev's decision to send missiles to Cuba. 'These missiles were not needed for deterrence', he explained. 'Our 300 were already more than enough to destroy the United States—more than enough. So it was a psychological thing. From my point of view, it was the first step to strategic parity'.

The Kennedy administration officials at the Cambridge conference admitted in retrospect that the Jupiter deployment had been provocative and unwise. Kennedy, it is apparent, had gone ahead with the deployment in spite of considerable opposition to it within State and Defense where the missiles were viewed as obsolescent and provocative. He did so because he was afraid that Khrushchev would misinterpret cancellation of the proposed deployment as a sign of his weakness and lack of resolve and become more emboldened in his challenges of Western interests in Berlin and elsewhere (Lebow, forthcoming).

Robert McNamara, secretary of defense during the Cuban crisis, was surprised that Khrushchev worried about a Cuban invasion. McNamara (1987: 59) assured the Russians 'that we had no plan to attack Cuba, and I would have opposed the idea strongly, if it ever came up'. But he acknowledged that he could understand why the Soviets could have concluded that an invasion was imminent. The covert military operations the administration was conducting against Castro's regime, he agreed, conveyed the wrong impression about American intentions. They were 'stupid but our intent was not to invade'. From the vantage point of a quarter-century, McNamara was struck by the irony of the situation. 'We thought those covert operations were terribly ineffective', he mused, 'and you thought they were ominous'.

McNamara and former national security advisor, McGeorge Bundy, were also surprised that the Soviets could have worried about a first strike. They knew that the administration had no intention of carrying one out! McNamara (1987: 76) asked Shaknazarov: 'Did your leaders actually believe that some of us thought it would be in our interest to launch a first strike?' Shaknazarov: 'Yes. That is why it seems to me

Khrushchev decided to put missiles in Cuba' (1987: 76). The Russians went on to explain that their fears of a first strike had been aroused by the Kennedy administration's strategic buildup, its stationing of first-strike weapons in Turkey, and claims by its defense and military leaders that they could destroy the Soviet Union without losing more than 25% of its own population in a counterblow.

Although none of the Soviets mentioned the Gilpatric speech, they all emphasized the extent to which American military preparations and assertions of strategic superiority exacerbated Soviet strategic insecurities and pushed Khrushchev toward more confrontational policies. From this it is clear the Gilpatric speech and related American attempts to manipulate the cost-calculus of Soviet leaders backfired. The Kennedy administration's efforts to increase the cost to the Soviet Union of any challenge had the real and undesired effect of making such a challenge more attractive to Soviet leaders.

The missile crisis indicates that deterrence, as practiced by *both* superpowers, was provocative instead of preventive. Khrushchev and other top Soviet leaders conceived of the Cuban missiles as a means of deterring American military and political threats to Cuba and the Soviet Union. The American actions that provoked Khrushchev had in turn been envisaged by President Kennedy as prudent, defensive measures against perceived Soviet threats. Both leaders, seeking to moderate the behavior of their adversary, helped to bring about the very kind of confrontation they were trying to prevent.

THE PRIMACY OF SELF

Deterrence purports to describe an interactive process between the defender of a commitment and a would-be challenger. The defending state is expected to define and publicize its commitment and do its best to make that commitment credible in the eyes of its adversary. Would-be challengers are expected to assess accurately the defender's capability and resolve. The repetitive cycle of test and challenge is expected to provide both sides with an increasingly sophisticated understanding of each other's interests, propensity for risk taking, threshold of provocation, and style of foreign policy behavior.

My analysis of adversarial relationships indicates that the expectations that deterrence has about deterrer and challenger bear little relationship to reality. Challengers frequently focus on their own needs and do not consider, or distort if they do, the needs, interests, and capabilities of their adversaries. Moreover, at times they are motivated not by 'opportunity', as deterrence theory expects, but rather by 'vulnerability' and perceived weakness. Deterrers, in turn, may interpret the motives or objectives of a challenger in a manner consistent with their expectations, with little regard to the competing expectations of the challenger. Both sides may also prove insensitive to each other's signals. Under these conditions, deterrence is likely to fail. Even recurrent deterrence episodes may not facilitate greater mutual understanding. On the contrary, experience may actually hinder learning to the extent that it encourages tautological confirmation of misleading or inappropriate lessons.

IMPLICATIONS FOR DETERRENCE THEORY

Some empiricists (Achen and Snidal 1988; Tetlock 1987; Huth and Russett 1984) contend that Stein and I misunderstand the purpose of social science theory. They argue that its goal is to predict human behavior, not necessarily to explain why that behavior occurs. With respect to deterrence, they insist that our sample, based only on deterrence failures, significantly biases our results. If we looked at deterrence successes, they argue, we would discover that deterrence is more successful than not. This would confirm the validity of deterrence theory as a predictor of state behavior.

These criticisms are methodologically and conceptually misguided. No analyst has yet succeeded, or ever will, in identifying the relevant universe of cases. Some of the reasons for this were made clear in the introduction of the chapter (see also Lebow and Stein 1987b). Chief among these is the difficulty of identifying deterrence successes. The more successful deterrence is, the fewer the behavioral traces it leaves behind. The assertion that deterrence theory is a better-than-average predictor of state behavior cannot be demonstrated. The several empirical studies that attempt to validate this claim do not come to grips with this and other methodological obstacles.

Because the universe of relevant deterrence cases can never be identified, the significance of the cases examined becomes critical. But aggregate data analyses have made no attempt to weight their cases in favor of those they deem the most important or critical. Instead, they treat them as equivalent in every respect. Analysts who use the case study approach, by contrast, make strenuous efforts to identify critical cases and to justify their choices. The case study literature on deterrence failure has now identified an impressive number of important deterrence failures. These cases, which led to major crises and wars, stand as a sharp challenge to the expectations of deterrence as a theory and its practice as a strategy.

These cases of deterrence failure reveal important common features. Flawed information gathering, evaluation, attribution, and decision making on the part of initiators were most often responsible for the miscalculations that defeated deterrence. These all-important processes cannot be captured by aggregate analysis. This requires in-depth study of individual cases of deterrence failure and success. As the old French saying goes, God is to be found in the details.

These same empiricists acknowledge the power of our argument about the importance of domestic politics and strategic vulnerabilities in pushing states toward military challenges. But they—and even some deterrence critics (George and Smoke 1974)—believe that deterrence theory could accommodate these considerations. To do so, they propose expanding it to incorporate a much wider range of political factors. Utility estimates could then take domestic politics, strategic vulnerabilities, and other factors into account instead of being based solely on narrow, and admittedly misleading, calculations of the relative military balance. This is easier said than done.

The incorporation of new variables would require an entirely new set of propositions to guide their weighing. Just how much importance, for example, should be given to national honor in comparison with the domestic political interests of leaders, ideological goals, or allied obligations? Deterrence theory provides no guidance for discriminating among these variables in order to construct a weighted model. For this reason, the Lebow-Stein critique of deterrence strikes at the theory, not only at deterrence as a real-world strategy.

Even if this problem could somehow be solved, deterrence theory would confront another insuperable obstacle. The incorporation of additional, more political variables would not help deterrence theory come to grips with the evidence that leaders deviate significantly from the process of rational choice in making critical foreign policy decisions. It is these deviations that largely account for deterrence failures. Models based on rational choice cannot therefore predict strategic decisions with any impressive degree of success. Analysts interested in improving the predictive capability of their models must abandon rational choice or, at the very least, incorporate significant elements of non-rational processes into their models. They cannot do this and retain the core of deterrence theory.

NOTES

This chapter is based on Part I of 'Beyond Deterrence', coauthored with Janice Gross Stein, *Journal of Social Issues* (Winter 1987) 43, no. 4, 5–71. Research and writing of the paper were supported by grants from the Carnegie Corporation of New York to Richard Ned Lebow and the Canadian Institute of Peace and Security to Janice Gross Stein.

1. For a fuller treatment of the detrimental effects of nuclear deterrence between the superpowers, see Lebow (1987a).
2. The definition of adequate communication and apparent resolve is difficult. Students of deterrence have traditionally assessed credibility with reference to bow a would-be challenger's leaders perceived the commitment in question. There is a serious problem with this approach; it risks making determinations of credibility tautological. If a commitment is challenged, it is assumed not to have been credible. This ignores the possibility that the commitment should have been seen as credible but was not for any one of a number of reasons independent of the defender's military capability or resolve. For this reason, the appropriate test of credibility must be the judgment of disinterested third parties and not that of the would-be challenger. As 1 will show, a challenger's receptivity to communications and its judgment about a commitment's credibility can be impaired by motivated biases. Thus, deterrent threats that appear credible to third parties can fail to be perceived as such by leaders intent on a challenge.
3. George and Smoke (1974: 519–520) argue that the outcome of a deterrence encounter can also be mixed. This occurs, in their opinion, when deterrence succeeds in dissuading a country's leaders from choosing certain options as too risky but does not prevent them from embarking upon another, less-risky challenge of the status quo. Such cases undoubtedly occur but I am not persuaded by the examples George and Smoke cite.
4. These cases are Fashoda (1898), Korea (1903–1904), Agadir (1911), July 1914, the Chinese entry into the Korean War (1950), Cuba (1962), the Sino-Indian crisis of 1962, and the Arab-Israeli wars of 1967, 1969, and 1973.

REFERENCES

Abel, E. 1966. *The Missile Crisis*, 28. Philadelphia: Lippincott.
Achen, C.H., and D. Snidal. 1988. Rational Deterrence Theory and Comparative Case Studies. *World Politics*, fall.
Allison, G. 1971. *Essence of Decision: Explaining the Cuban Missile Crisis*, 52–56, 237–244. Boston: Little, Brown.
Borg, D., and S. Okamoto (eds.). 1973. *Pearl Harbor as History: Japanese-American Relations, 1931–1941*. New York: Columbia University Press.
Brodie, B. 1959. The Anatomy of Deterrence. *World Politics* 11: 173–192.
Burlatsky, F. 1987a. *Proceedings of the Cambridge Conference on the Cuban Missile Crisis*. Cambridge, Mass, 11–12 October 1987, mimeograph.
Burlatsky, F. 1987b. The Caribbean Crisis and Its Lessons. *Literaturnaya Gazeta*, 11 November 1987: 14.
Butow, R. 1961. *Tojo and the Coming of the War*. Stanford: Stanford University Press.
George, A.L., and R. Smoke. 1974. *Deterrence in American Foreign Policy: Theory and Practice*. New York: Columbia University Press.
Gromyko, A.A. 1971. The Caribbean Crisis, 2 Parts. *Voprosy istorii* Nos. 4 & 8, English translation in Ronald R. Pope, *Soviet Views on the Cuban Crisis: Myth and Reality in Foreign Policy Analysis*, 161–226. Lanham, Md: University Press of America, 1982.
Heller, M.A. 1984. *The Iran-Iraq War: Implications for Third Parties*. JCSS Paper No. 23. Tel Aviv and Cambridge: Jaffee Center for Strategic Studies and Harvard University Center for International Affairs.
Hilsman, R. 1967. *To Move a Nation*, 164: 200–220. Garden City, NY: Doubleday.
Horelick, A., and M. Rush. 1966. *Strategic Power and Soviet Foreign Policy*, 141. Chicago: University of Chicago Press.
Hosoya, C. 1968. Miscalculation in Deterrence Policy: Japanese-U.S. Relations, 1938–1941. *Journal of Peace Research* 2: 79–115.
Huth, P., and B. Russett. 1984. What makes deterrence work? Cases from 1900 to 1980. *World Politics* 36 (4): 496–526.
Ienaga, S. 1978. *The Pacific War, 1931–1945*. New York: Pantheon.
Ike, N. 1967. *Japan's Decision for War, Records of 1941: Policy Conferences*. Stanford: Stanford University Press.
Janis, I., and L. Mann. 1977. *Decision Making: A Psychological Analysis of Conflict, Choice, and Commitment*. New York: Free Press.
Jervis, R. 1979. Deterrence theory revisited. *World Politics*, 31: 289–324.
Jervis, R., R.N. Lebow., and J.G. Stein. 1985. *Psychology and Deterrence*. Baltimore: Johns Hopkins University Press.

Kaplan, M.A. 1958. The Calculus of Deterrence. *World Politics* 11: 20–44.

Kaufmann, W.W. 1954. *The Requirements of Deterrence*. Princeton, NJ: Center of International Studies.

Kissinger, H.A. 1960. *The Necessity of Choice*, 40–41. New York: Harper.

Khrushchev, N.S. 1970, 1974. *Khrushchev Remembers*. 2 vols, trans. ed. Strobe Talbott, 488–505, 509–514. Boston: Little, Brown.

Lebow, R.N. 1981. *Between Peace and War: The Nature of International* Crisis, 26–29, 48–51, 101–228. Baltimore: Johns Hopkins University Press.

Lebow, R.N. 1984. Windows of Opportunity: Do States Jump Through Them? *International Security* 9: 147–186.

Lebow, R.N. 1985. Conclusions. *Psychology and Deterrence*, 204–211. Baltimore: Johns Hopkins University Press.

Lebow, R.N. 1987a. Conventional and Nuclear Deterrence: Are the Lessons Transferable. *Journal of Social Issues* 43 (4): 171–191.

Lebow, R.N. 1987b. Deterrence Failure Revisited. *International Security*, 12: 197–213.

Lebow, R.N. Forthcoming. The Turkish Missile Deployment and the Origins of the Cuban Missile Crisis.

Lebow, R.N., and J.G. Stein. 1987a. Beyond Deterrence. *Journal of Social Issues* 43 (4): 5–71.

Lebow, R.N., and J.G. Stein. 1987b. Beyond Deterrence: Building Better Theory. *Journal of Social Issues* 43 (4): 155–169.

McNamara, R. 1987. *Proceedings of the Cambridge Conference on the Cuban Missile Crisis*. Cambridge, Mass, 11–12 October 1987, mimeograph.

Mikoyan, S., 1987. *Proceedings of the Cambridge Conference on the Cuban Missile Crisis*. Cambridge, Mass, 11–12 October 1987, mimeograph.

Milburn, T.W. 1959. What Constitutes Effective Deterrence? *Journal of Conflict Resolution* 3: 138–146.

Orme, J. 1987. Deterrence Failures: A Second Look. International Security: 16–124.

Quester, G. 1966. *Deterrence Before Hiroshima: The Airpower Background to Modern Strategy*. New York: Wiley.

Russett, B. 1967. Pearl Harbor: Deterrence Theory and Decision Theory. *Journal of Peace Research* 4 (2): 89–105.

Schelling, T. 1966. *Arms and Influence*, 374. New Haven, CT: Yale University Press.

Shaknazarov, G. 1987. *Proceedings of the Cambridge Conference on the Cuban Missile Crisis*. Cambridge, Mass, 11–12 October 1987, mimeograph.

Snyder, G.H., and P. Diesing. 1977. *Conflict Among Nations: Bargaining, Decision Making and System Structure in International Crisis*. Princeton, NJ: Princeton University Press.

Snyder, J. 1985. Perceptions of the Security Dilemma in 1914. In *Psychology and Deterrence*, eds. R. Jervis, R.N. Lebow, and J.G. Stein, 153–179. Baltimore: Johns Hopkins University Press.

Stein, J.G. 1985a. Calculation, Miscalculation, and Conventional Deterrence I: The View from Cairo. In *Psychology and Deterrence*, ed. R. Jervis, R.N. Lebow, and J.G. Stein, 34–59. Baltimore: Johns Hopkins University Press.

Stein, J.G. 1985b. Calculation, Miscalculation, and Conventional Deterrence II: The View from Jerusalem. In *Psychology and Deterrence*, ed. R. Jervis, R.N. Lebow, and J.G. Stein, 60–88. Baltimore: Johns Hopkins University Press.

Tatu, M. 1968. Power in the Kremlin: From Khrushchev s Decline to Collective Leadership, trans. ed. H. Katel. London: Collins.

Tetlock, P.E. 1987. Testing Deterrence Theory: Some Conceptual and Methodological Issues. *Journal of Social Issues* 43 (4): 85–92.

Tripp, C. 1986. Iraq—Ambitions Checked. Survival 28(November–December): 495–508.

CHAPTER 4

Lessons of World War I

World War I was a catalyst of international relations (IR) theory, which arose in its aftermath and came to maturity after World War II.[1] Many theorists wanted to prevent future wars by learning more about the causes of previous ones. A century on, we have a diverse set of theories and propositions about the origins of war and international relations more generally. Today's optimists—mostly liberals and constructivists—insist that theorists and policymakers alike have learned much from 1914 to 1939. They point to the post-1945 success of the North Atlantic community and the European Union, both of which have made war unthinkable among an expanding circle of nations. Today's pessimists—for the most part realists—believe that little has changed and not that much has been learned about international relations since Thucydides, Machiavelli and Hobbes.

I believe it possible to learn from the past, but only if we are open-minded, make use of multiple competing perspectives, engage relevant historical evidence, acknowledge the importance of agency and context, and avoid facile comparisons between past and present. This mind-set cannot be brought about by new information or exhortations, but reading history can certainly encourage it. Ideographic narratives of events on

Richard Ned Lebow, 'What can international relations theory learn from the origins of World War I?', International Relations, 2014, Vol. 28, No. 4, pp. 387-410. Copyright © 2014 SAGE Publications. Reprinted by permission of SAGE Publications. The online version of this article can be found at: http://journals.sagepub.com/doi/abs/10.1177/0047117814556157.

© The Author(s) 2018
R.N. Lebow, *Avoiding War, Making Peace*,
DOI 10.1007/978-3-319-56093-9_4

which theories are based or purport to explain can highlight omissions, tensions, and other problems. I offer my review of the recent historical literature on the origins of World War I with these ends in mind.

The two World Wars are the central case for much of international relations theory concerned with questions of war and peace. They encouraged elaboration of the liberal and realist paradigms and their implications for war prevention. They strengthened the predisposition to look for underlying causes of war but also brought about a new focus on crisis management. They not only inspired strategic bargaining models on the assumption that leaders were rational but also heightened awareness of the irrational and the possibility of unintended war. Interpretations of the origins of these wars lie at the heart of balance of power theories, deterrence, power transition theory, rationalist approaches that stress the importance of information, Marxist theories of imperialism, organizational and bureaucratic explanations of war, and constructivist theories that emphasize the character and robustness of regional and international societies.

The origins of both World Wars, but especially World War I, have been hotly contested by generations of historians. Some theories of war and its prevention build on particular interpretations of its origins, but there is a growing consensus among historians that there is no single, or even dominant, cause of this war. Rather, it was the result of a suite of interactive and reinforcing causes, although there is no consensus about which of these was the most important. The centenary of the Great War has encouraged a spate of new studies that build on some new primary documents but mostly represent a rethinking of the origins due to a collective shift away from the question of what country was most responsible for war to how such a catastrophe could happen. The focus of historical research has accordingly drawn closer to questions of interest to international relations scholars, and our field has something to learn from the new research.

The new literature offers evidence and arguments relevant to the claims of balance of power, power transition, and deterrence theories. It suggests the importance of immediate causes of war, which can be independent of underlying causes and cannot be taken for granted. It highlights the role of agency and the ways in which policy can be driven by idiosyncratic or seemingly inappropriate goals, based on erroneous understandings of other actors and threat assessments and have consequences not expected, and sometimes, not even unimagined by actors. At a more fundamental level, it raises questions about approaches that assume rational actors are fundamentally interchangeable and driven by relatively objective assessments of constraints and opportunities. Most importantly, the new research should make us question the conceit that any parsimonious theory of war can tell us much about any single war or the phenomenon of war more generally.

HISTORIANS AND WORLD WAR I

Historians of World War I initially focused on the relative responsibility of the great powers and only later sought to understand how such a conflict could come about. In the early postwar period, the question of war guilt was given special impetus by article 231 of the Treaty of Versailles that justified German reparations to Belgium, France, and Britain on the basis of Germany's responsibility for the war. Most foreign ministries published documents, and in the German case, heavily edited to support their country's claim of innocence. Former officials from all the great powers published memoirs, most of them patently self-serving. We now know that the 40-volume German collection of documents on European politics—*Die Große Politik der Europäischen Kabinette, 1871–1914*—was very selective and documents excluded that suggested an aggressive role for Germany.[2] Not surprisingly, most British and French scholars held Germany and Austria responsible for the war. Their German counterparts and some American revisionists portrayed Germany as their victim or thought responsibility equally divided among the great powers.[3] The debate about the origins of the war found a parallel in that over the consequences of the Treaty of Versailles and reparations.[4] The war guilt controversy produced considerable scholarship on Germany and very little, by contrast, on the other great powers.

The publication in 1942 of Luigi Albertini's magisterial three-volume study of the origins of World War I—which appeared in English translation a decade later—represented a major turning point.[5] It documented in a thorough and dispassionate way the prime responsibility of Germany and Austria for war and how the decisions of their leaders were embedded in a decade-long struggle among the great powers that created an atmosphere in which risk taking and offensive military doctrines became dominant. For several decades, many scholars regarded this work as close to definitive.

In Germany, little changed until the 1960s. The older school of German historians, led by Gerhard Ritter, himself a veteran of the war, continued to deny that Germany had sought or planned a war. They were challenged by Fritz Fischer, whose *Griff nach der Weltmacht* (Grasping Out for World Power) appeared in November 1961 offered extensive documentation for what he argued was Germany's push for war in 1914 and pursuit of hegemonic goals.[6] By implication, Hitler and World War II were not some *Betriebsunfall* (accident) of German history as the conservative historians alleged but an extension of Imperial Germany's foreign policy goals. Fischer was shunned by the *Zunft* (the guild of historians), some of whose members accused him of 'treason' and violation of a national taboo. *Griff nach der Weltmacht* appeared against the background of the Eichmann trial, the construction of the Berlin Wall, and a major Cold War crisis over the status of that city. It provoked a national controversy that spread to the popular press and resulted in the withdrawal of official funding for Fischer's scheduled lecture tour in the USA.[7]

Fischer's argument drew support from a contemporaneous expose of the extent to which the national commission that had edited and published the 40-volume German documents on the war in the 1920s had excluded anything inimical to German claims of innocence. The book also spoke to a younger generation of Germans who sought to come to terms with the past (*Vergangenheitsbeweltigung*) through scholarship, commemoration, memorials, and school curricula.[8] By these means, they distanced themselves from earlier generations, felt more comfortable about being German, and gained the respect of other Europeans. Ultimately, the Fischer thesis became the conventional wisdom in Germany. In retrospect, it is apparent that Fischer exaggerated the extent to which the Imperial War Council Meeting of December 1912 made a decision for a preventive war. The Fischer thesis also rests on the questionable claim that the so-called September Program—the list of war aims prepared by German industrialists in September 1914—is evidence of Germany's motives for an aggressive war. It was prepared at the request of the foreign ministry at the moment when the German army was invading France and victory appeared imminent. It was a response to expected victory, not a plan for war. *Griff Nach der Weltmacht* nevertheless had a positive legacy by focusing historical debates on documents and freeing the German historical profession of its self-imposed and rather brutally enforced political orthodoxy. At the same time, it kept alive the war-guilt question, which is no longer relevant to contemporary political concerns or intellectual efforts to understand and prevent great power war.[9]

In subsequent decades, most accounts of the origins of the war have been less partisan in nature and more detached from contemporary controversies. While there is a decided shift away from *Kriegschuldfrage*, it never goes away. Recent works by Sean McMeekin and Max Hastings have revived this controversy.[10] McMeekin blames Russia for the war, arguing that its leaders deliberately provoked it in the hope of gaining control over Constantinople and the Straits. Historians have been very critical of his account which they describe as highly selective in its use of evidence to support an exaggerated and unconvincing account of Russian responsibility for the war.[11] Hastings is unremitting in holding Germany responsible for the war, and some critics consider his account vengeful.[12] Hew Strachan largely subscribes to Fischer thesis of German preventive war and blames Austria and Serbia.[13] Thomas Otte describes the blunders of German leaders more responsible than anything else for the war.[14] Margaret MacMillan distributes responsibility almost equally among Germany, Austria, and Serbia.[15]

Christopher Clark's *The Sleepwalkers* has attracted the most attention from scholars and the reading public. He finds multiple structural causes for war and stresses the lack of insight and judgment of leaders, even given the constraints under which they operated. These included fragmented centers of power, lack of transparency, and difficulties in signaling intentions. Like MacMillan and Strachan, he offers a continent-wide perspective on events, and he also benefits from knowledge of decision-making theory. Some have hailed his work as a worthy successor to Albertini.[16] Clark is less interested than some in assigning responsibility than most other historians, although he is more sympathetic to Germany Austria-Hungary than most and more critical of the entente powers.[17] For a revisionist account, it is very balanced. Clark's provocative title suggests that European leaders stumbled into a war that all were prepared to fight, that some were willing to risk, but that none wished to start. It has been a best seller in Germany, in large part for this reason judging from the press commentary. On the whole, German historians remain more convinced than others of their country's primary responsibility for the war. They include German historians like John Rohl, Annika Mombauer, and Volker Berghahn who work and live in the UK or the USA.

Recent scholarship has been greatly benefitted by access to archives formerly in East Germany and the Soviet Union that were largely closed to Western scholars. New work on Russia's role in the July crisis; biographies of the Kaiser, Moltke, and Falkenhayn; a controversial book and new documents; and debate about the Schlieffen Plan have led to a more complete understanding of the motives of these actors.[18] So too have publications on Austro-Hungarian policy and its leaders, Serbian politics, and Austro-Serbian relations.[19]

There has been a shift in focus in the last decade from national responsibility to shared features of the European political, economic, and cultural environment, and with it, an attempt to understanding the 'moods' and 'mentalities' of leaders and peoples. Jay Winter notes in his introduction to *The Cambridge History of the First World War* that the 'tragic interpretation' of World War I has become increasingly dominant. Clark, Macmillan, and Wawro are outstanding examples. There is also extensive new research and writing on the conduct of the war (the home front, the aftermath, and its memorialization and representation in literature).[20]

None of these works was written with IR theory in mind. Many of them address questions that seem far removed from the concerns of such theories and explore almost everything in finer detail than considered necessary by those interested in nomothetic forms of knowledge. The recent crop of histories of World War I is nevertheless more adventurous than past works by virtue of its comparative analysis. Most of the general accounts of the outbreak of the war explore policymaking in all the great powers, and in this connection, Serbia has been given a more prominent role than in the past.[21]

Recent historical works have important implications for IR theory. They offer more fully documented analyses of the motives, fears, and expectations of leading policymakers, explore connections between underlying and immediate causes of war, and highlight the importance of agents and contingency.

Representativeness

The two World Wars are the most important cases for most realist theories. Realists assume that these wars are typical of wars in general or at least those among the great powers. Historians stress what is different, even unique, about wars and the epochs in which they occurred. This difference reflects the different goals of history and social science. Ideally, both should be interested in the general and the particular. It is necessary to know something about the general to identify and describe the particular, and knowledge of particulars to generalize. Comparisons across cases, on which most IR theory rests, assume that they share enough important features to justify this research strategy. How do we know? And how do we know which features are important?

To find defensible answers to these questions, IR scholars must read history to develop a sophisticated understanding of the contexts in which events of interest took place. World War I broke out in a Europe characterized by rapid economic development, the rise of new classes, and the spread of new ideas, including nationalism, all of which put enormous stress on existing political institutions and practices. Recent works on the origins of World War I see these developments as fundamental underlying causes in the sense that they made leaders of the great continental powers more insecure, more aggressive, and more favorably disposed, if not to war, to the kind of risk taking that made war more likely.[22] The Austrian, Russian, German, French, and British responses to the assassination and events that followed were very much context dependent. This consensus does not rule out generalizing across cases but does mean that IR scholars must carefully construct their propositions and data sets to take this context and some of its most important features into account. They will complicate comparisons and dictate what kinds of comparisons are appropriate. They may rule out some comparisons or require particular features to be controlled for in making comparisons.

The cumulative analyses of World War I create a second, related problem. Historians have identified what they consider to be a number of political, military, social, and ideational causes of war. They include nationalism, alliance systems, commitments to preserving honor, and social Darwinism. The most recent accounts of the origin of the war do not significantly disagree with earlier ones in this regard. Nobody proposes a 'cause' that has not previously been mooted, and there is a relatively minor reevaluation of the relative importance of what has traditionally been considered the most important underlying ones. Historians tend not to rank underlying causes, but they invariably describe them as reinforcing. Some only have an effect, or have a greater effect, in the presence of others. And this relationship is often country specific. In Germany, Social Darwinism, fear of domestic change, strategic insecurity, and status concerns interacted synergistically but seemingly not at all in Britain. They helped to make German leaders more risk prone. In Britain, these considerations were not present or less muted and help to explain why British leaders were risk averse.

Underlying causes resemble genes in that they must be turned on to have an effect, and this often depends on the presence of other genes and chemical, even environmental triggers. This is also true for many so-called underlying causes. Their effect can depend on the presence of other underlying causes or external conditions, and multiple causes can interact in ways that amplify their effects. So the simple identification of the presence or absence of a theorized underlying cause or causes is only a first step in determining their consequences and the similarities between this war and others. In effect, one needs to create causal maps for purposes of comparison.[23]

Existing international relations theories explain wars do so in terms of their underlying causes. Many assume that immediate or precipitating causes are unproblematic; that something will happen to trigger war when the conditions are ripe. One of the prominent features of the newer works on World War I is their emphasis on agency, a subject I address in the next section. For the moment, let us consider one of the important implications of agency for comparative analysis of the origins or conduct of wars. With different leaders, war might not have occurred in 1914, or on other occasions, and might have broken out when it did not historically. The Sarajevo assassinations removed Archduke Franz Ferdinand from the scene. By all accounts, he was peacefully inclined and believed that war between Austria-Hungary and Russia could spell the death knell of both empires. He was committed to a program of domestic reforms, which also required peace. Some other pretext for war probably would not have been exploited had he remained alive and a major player.

Absent the right pretext and leaders willing to exploit it, war may not happen. If so, theories of war and data sets used to test them are incomplete, if not misleading, in the absence of efforts to theorize and code for the presence of triggers. Some conflicts need very particular pretexts and catalysts, and World War I was one of them. The assassinations at Sarajevo met six conditions without which the Austrians would not have decided on a war against Serbia nor the Germans supported them if they had. It removed Franz Ferdinand, allowed Conrad von Hotzendorf, the bellicose Austrian chief-of-staff, to remain in power; made it possible for the Kaiser and his chancellor Bethmann-Hollweg to convince themselves that they would not be responsible for war if the Russians intervened and the crisis escalated; and convinced Bethmann-Hollweg to risk war because Russia could be made to appear responsible, thus ensuring the essential support of Germany's socialists.[24]

CONTINGENCY

Theories of war largely treat World War as overdetermined and buy into the cliché that Europe was dry kindling waiting for a spark to set it alight. Theories that build on or address World War II regard it as highly contingent. Deterrence theorists assume that war in Europe could have been prevented the 1930s if France, Britain, and the Soviet Union had been more military powerful or responded in a more timely way to the threat to peace posed by a revanchist, Hitler-led Germany.[25] There is nevertheless a consensus among historians that Hitler and Japanese leaders wanted war and exploited and invented pretexts to serve their purposes.

Theories of war are for the most not determinist but at the same time downplay contingency. To recognize the stochastic nature of much political life, and especially the outbreak of particular wars, would threaten the generalizability of any theory. At the same time, as noted above, IR scholars assess the contingency of the World Wars differently and often disagree among themselves in this regard. Those who focus on deterrence need to make the case for contingency. IR theorists do not ask why one systemic war is seemingly overdetermined and its successor possibly contingent. Nor do they inquire what these differences mean for the project of theory building.

With regard to World War I, there has been a significant shift in opinion among historians away from inevitability toward contingency.[26] Christopher Clark describes the July crisis as a story saturated with agency. War was the product of a chain of decisions, each of which might have been different. Other futures are accordingly 'easy to imagine'.[27] According to Margaret MacMillan, it is 'Easy to throw up one's hands and say the Great War was inevitable, but that is dangerous thinking'.[28] Europe, she insists, did not have to go to war in 1914. It was the result of military planning in a political vacuum, poor civilian–military communication before and during the crisis, and above all, woefully inadequate political and military leadership in July 1914.[29] Afflerbach, Afflerbach and Stevenson, Kiessling, Strachan, Clark, Becker and Krumeich, Mulligan, Martel, and Otte all argue for the contingency of World War I, although they offer varying assessments of its probability.[30]

Earlier generations of historians focused almost entirely on the developments and events that were seemingly responsible for war and made much of the alleged outpouring of enthusiasm in the capitals of all the participants once war was declared. Recent accounts devote considerable space to developments and events that promoted peace and expectations of peace. These authors challenge the myth of universal support for war once it was declared and document the extent to which there were antiwar protests.[31] In Berlin, some 100,000 people took to the streets to demonstrate for peace, more than had turned out for pro-war marches.[32]

Recent accounts note the extent to which war took most European leaders by surprise. They did not believe that yet another Balkan crisis had a serious potential to threaten the general peace. Balkan and other crises had repeatedly engaged the attention of the great powers; they had consistently acted collectively to limit their consequences. Many leaders went on or remained on holiday after the Sarajevo assassinations, as there was little sense of urgency in most capitals at the outset. Most received updates and returned to their respective capitals after receiving word on 24 July of the Austrian ultimatum to Serbia.[33] Even then, British foreign minister Grey assumed that the usual scenario would play out: rising tensions, a European conference, and a diplomatic settlement as all major powers had an interest in preserving the peace. Alarm bells sounded only when the details of the Austrian ultimatum became available.[34]

We cannot equate surprise with contingency. Death, when it comes, takes most people by surprise, although for all it is inevitable. We must interrogate the arguments offered in support of contingency. Those concerning agency are the most important. There is a general consensus that the quality of decision making was uniformly low, in part due to the inexperience of some leaders but more importantly due to their intellectual and psychological inadequacy. I treat this issue in more detail in my later discussion of rationalist models. Here, let me accept these claims and briefly discuss their implications for contingency. The striking uniformity of bad leadership suggests that it was probably a structural feature. Military organizations were run almost everywhere by aristocrats who attained their positions more by virtue of their social connections than their competence. In Germany, the quality of leadership was low for other reasons; generals were committed to war for reasons that little to do with security, failed to think through even the military implications of their war plans, and engaged in denial instead of confronting difficult choices.[35] Diplomats and political officials in turn were slow to recognize the gravity of the situation, largely insensitive to the consequences of their actions for other actors and, British Foreign Secretary Sir Edward Grey aside, unwilling to take any risks to preserve the peace.

Is there any reason to suspect that different diplomats and political leaders would have made a difference? Toward this end, several historians offer counterfactuals. The most common one concerns Franz Ferdinand, whose assassination might easily have been prevented.[36] He was deeply committed to peace with Russia and would have opposed those like Conrad who pushed for war against Serbia on the grounds that it was likely to escalate into a wider war. Conrad had demanded war in 1906, 1908–1909, and 1912–Between January 1913 and January 1914, he proposed war against Serbia 25 times. Franz Ferdinand intended to remove Conrad from the position as chief of the general staff upon his return from Sarajevo. Franz Ferdinand's survival and Conrad's forced retirement would have significantly changed the balance of power in Vienna and deprived the hawks of their much-desired pretext. Margaret MacMillan suggests that if Alfred von Kiderlen-Wächter, foreign secretary from 1910 to 1912, had remained in office, he would have been more likely than Bethmann-Hollweg to stand up to the Kaiser and Moltke.[37] However, it is more difficult to conjure up reasons for a prolonged tenure in the foreign office for Kiderlen.

The other common counterfactual concerns the timing of the Austrian ultimatum to Serbia. The Germans thought earlier action by Austria would have capitalized on the sympathy felt everywhere in Europe after the assassinations and the widespread belief that Serbia had in some way been complicit. However, there is no compelling argument for why Russia would have been more constrained; a prior Austrian foreign policy review commissioned by foreign minister Leopold Berchtold concluded that Russia would not stand aside if Serbia was attacked.[38] There was also no reason to think that Austria could act with dispatch given the initial Hungarian opposition to war and the need to secure German backing. Conrad also delayed war because of the harvest and slow pace of Austrian military preparations.

None of the recent historians consider what might have happened if the Sarajevo tragedy had been averted. To be sure, there would have been no July crisis and war in August 1914. Structural theories assume that some other catalyst would have come along before long. A 'second-order' counterfactual would have put history more or less back on track. I consider this unlikely because, as noted, Sarajevo was a cause in its own right. In the absence of the six conditions it fulfilled, it is unlikely that Austria would have attacked Serbia or Germany risked war with Russia by backing Austria. It is also hard to imagine any other set of countries starting a war or implementing initiatives that made it likely. I further contend that by 1917, leaders in Vienna, Berlin, and St. Petersburg would have become increasingly risk averse for different reasons. There was a narrow window in which war was possible, and it required a very special kind of catalyst.[39]

I close this section by returning to the forces working for peace. In the decade before France and Germany had resolved their differences over Morocco. Britain and Germany had come to an agreement about Persia and the Baghdad railway, were coming to grips with naval race, and negotiating the possible distribution of Portuguese colonies in Africa. Prior crises had created real tensions but had all been peacefully resolved. Recent accounts of the July crisis note the existence of large peace movements and trade union opposition to war. Governments everywhere were surprised that there were no general strikes or interference with mobilization.[40]

Economic development was another powerful force for peace. It was widely believed that war would threaten European civilization because of the havoc it would wreck on every national economy. This expectation was shared by soldiers and civilians, and most of them expected—or at least hoped for—a short war. Otherwise, markets and loans were expected to dry up and investment to all but cease, triggering a downward economic spiral. Bankers, businessmen, and politicians alike thought it impossible to fund a large war. They missed the economic lessons of the American Civil War and Russo-Japanese War, just as the generals were blind to their military lessons.[41] All the German industrialists and bankers consulted by the Kaiser urged peace; it was also very much wanted by City of London. In a few more years, these forces would have become stronger, and perhaps, German leaders would have become more open to their arguments. Nobody imagined anything like Verdun or the Somme or German efforts to strangle Britain with submarine warfare. To his credit, the Elder Moltke, who died in 1891, recognized that a short war was all but impossible in an era of multimillion man armies. He became enamored of peace for this reason and designed his eponymous war plan to win a campaign rather than a war.[42] The British were alone in planning for long-economic warfare and a blockade of their adversaries.[43] The German thought the British would abide by the rules of war in terms of engagements between battle fleets.[44]

These misjudgments hold an important lesson for IR theory. Everywhere, generals, politicians, bankers, and businessmen made decisions based on false premises and erroneous expectations. Generals believed that the offensive would triumph, politicians and diplomats that time was working against their countries, and bankers and businessmen that war might lead to economic collapse. Balance of power, deterrence, and rationalist theories all assume that leaders have a reasonable understanding of the environments in which they operate, a thoroughly unwarranted assumption in the case of 1914. The World War I arguably came about because of these illusions. If political and military leaders had had better understandings of critical features of political, military, and economic contexts, they would surely have been more cautious.

World War I is not unique in this regard. Between 1648 and the present, initiators of wars that involved at least one great or rising power on each side won slightly less than half of these conflict. From 1945 to the present, initiators fought 31 wars and achieved their political goals in only 7 or 26% of them and attained a military victory in only 10 or 32% of them.[45] This is not at all impressive given that the choice of war or peace, and the timing of any war, was up to the initiator in the overwhelming number of cases. Balance of power theory and other realist and rationalist approaches to foreign policy assume that leaders will only initiate war when they expect to win, or at least, not to lose. This expectation flies in the face of empirical evidence because leaders often undertake war for reasons of honor and revenge, not security or material gain.[46] Nor do they necessarily undertake a careful analysis of cost and risk beforehand. To understand World War I—and many other conflicts—we need to ask why policymakers ignore critical and readily available information and take refuge in comforting illusions.

BALANCE OF POWER

The balance of power has been the core mechanism of realist theories of international relations. In a multipolar world, balance of power theorists assume that balancing generally involves alliances, and this in turn requires early recognition of threats and effective diplomacy. It implicitly entails the active practice of deterrence, although balance of power theorists are largely mute on this subject. Would-be aggressors are expected to make a reasonable estimate of alliance cohesion and the military balance and act in a restrained manner when they confront an unfavorable balance of power.

In 1914, balance of power failed to prevent war. Balance of power theorists assume that the balance is not all that difficult to estimate, although alliance cohesion, an important component of that assessment, can be problematic. On the eve of war, there was striking variation across and within countries about the present and likely future military balance.[47] Estimates of the balance were highly motivated. German military leaders were not at all confident about their ability to wage a victorious war on two fronts. Moltke and Falkenhayn were quite pessimistic, although Moltke was much more confident when attempting to persuade the Kaiser and chancellor to risk war.[48]

Conrad von Hotzendorf was committed to attack Serbia but not optimistic about Austrian army's ability to crush Serbia and fend off a Russian attack in Galicia. At the outset, the Russians had 50 plus divisions, with many more in reserve, and the Serbians 11. Against these forces, Austria-Hungary could marshal 48 and had an inferior railway system.[49] To attain a victory, they would have to overrun Serbia quickly with the 14 divisions Conrad earmarked for this purpose while holding off the Russian steamroller in Galicia. Yet, war games revealed that the Serbs could defend themselves effectively against an Austrian attack, as indeed they did. On the eve of war, Conrad deluded himself into believing that 'a brisk, brave attack' would nevertheless succeed. His 'willful blindness was remarkable.'[50] Franz Josef to his credit was deeply pessimistic about a two-front war. Russian military and political officials were, if anything, more unrealistic than their German and Austrian counterparts in thinking they could launch offensive against two adversaries at the same time. In Vienna and Berlin, expectations about the future state of the balance of power were in many ways decisive. Austrian officials worried that Serbia would get stronger, that Romania would become hostile and Russian influence grow in the Balkans. These expectations were probably warranted, but we must note that Austria had behaved in ways to make them at least in part self-fulfilling.[51]

By 1914, German military and political leaders were convinced that Russian railway building would render the Schlieffen Plan unworkable by 1917. They also worried about the possible loss of Austria as a reliable ally. For these reasons, Moltke and General Erich von Falkenhayn favored a preventive war and did their best to convince the otherwise peacefully inclined chancellor to assume the risk of war.[52] German fear of Russia was greatly exaggerated, if not altogether misplaced, as the opening campaign in the east soon revealed that the Russian army was in no condition to conduct a successful offensive against Germany. The July crisis indicates that the balance of power is a highly subjective judgment and readily influenced by the goals and psychological state of leaders; Austrian, German, and Russian leaders saw what they wanted to see and what they feared to see. The balance may also be less important than actor expectations about its likely direction and pace of change.

It therefore makes no sense for theorists to use their own assessments of the balance, as they so often do. These must be reconstructed through the eyes of relevant actors.[53]

The balance of power was also problematic in 1914 because of the motives of Austrian, Russian, and German leaders. Conrad, Berchtold, Hoyos, and the other hawks in the foreign ministry were keen to uphold the honor of the Empire and believed that any moderate response to the assassinations would undermine its standing.[54] Conrad confided to his mistress that Russia and Serbia would be 'the coffin nails' of Austria-Hungary but that war was necessary 'because such an ancient monarchy and such an ancient army cannot perish ungloriously [sic]'.[55] Moltke and the Kaiser were equally moved by considerations of honor, and the Kaiser defined his role as the Austrian Emperor's 'second' in his duel with Serbia.[56] A balance of power cannot deter in these circumstances because losing a war will not be seen by leaders as worse than not fighting one because of the shame this is understood to entail; and it is always possible to delude oneself into believing that victory is possible. On the eve of the war, Conrad confided to his mistress: 'It will be a hopeless struggle, but it must be pursued because so old a Monarchy and so glorious an army cannot go down ingloriously.'[57] Count Alexander Hoyos, permanent head of the foreign ministry, exclaimed: 'We are still capable of resolve! We do not want to or ought to be a sick man. Better to be destroyed quickly.'[58]

The balance of power did not prevent war but did forestall German hegemony. Britain declared war on Germany when it invaded Belgium and the USA intervened decisively in April 1917. The history of the European state system offers additional evidence that balances of power have consistently prevented hegemony but not war.

In contrast to most balance of power theories, power transition theory emphasizes perceptions of changes in the balance. Its advocates attribute systemic wars to conflicts between rising and dominant powers. Rising powers attack dominant powers when they feel strong enough to win and reorder the international system to their advantage.[59] Alternatively, dominant powers launch preventive wars against rising powers to forestall this outcome.[60] Power transition theorists routinely offer World War I in support of one or the other variant.

Was 1914 a preventive war? Much of the German historical community finds the Fischer thesis extreme but generally accepts that 1914 had features of a preventive war.[61] Certainly, Moltke was pushing for military action from the outset.[62] Margaret MacMillan offers a more restrained judgment about Bethmann-Hollweg—he:

> may not have deliberately started the Great War ... Nevertheless, by taking its coming for granted, as something desirable even, by issuing the blank cheque to Austria-Hungary, and by sticking to a war plan which made it inevitable that Germany would fight on two fronts, Germany's leaders allowed it to happen.[63]

It is still quite a stretch to explain German policy in terms of power transition theory. The dominant power by any metric in 1914 was the USA, and it did not figure at all into German calculations. On the continent, Germany was the leading power and growing stronger every year. This is why every banker, industrialist, and shipping magnate consulted by the Kaiser urged him to pursue a peaceful foreign policy. Russia was developing rapidly but still a very backward country; it could mobilize impressive manpower but its effective use required good training, equipment, and leadership, which Russia lacked. Moltke's concern for Russia and its railway reforms was driven in the first instance by his paranoia and projection.[64] He and the Kaiser worried about Asiatic hordes overrunning Germany and putting an end to Western civilization. Moltke and the generals also wanted war sooner rather than later because of their commitment to the offensive and its ultimate expression in the Schlieffen Plan.[65] Moltke knew from war games that Germany could easily fight a defensive war on both fronts but rejected a defensive strategy out of hand. If power transition was a motive, Germany would surely have waged a defensive in the west and an offensive in the east against Russia, considered to be the rising power.

DETERRENCE

Deterrence is a strategy that aims to prevent undesirable behavior by promising to punish the actor who carries it out. It assumes that actors carefully evaluate the expected gains, costs, and risks of their initiatives and that this cost calculus can be influenced from the outside. Deterrence attempts to raise the costs associated with a specific behavior to make them outweigh any possible gains by means of credible threats of certain punishment. Deterrence theory stipulates would-be deterrers must define their commitments, communicate them to would-be challengers, possess the military capability to defend them or otherwise punish transgressors, and impart credibility to their threats.[66]

Deterrence has a long history in conventional conflicts but was extensively theorized during the Cold War when nuclear weapons made the prospect of war increasingly catastrophic.[67] Deterrence advocates sought to justify the strategy by counterfactual arguments about both World Wars. They described World War I as a deterrence failure on the grounds that Britain failed to convey its resolve to Germany in a timely way that it would intervene on the side of France if Germany invaded Belgium. World War II was also considered a deterrence failure because of appeasement. It is commonly asserted that Hitler's reoccupation of the Rhineland and invasion of Austria could have been prevented by effective deterrence or his later aggressions by prompt retaliation. Cold War crises were also interpreted retrospectively to validate deterrence. Alexander George and Richard Smoke, among others, categorized the several Berlin crises as deterrence successes.[68] The Cuban missile crisis was widely acknowledged as a deterrence failure. However, the fault was not attributed to the strategy but to Kennedy's alleged failure to perform it effectively. With the end of the Cold War, enough evidence became available from the Soviet side to decisively discredit these interpretations. The Berlin crises could not be considered deterrence successes because neither Stalin nor Khrushchev intended to occupy West Berlin. Khrushchev never doubted Kennedy's resolve but rather thought him brash and unconstrained and refused to deploy missiles openly in Cuba, as the Castro brothers wished, because he was convinced that Kennedy would send out the navy and stop or sink his ships.[69] Throughout the Cold War, Soviet leaders never doubted American resolve but rather worried that they were reckless and trigger-happy.[70]

Realists and deterrence supporters argued that deterrence failed in 1914, not because it was a flawed strategy but because it had not been practiced effectively.[71] Had British leaders effectively put Germany on notice that they would intervene in support of France, German leaders might have restrained instead of encouraged Austria. Historians reject this contention outright. They contend that there was ample evidence that Britain would come to France's aid if Germany invaded Belgium, and that this was known to the Kaiser, Bethmann-Hollweg, and Jagow and Zimmermann in the foreign office. They reject the speculation that an earlier and firmer British commitment would have made any difference.[72] Speaking for a consensus among German historians, Volker

Berghahn maintains that Moltke wanted a preventive war as did Conrad and that the former had long ago discounted the military significance of British intervention. So, timely demonstrations of credibility were not the issue in 1914.[73]

Critics of deterrence have long maintained that it has the potential to make war more rather than less likely, an argument originally developed by revisionist historians between the wars. Hew Strachan is among the most recent historians to document the downside of deterrence in 1914.[74] French President Poincaré believed that robust alliances with Russia and Britain would restrain Germany. However, Germany could only be deterred 'if it had a mind to be deterred', and it did not. Germany and Austria in turn calculated that their alliance would keep Russia quiescent or, failing that, France from coming to Russia's aid. In practice, both alliances intensified conflict and encouraged worst-case analysis and preemption, the latter because of the nearly universal belief in the value of offense and need for speed. Strachan maintains that alliances were sought as much for reasons of status as for security, and this too provided incentives to act in the face of credible deterrence threats. Russia had to support Serbia because it had not done so in 1909; Germany had to support Austria-Hungary because it had opposed its adventurism in 1913; France had to honor its commitments to Russia because it had not done so in 1909. The 'statesmen of 1914 were pygmies'.[75] Only Britain was careful about making military commitments, and foreign secretary Grey prepared to take risks for peace.

Janice Stein and I have argued that deterrence often fails for two other sets of reasons.[76] Leaders facing a combination of domestic and foreign threats they believe can only be overcome through an aggressive foreign policy become more sensitive to the threats of inaction than of action. Once committed to challenging a commitment of an adversary, they readily succumb to motivated bias and ignore, deny, distort, or explain away information that threatens the success of their initiatives, and this includes efforts by defenders to buttress their commitments and resolve. Deterrence often finds expression in threatening rhetoric, arms buildups, and forward deployments, actions that are readily interpreted as intimidation by target actors and make the would-be deterrer appear a would-be aggressor. In the Cold War, it led to a series of escalating crises, culminating in the Cuban missile crisis that threatened a war that superpowers were desperate to avoid.

There is compelling evidence that a similar process characterized the run up to World War I. Deterrence took the form of alliances and military buildups in weapons, armies, and fleet and encouraged worst-case analysis and behavior that made those expectations self-fulfilling. Most striking according to recent historians is the extent to which leaders were sensitive to the threats posed by would-be adversaries but utterly insensitive to the effects of their initiatives on their leaders.[77] This was most evident in the case of Germany, whose leaders felt encircled but were blind to the ways they had helped to bring this situation about. Field Marshal Alfred von Waldersee and Moltke, his successor as chief of the general staff, talked of Germany's need to fight for third existence as people.[78] Thomas Otte paraphrases the Lebow-Stein argument in the context of 1914. 'To some extent', he writes:

> all the powers, with the exception of Britain, were driven by a sense of weakness, which made it difficult for them to pull back from the abyss of war. The certainty of diplomatic defeat, and its foreseeable adverse effects in the short term, proved a more powerful spur not to compromise than the incalculable, because more distant, consequences of military conflict.[79]

CRISIS MANAGEMENT

The Cold War provided a new lens through which to reexamine World War I and its origins. A key text in this connection was Barbara Tuchman's *Guns of August,* published in 1962.[80] It made the case for accidental war arising from the rigid nature of mobilization plans and ignorance of them by political leaders who did not understand that mobilization meant war—a claim since shown by historians to be incorrect. President Kennedy was riveted by the book and later confessed that it was very much in his mind during the Cuban missile crisis. International relations scholars also began to explore the problem of unintended escalation, inspired in large part by the Berlin and Cuban missile crises, in which accidental war seemed a real possibility.

The focus of crisis management has given rise to interesting controversies chief among them is the importance scholars assign to decision-making procedures. Alexander George and Irving Janis both argued that good decision making would lead to better crisis outcomes and sought to develop procedures toward this end, among them use of a devil's advocate in policy deliberations.[81] Critics, including the author, countered that what really matters are the assumptions leaders bring to the table. When these are shared, they are unlikely to be acknowledged, let alone debated. Faulty or inappropriate assumptions will lead to ineffective, even counterproductive, policies regardless of the quality of the decision-making process. The July crisis and more recent ones were mobilized by opponents of decision-making procedures and their critics in support of their respective arguments and led to a general debate about whether intelligence failures could be significantly reduced.[82]

There can be little doubt that decision making in every capital in 1914 was woefully inadequate and for multiple reasons. The poor performance of leaders, diplomats, and generals offers support to both sides in this controversy. In Serbia, authority was fragmented. Chief of the intelligence department of the general staff Dragutin Dimitrijevic, known as Apis, sent three members of the Black Hand to assassinate Franz Ferdinand when he learned of his impending visit to Sarajevo. Higher-ranking Serbian officials were too intimidated or powerless to stop him or provide effective warnings to Vienna.[83] Among the great powers, there was little consultation between political and military leaders. In France and Britain, the only two countries with parliamentary committees intended to encourage consultation, little to no exchange of views occurred. In Austria-Hungary, political leaders were aware of Conrad's intention to earmark 15 divisions to attack Serbia, reducing the forces available to protect Galicia against the expected Russian attack. Most made no effort to persuade him to the contrary.[84]

Hardly anybody sensed the seriousness of the crisis until late in the day. Franz Ferdinand's visit to Sarajevo was deliberately provocative because it was scheduled for the feast day of St Vitus, when Serbs commemorated their defeat by the Ottomans on 28 June 1389. The local Austrian authorities paid less attention to the Archduke's security than they did to choosing wines and trying to ascertain if he liked to listen to music at lunch. Private motives often replaced or equaled public ones. Conrad wanted war because he hoped that victory would allow him to circumvent convention and marry his already married mistress Gina.[85] The assassinations aroused emotions throughout Europe but especially in Franz Josef and the Kaiser, both of whom became more disposed to war.

German leaders deluded themselves into believing that their 'blank cheque' would not provoke a continental war; they expected to Russia to stand aside, especially if Austria acted quickly. Falkenhayn and Bethmann-Hollweg had their doubts about whether Austria would follow through on its ultimatum to Serbia. Bethmann-Hollweg had no inkling of the contents of the ultimatum. Nor did Conrad apprise his German ally of just how long it would take to begin operations against Serbia. The Kaiser failed to provide overall guidance and continuity to German policy. At the height of the crisis, he was in Potsdam where he had a dissociative reaction for 24 h and was out of reach and out of touch with everyone.[86] In Berlin, Moltke and Bethmann-Hollweg sent opposing signals to Austrian political and military leaders.[87] All the German leaders convinced themselves that they could win a short war because they doubted they could fight or win a long one.[88]

Political and military leaders across Europe repeatedly stressed the constraints under which they operated and ignored those faced by others. They were so convinced of the rectitude of their respective cases that they failed to consider the interests and likely responses of other powers. They succumbed to a 'dangerous feeling of helplessness in the face of doom' in contrast to John Kennedy and Nikita S. Khrushchev in the Cuban missile crisis who took strategic and political risks to preserve the peace.[89] Throughout the crisis, Bethmann-Hollweg was depressed and deeply pessimistic as a result of his wife's death in May.[90] He convinced himself that a 'fate greater than human power hangs over the situation in Europe and over the German People'.[91] He supported Austria's desire to settle scores with Serbia even though he recognized that it was likely to provoke a continental war, and one, he wrote Moltke, that would have catastrophic results. 'The culture of almost all of Europe will be destroyed for decades to come.'[92] The Kaiser also denied personal responsibility by asserting that the affairs of nations were now 'in the hands of god'.[93] Christopher Clark contends that these kinds of self-serving narratives 'enabled decision-makers to hide, even from themselves, their responsibility for the outcomes of their actions. If the future was already mapped out, then politics no longer meant choosing among options, each of which implied a different future'.[94]

Almost everyone operated on the basis of false assumptions. Past Balkan and European crises had been resolved when other powers became involved because nobody wanted war. The July crisis escalated out of control because Austria wanted a local war and German leaders were not adverse to a general one. German diplomacy sought to limit war, not to prevent it. Yet, the German military had only considered and planned for a two-front continental war. Bethmann-Hollweg was not adverse to this prospect because his vision of war was Sadowa and Sedan, not Verdun or the Somme. Germany made no preparations for a long war although this is what Moltke feared. He and Falkenhayn believed that a long war would be impossible to fight, let alone win and desperately wanted to believe in the possibility of a shorter one.[95] The general staff tried to place orders for grain in Holland on the eve of Belgium invasion, but the treasury would not authorize the expenditure. In Vienna, Austrian hawks argued that they could fight a localized war against Serbia and that with German support Russia would back down again as it had in 1909. The Kaiser and Bethmann-Hollweg also expected Russian to remain quiescent, while Moltke appears to have hoped they would not. He desperately wanted war with France but was by no means confident of victory.[96] The French misjudged the value of Russian entry into the war and falsely assumed that their offensive would be directed against Germany, not against Austria-Hungary as well. British foreign secretary Grey believed until late in the crisis that Germany would restrain Austria, not egg it on.[97]

Rationalist models came increasingly into vogue in IR theory the 1980s, and much of their focus was war initiation.[98] They link alleged structural features to agent behavior. Many start from the assumption that war is the result of incomplete information: opposing sides cannot find an agreement they would both settle for or cannot know the outcome of a war between them. In the later circumstance, one or both parties may consider war preferable to an unsatisfactory settlement. Uncertainty about the outcome of war was high in 1914, but there is little evidence that leaders among the leading protagonists engaged in the kind of cost calculus that rationalist models expect. Rather than trying to reduce uncertainty by searching for new information and carefully analyzing that which they had, Austrian, German, and Russian leaders sought refuge in their illusions. Historians from Luigi Albertini to the present agree that the most striking feature about 1914 was the unreflective, ill-considered, and emotional nature of decisions for mobilization and war in Austria-Hungary, Berlin, and St. Petersburg.

WHY THE ALLIES WON

As the preceding discussion indicates, the origins of World War I, not its course or outcome, have been the primary focus of IR research. There has been some theorizing about the differential success of regime types, the reasons why wars drag on or end, and the kinds of postwar regimes that are established in hope of preventing a recurrence of system-level war.[99] Most of this research is comparative in focus and quantitative in method. Research on war termination and postwar management has relied more on case studies.

Stam and Reiter, among others, insist that democracies are more successful because they are more legitimate, better able to mobilize people and resources, and more likely to have capable leaders.[100] These theorists cite both World Wars in support of their claims. The one historian to engage this question directly is Christopher Mick, who contributed the chapter on victory to *The Cambridge History of The First World War*.[101] He dismisses the supposed success of democracies as an ideological claim that cannot be substantiated on the basis of the empirical record. Without Russia, he insists, the allies would have lost. Germany would not have had to fight a two-front war and could have mobilized all of its army against Belgium and France from the outset. It would likely have outflanked the British Expeditionary Force and possibly won the Battle of France in 1914. Germany and Austria-Hungary, he insists, were not disadvantaged by their form of government but by their domestic political–institutional structures. Both countries were federal in nature with considerable power reserved to states or regions. This made it correspondingly more difficult than it was in Britain or France to raise taxes at the national level or impose them of sub-units.

In leadership, the democracies had an advantage. Conrad was an incompetent chief of staff. Ludendorff was a good tactician but an 'inept and short-sighted politician'. German generalship was excellent and the Germans pioneered new tactics that proved very effective in the 1918 Spring offensive. German morale remained high until the failure of this offensive, which was waged at great cost. The biggest difference between the two blocs was their economies. The Gross Domestic Product (GDP) of the Central Powers was only 65% of that of the allies. Britain and France could also draw on enormous reserves of manpower and raw materials from overseas and colonies. Here, sea power played a vital role and was a function of Britain's geographical position and history, not of its democracy. The USA really swung the balance and was key to the allies from the outset in the loans and food it provided. The arrival of American troops in France in the autumn of 1917 did wonders for allied morale and resolve.[102]

In 1914, Germany was not an authoritarian regime by the standards of the day. It had a free press, a parliament elected by universal male suffrage, and an independent judiciary. But war quickly brought about dictatorship. In contrast to Britain and France, military and foreign policy were the private preserve of the Kaiser and the only authority the Reichstag had over them was the power of the purse. Once the socialists voted the *Burgfrieden* (domestic political truce) at the outset of hostilities, they were marginalized. This paved the way for a military dictatorship, which exercised de facto power after Bethmann-Hollweg resigned in January 1917 in opposition to the Kaiser's authorization of unrestricted submarine warfare. If we consider the counterfactual that the socialists had behaved differently and had more input in policy, there is no reason to think that this would have affected the final outcome. Germany should not have gone to war, should have waged a defensive war on both fronts if it did, and should have sought a negotiated peace on the basis of the status quo ante bellum once its initial offensive in the West failed. There is no evidence that a more democratic Germany would have behaved this way.

CONCLUSION

Theory loses its value when it does not engage empirical evidence or does so in a self-serving and selective way. Karl Deutsch identified the preference for internal or external feedback as the principal cause for the failure of social and political systems.[103] Such behavior encourages leaders and peoples to avoid confronting uncomfortable facts, making difficult choices in trade-offs and revising their beliefs and routines to suit evolving needs. This essay suggests that some IR theorists confront the same problem. Their highly abstract formulations are largely self-referential and they cherry-pick evidence that is, or can be made to appear, supportive of their theories.

The new research on World War I raises other issues for IR theories. Historians make a compelling case that the particular matters. Context was everything in 1914. The values and ideas of leaders determined the degree to which they envisaged war as an opportunity, necessity, or catastrophe. It influenced their reading of the balance of power and its importance, the choices open to themselves and their adversaries, and where they thought diplomacy would gave way to war.

Context encompasses agency, and historians agree it was decisive in World War I. The quality of policymaking was deplorable and almost all of the historians offer counterfactuals to buttress their contention that war was not inevitable. The survival of Franz Ferdinand and his removal from office of Conrad or a more self-confident leader like Kiderlen in Berlin or a different foreign or war minister in St. Petersburg could have made all the difference.[104] In the words of Thomas Otte, 'the "balance of power" or the "alliance system" did not cause Europe's descent into war... individuals acting in response to external and internal stimuli, and to perceived opportunities and threats, were central to the developments of July 1914'.[105]

Context also includes confluence, and I have made the case that World War I was the result of three independent and highly contingent chains of causation that came into confluence in 1914 and made leaders in Vienna, Berlin, and St. Petersburg more risk prone. By 1917, these leaders or their successors would have become more risk averse for different sets of reasons. In the absence of Sarajevo, Europe might have made to 1917 without war and a continental conflict might have become increasingly less likely in subsequent years.[106]

It follows that structural theories and rationalist accounts, which by definition, exclude ideas, agency, path dependence, confluence, and emergence from their analysis can never be more than starting points for causal narratives in which the particular must be combined with the general. Max Weber was alert to this truth. He describes 'purposefully' rational action as an ideal type, which he calls 'right rationality' (*Richtigskeitstypus*). It is rarely found in practice but offers a useful benchmark for understanding deviations from it, and thus cause, in singular events. Weber also understood that rationality was context dependent. Different motives and goals would prompt different assessments of what was rational.[107] International relations scholars must recognize this truth and give up the goal of parsimonious, predictive theory.

The most important lesson of historical research on World War I is not its implications for any particular paradigm or theory but rather for how we think of theory and its utility. The literature on other wars, crises, and accommodations that have been extensively studied offers additional confirmation of Weber's characterization of many, if not most, developments of interest to us as singular in nature. Explanation or forecasting is a two-step process. We make use of theories or other abstractions to order these events in terms of categories and to tell us how perfectly rational actors would behave unconstrained by incomplete information, domestic politics and pressures, and other policy problems they confront. These theories, of course, must provide substance to the concept of rationality. Weber defines it as an ends–means relationship and insists that the ends are chosen by actors and cannot be imposed or assumed from the outside by analysts or theorists.[108] We must try to reconstruct actor goals or gather information about them of forecasting and then use our theories as a first step in creating a narrative that takes actors and context into account. Repeated analytical experience of this kind will help us reformulate our theories to make them more useful starting points for explanation and forecasting, which is the goal of theory in the social sciences.

Funding
This research received no specific grant from any funding agency in the public, commercial, or not-for-profit sectors.

NOTES

1. I would like to thank Ken Booth and the anonymous reviewers for their helpful comments.
2. Germany, Foreign Ministry, *Die Große Politik der Europäischen Kabinette, 1871–1914*, 40 vols, ed Johannes Lepsius and Albrecht Mendelssohn Bartholdy (Berlin: Deutsche Verlagsgesellschaft, 1922–1927); Holger H. Herwig, 'Clio Deceived: Patriotic Self-Censorship in Germany after the Great War', *International Security*, 12(2), 1987, pp. 5–44.
3. Sidney Fay, *The Origins of the World War*, 2nd ed., rev. 2 vols (New York: Macmillan, 1938 [1928]).
4. John Maynard Keynes, *The Economic Consequences of the Peace* (London: Macmillan, 1919); Etienne Mantoux, *The Carthaginian Peace: Or, the Consequences of Mr. Keynes* (Oxford: Oxford University Press, 1946), written in English.
5. Luigi Albertini, *The Origins of the War of 1914*, 3 vols, trans. by Isabella M. Massey (Oxford: Oxford University Press, 1952).
6. Fritz Fischer, *Griff nach der Weltmacht: die Kriegszielpolitik des kaiserlichen Deutschland 1914–1918* (Düsseldorf: Droste, 1962). English translation, *Germany's Aims in the First World War*, published by Norton in 1967. Fischer followed up with a second volume *Krieg der Illusionen; die deutsche Politik von 1911 bis 1914*, trans. into English (Berlin: Droste, 1969).
7. Hartmut Pogge von Strandtmann, 'The Political and Historical Significance of the Fischer Controversy', *Journal of Contemporary History*, 48(2), 2014, pp. 251–270; Annika Mombauer, 'The Fischer

Controversy, Documents and the "Truth" about the Origins of the First World War', *Journal of Contemporary History*, 48(2), 2014, pp. 290–314.

8. Wulf Kansteiner, *In Pursuit of German Memory: History, Television, and Politics after Auschwitz* (Athens, OH: University of Ohio Press, 2006).

9. Jonathan Steinberg, 'Old Knowledge and New Research: A Summary of the Conference on the Fischer Controversy 50 Years On', *Journal of Contemporary History*, 48(2), 2014, pp. 241–250.

10. Notable exceptions are Sean McMeekin, *The Russian Origins of the First World War* (Cambridge, MA: Harvard University Press, 2011) and Max Hastings, *Catastrophe 1914: Europe Goes to War* (London: Collins, 2013). Both authors have been severely criticized for their focus on guilt. McMeekin has also encountered serious criticism for the substance of his argument.

11. *BBC News*, 'World War One: Ten Interpretations of Who Started WWI', 12 February 2014, available at: http://www.bbc.co.uk/news/magazine-26048324; a more reliable recent account is Marina Soroka, *Britain, Russia, and the Road to the First World War: The Fateful Embassy of Count Alexander Benckendorff* (Farnham: Ashgate, 2011).

12. William Mulligan, 'The Trial Continues: New Directives in the Study of the Origins of the First World War', *English Historical Review*, 129(538), 2014, pp. 639–666; Richard J. Evans, 'The Road to Slaughter', *New Republic*, 5 December 2011, available at: http://www.newrepublic.com/book/review/the-road-slaughter (Accessed 8 August 2014); Lucian J. Frary, *H-Russia*, February 2012, available at: http://www.h-net.org/reviews/showrev.php?id=34716 (Accessed 10 August 2014).

13. Hew Strachan, *The First World War: To Arms* (Oxford: Oxford University Press, 2013).

14. Thomas G. Otte, *July Crisis: The World's Descent into War, Summer 1914* (Cambridge: Cambridge University Press, 2014), pp. 518–519.

15. *Margaret MacMillan, The War that Ended Peace: How Europe Abandoned Peace for the First World War* (London: Profile Books, 2013).

16. Christopher Clark, *The Sleepwalkers* (London: Allen Lane, 2013).

17. For France and Russia, Clark relies heavily on Stefan Schmidt's *Frankreichs Außenpolitik in der Julikrise 1914* (Munich: Oldenbourg, 2009) that argues convincingly that France was not a passive player but supportive of Russian risk taking in the July crisis.

18. McMeekin, *Russian Origins;* John C. Röhl, *The Kaiser and His Court: Wilhelm II and the Government of Germany* (Cambridge: Cambridge University Press, 1994); Annika Mombauer, *Helmuth von Moltke and*

the Origins of the First World War (Cambridge: Cambridge University Press, 2001) and Annika Mombauer, 'Of War Plans and War Guilt: The Debacle Surrounding the Schlieffen Plan', *Journal of Strategic Studies*, 28(5), 2005, pp. 857–855; Holger Afflerbach, *Falkenhayn: Politisches Denken und Handeln in Kaiserreich* (Munich: Oldenbourg, 1994); Terence Zuber, *Inventing the Schlieffen Plan: German War Planning, 1871–1914* (Oxford: Oxford University Press, 2002) and Terence Zuber, *The Real German War Plan*, 1904–1914 (London: History Press, 2011).

19. Holger H. Herwig, *The First World War: Germany and Austria-Hungary, 1914–1918* (London: Arnold, 1998); Lawrence Sondhaus, *Franz Conrad von Hötzendorf: Architect of the Apocalypse* (Boston: Humanities Press, 2000); Günther Kronenbitter, *Krieg im Frieden: die Führung der k.u.k. Armee und die Grossmachtpolitik Österreich-Ungarns 1906–1914* (Munich: Oldenbourg, 2003); Clark, *Sleepwalkers*; Manfred Rauchensteiner, *Der erste Weltkrieg und das Ende der Habsburger-Monarchie* (Vienna: Böhlau Verlag, 2013); Wolfram Domik, *Des Kaisers Falke: Wirken and Nach-Wirken von Franz Conrad von Hötzendorf* (Innsbruck: Studien Verlag, 2013); Geoffrey Wawro, *A Mad Catastrophe: The Outbreak of World War I and the Collapse of the Habsburg Empire* (New York: Basic Books, 2014).

20. Jay Winter (ed.), *The Cambridge History of the First World War: Global War*, vol. I (Cambridge: Cambridge University Press, 2014); Hew Strachan, *The First World War* (London: Penguin Books, 2005); Holger Afflerbach, *Der Dreibund: Europäische Grossmacht-und-Allianzpolitik vor dem Ersten Weltkrieg* (Vienna: Böhlau Verlag, 2002); Holger Afflerbach and David Stevenson (eds), *An Improbable War: The Outbreak of World War I and European Political Culture before 1914* (New York: Berghahn Books, 2007); Rauchensteiner, *Der erste Weltkrieg und das Ende*; Dornik, *Des Kaisers Falke*; Wawro, *A Mad Catastrophe*; David Reynolds, *The Long Shadow: The Great War and the Twentieth Century* (London: Simon & Schuster, 2013).

21. Strachan, *The First World War*; Clark, *Sleepwalkers*; Hastings, *Catastrophe 1914*; Wawro, *A Mad Catastrophe*; MacMillan, *The War that Ended Peace*.

22. Strachan, *The First World War*; Clark, *Sleepwalkers*; Wawro, *A Mad Catastrophe*; Rauchensteiner, *Der erste Weltkrieg und das Ende*; Macmillan, *The War that Ended Peace*; Gerd Krumeich, *Juli 1914: Eine Bilanz* (Paderborn: Ferdinand Schöningh, 2014).

23. Richard Ned Lebow, *Constructing Cause in International Relations* (Cambridge: Cambridge University Press, 2014), for an elaboration of this process.

24. Richard Ned Lebow, *A Cultural Theory of International Relations* (Cambridge: Cambridge University Press, 2010), ch. 7.
25. For example, Robert E. Osgood and Robert W. Tucker, *Force, Order, and Justice* (Baltimore, MD: Johns Hopkins University Press, 1967).
26. Wawro, *A Mad Catastrophe*, p. 98, is an important exception.
27. Clark, *Sleepwalkers*, pp. 361–366.
28. MacMillan, *The War that Ended Peace*, p. xxviii.
29. Ibid, p. xxv.
30. Karl Wilsberg, *Terrible Ami - amiable enemies: Kooperation und Konflikt in dem deutsch-französischen Beziehungen, 1911–1914* (Bonn: Bouvier, 1998); Afflerbach, *Der Dreibund;* Afflerbach and Stevenson, *An Improbable War;* Friedrich Kiessling, *Gegen den grossen Krieg? Entspannung in den internationalen Beziehungen, 1911–1914* (Munich: Oldenbourg, 2002); Strachan, *The First World War;* Clark, *Sleepwalkers,* pp. 361–366; Jean-Jacques Becker and Gerd Krumeich, '1914: Outbreak', in Jay Winter (ed.), *The Cambridge History of the First World War*, I (Cambridge: Cambridge University Press, 2014), pp. 39–64; William Mulligan, *The Origins of the First World War* (Cambridge: Cambridge University Press, 2010); Gordon Martel, *The Month That Changed the World, July 1914* (Oxford: Oxford University Press, 2014); Otte, *July Crisis.*
31. See especially, Afflerbach and Stevenson, *An Improbable War.*
32. Macmillan, *The War that Ended Peace*, p. 570 citing Konrad Jarausch, *The Enigmatic Chancellor: Bethmann Hollweg and the Hubris of Imperial Germany* (New Haven, CT: Yale University Press, 1973), pp. 151–152, 164.
33. Otte, *July Crisis,* offers good evidence of the extent to which the ultimatum was perceived as a watershed.
34. MacMillan, *The War that Ended Peace*, pp. 511–512.
35. Albertini, *The Origins of the War*, vol. III, chs 1 and 5; Jack Snyder, *Ideology of the Offensive: Military Decision Making and the Disaster of 1914* (Ithaca, NY: Cornell University Press, 1984); Mombauer, *Helmuth von Moltke;* Strachan, *The First World War;* Dornik, *Des Kaisers Falke;* Sondhaus, *Franz Conrad von Hötzendorf;* Kronenbitter, *Krieg im Frieden;* Wawro, *A Mad Catastrophe.*
36. Samuel R. Williamson, Jr, 'Influence, Power, and the Policy Process: The Case of Franz Ferdinand', *The Historical Journal*, 17, 1974, pp. 417–434; Clark, *Sleepwalkers*, pp. 116–117; Jean-Paul Bild, *François Ferdinand d'Autriche* (Paris: Editions Tallandier, 2002), pp. 293–297; Richard Ned Lebow, *Archduke Franz Ferdinand Lives: A World without World War I* (New York: Palgrave Macmillan, 2014), ch. 3.
37. MacMillan, *The War that Ended Peace*, p. 545.

38. Wawro, *A Mad Catastrophe*, p. 95.
39. Richard Ned Lebow, *Forbidden Fruit: Counterfactuals and International Relations* (Princeton, NJ: Princeton University Press, 2010), ch. 3.
40. Strachan, *The First World War*, pp. 143–144, 162–163.
41. Olivier Cosson, *Préparer la Grande GuerreL L'Armée française et la guerre russo-japonaise (1899–1914)* (Paris: Les Indes Savantes, 2013), who contends that French observers learned only what supported their understandings of their country's military strengths.
42. David Stevenson, *Anticipating Total War, 1870–1914* (Cambridge: Cambridge University Press, 2006).
43. The British navy did plan beforehand for a blockade. Matthew Seligmann, *The Royal Navy and the German Threat, 1901–1914* (Oxford: Oxford University Press, 1012); Stephen Cobb, *Preparing for Blockade: Naval Contingency for Economic Warfare, 1885–1914* (Farnham: Ashgate, 2013); Nicholas A. Lambert, *Planning Armageddon: British Economic Warfare and the First World War* (Cambridge, MA: Harvard University Press, 2012).
44. Dirk Bönker, *Militarism in a Global Age: Naval Ambitions in Germany and the United States* (Ithaca, NY: Cornell University Press, 2012), pp. 27–36, 101–104, 146.
45. Richard Ned Lebow, *Why Nations Fight: Past and Future Motives for War* (Cambridge: Cambridge University Press, 2010), chs 2 and 4.
46. Lebow, *Why Nations Fight*; Lebow, *A Cultural Theory of International*, chs 4–9 for documentation.
47. William H. Wohlforth, 'The Perception of Power: Russian in the Pre-1914 Balance', *World Politics*, 38, 1987, pp. 353–381.
48. Mombauer, *Helmuth von Moltke*, pp. 188–189, 201–202; Afflerbach, *Falkenhayn*, pp. 147–171.
49. Wawro, *A Mad Catastrophe*, p. 101.
50. Ibid, pp. 102, 117.
51. Herwig, *The First World War*, pp. 6–17; Dornik, *Des Kaisers Falke*, pp. 126–134; Clark, *Sleepwalkers*, pp. 451–452.
52. Mombauer, *Helmuth von Moltke*, pp. 180–181; Dieter Hoffmann, *Der Sprung ins Dunkle oder wie er 1. Weltkrieg entfesselt wurde* (Leipzig, Militzke, 2010), pp. 325–330.
53. David Stevenson, *Armaments and the Coming of War: Europe, 1900–1914* (New York: Oxford University Press, 1996); David Hermann, *The Arming of Europe and the Making of the First World War* (Princeton: Princeton University Press, 1996), deserve credit for reconstructing participant understandings of the military balance and its direction of change.

54. Herwig, *The First World War,* p. 11; Becker and Krumeich, '1914: Outbreak'; Lebow, *A Cultural Theory of International,* pp. 208, 349–365; Clark, *Sleepwalkers,* pp. 391–404.
55. Wawro, *A Mad Catastrophe,* p. 121.
56. Avner Offer, 'Going to War in 1914: A Matter of Honour?', *Politics & Society,* 23, 1995, pp. 213–241; Sondhaus, *Franz Conrad von Hötzendorf,* pp. 139–141.
57. Sondhaus, *Franz Conrad von Hötzendorf,* p. 140.
58. Alexander Musilin, *Das Haus am Ballplatz. Erinnerungen eines Östereich-Ungarischen Diplomaten* (Munich: Verlag für Kulturpolitik, 1924), p. 226.
59. A. F. K. Organski and Jacek Kugler, *The War Ledger* (Chicago, IL: University of Chicago Press, 1980).
60. Robert Gilpin, *War and Change in International Relation* (Cambridge: Cambridge University Press, 1981); Dale Copeland, *The Origins of Major War* (Ithaca, NY: Cornell University Press, 2000).
61. Steinberg, 'Old Knowledge and New Research'; Mombauer, 'The Fischer Controversy'.
62. Mombauer, *Helmuth von Moltke,* pp. 188–189; Hoffmann, *Der Sprung ins Dunkle,* pp. 325–330.
63. MacMillan, *The War that Ended Peace,* p. 527.
64. Mombauer, *Helmuth von Moltke,* pp. 145, 211, 281; MacMillan, *The War that Ended Peace,* p. 526.
65. Mombauer, *Helmuth von Moltke,* pp. 188–189, 210.
66. Richard Ned Lebow, *Between Peace and War: The Nature of International Crisis* (Baltimore, MD: Johns Hopkins University Press, 1981), pp. 82–97.
67. For example, Thomas Schelling, *Arms and Influence* (New Haven, CT: Yale University Press, 1966).
68. Alexander L. George and Richard Smoke, *Deterrence in American Foreign Policy: Theory and Practice* (New York: Columbia University Press, 1974).
69. Richard Ned Lebow and Janice Gross Stein, *We All Lost the Cold War* (Princeton, NJ: Princeton University Press, 1994), pp. 73–77.
70. Ted Hopf, *Peripheral Visions: Deterrence Theory and American Foreign Policy in the Third World, 1965–1990* (Ann Arbor, MI: University of Michigan Press, 1994).
71. Sean M. Lynn-Jones, 'Détente and Deterrence: Anglo-German Relations, 1911–1914', *International Security,* 11, 1986, pp. 121–150; Scott D. Sagan, '1914 Revisited: Allies, Offense an Instability', *International Security,* 11, 1986, pp. 51–75.

72. Keith Wilson, 'Britain', in F. H. Hinsley and Keith Wilson (eds), *Decisions for War, 1914* (London: St Martin's Press, 1995), pp. 175–208; Kumeich, *Juli 1914;* Becker and Krumeich, '1914: Outbreak'; Berghahn, 'Origins', in Jay Winter (ed.), *The Cambridge History of the First World War* (Cambridge: Cambridge University Press, 2014), pp. 16–38; Strachan, *The First World War,* pp. 124–125.

73. Berghahn, 'Origins'; Otte, *July Crisis,* pp. 520–521.

74. Ibid, pp. 124–125.

75. Ibid, pp. 126–128. See also Clark, *Sleepwalkers,* pp. 356–68.

76. Lebow, *Between Peace and War,* ch. 5; Robert Jervis, Richard Ned Lebow and Janice Stein, *Psychology and Deterrence* (Baltimore, MD: John Hopkins University Press, 1984); Lebow and Stein, *We All Lost,* chs 4, 7 and 13.

77. Strachan, *The First World War;* Clark, *Sleepwalker;* MacMillan, *The War that Ended Peace;* Becker and Krumeich, '1914: Outbreak'.

78. Steinberg, 'Old Knowledge and New Research'; MacMillan, *The War that Ended Peace,* p. 523.

79. Otte, *July Crisis,* p. 508.

80. Barbara Tuchman, *The Guns of August* (New York: Macmillan, 1962).

81. Alexander L. George, *Presidential Decisionmaking in Foreign Policy: The Effective Use of Information and Advice* (Boulder, CO: Westview Press, 1980); Irving L. Janis, *Victims of Group Think* (Boston, MA: Houghton, Mifflin, 1972).

82. Richard K. Betts and Thomas G. Mahnken, *Paradoxes of Strategic Intelligence* (Portland, OR: Frank Cass, 2003).

83. Clark, *Sleepwalkers,* pp. 47–64.

84. Herwig, *The First World War,* pp. 6–18; Samuel R. Williamson, Jr, *Austria-Hungary and the Coming of the First World War* (London: Macmillan, 1990), pp. 212–263.

85. Dornik, *Des Kaisers Falke,* pp. 75–79.

86. Lebow, *Between Peace and War,* pp. 115–118, 139–45, 283–285.

87. Mombauer, *Helmuth von Moltke,* pp. 208–216.

88. On the short war 'myth', Stig Förster, 'Der deutsche Generalstab und die Illusionen des kurzen Krieges, 1871–1914: Metakritik eines Mythos', *Militärgeschichtliche Mitteilunen,* 1995, pp. 61–95.

89. MacMillan, *The War that Ended Peace,* p. 565.

90. Kurt Riezler, *Kurt Riezler. Tagebücher, Aufsätze, Dokumente,* ed Karl Dietrich Erdman (Göttingen: Vandenhock & Ruprecht, 1972), Diary Entry, 7–8 July 1914.

91. Riezler, *Kurt Riezler,* Diary Entry, 27 July 1914.

92. Mombauer, *Helmuth von Moltke,* pp. 106–107.

93. John A. Moses, 'The British and German Churches and the Perception of War, 1908–1914', *War & Society,* 5, 1987, pp. 23–44.

94. Clark, *Sleepwalkers*, p. 350.
95. Herwig, *The First World War*, pp. 36, 49; Mombauer, *Helmuth von Moltke*, p. 211.
96. Mombauer, *Helmuth von Moltke*, pp. 28, 145, 211.
97. MacMillan, *The War that Ended Peace*, pp. 556–558.
98. Bruce Bueno de Mesquita, *The War Trap* (New Haven, CT: Yale University Press, 1986); Bruce Bueno de Mesquita and David Lalman, 'Reason and War', *American Political Science Review*, 80, 1986, pp. 1113–1130; James D. Fearon, 'Rationalist Explanations for War', *International Organization*, 49, 1995, pp. 379–414.
99. Allan C. Stam and Dan Reiter, *Democracies at War* (Princeton, NJ: Princeton University Press, 2002); Hein Goemans, *War and Punishment: The Causes of War Termination and the First World War* (Princeton, NJ: Princeton University Press, 2000).
100. Goemans, *War and Punishment;* Michael E. Brown, Owen R. Coté, Sean M. Lynn-Jones and Steven E. Miller (eds), *Do Democracies Win Their Wars?* (Cambridge, MA: The MIT Press, 2011).
101. Christopher Mick, '1918: Endgame', in Jay Winter (ed.), *The Cambridge History of the First World War* (Cambridge: Cambridge University Press, 2014), pp. 133–1371.
102. Mick, '1918: Endgame'.
103. Karl W. Deutsch, *Nerves of Government* (New York: Free Press, 1964), pp. 214–227.
104. Lebow, *Archduke Franz Ferdinand Lives*, pp. 19–20: Clark, *Sleepwalkers*, p. 395; MacMillan, *The War that Ended Peace*, p. 545.
105. Otte, *July Crisis*, p. 506.
106. Lebow, *Forbidden Fruit*, ch. 3.
107. Max Weber, *'Objectivität'*, and 'Kritische Studien' in *Gesammelte Aufsätze zur Wissens-chaftslehre,* ed Johannes Winckelmann, 3rd ed. (Tübingen: J. C. B. Mohr (Paul Siebeck), 1968), pp. 170–172, 276–280. English translations in Hans Henrik Brunn and Sam Whimster (eds), *Max Weber: Collected Methodological Writings* (London: Routledge, 2012).
108. Weber, *'Objectivität.'*.

CHAPTER 5

Lessons of the Cold War

NUCLEAR THREATS AND NUCLEAR WEAPONS

The role of nuclear weapons in Soviet-American relations has been hotly debated. Politicians, generals, and most academic strategists believe that America's nuclear arsenal restrained the Soviet Union throughout the Cold War. Critics maintain that nuclear weapons were a root cause of superpower conflict and a threat to peace. Controversy also surrounds the number and kinds of weapons necessary to deter, the political implications of the strategic balance, and the role of nuclear deterrence in hastening the collapse of the Soviet imperium.

These debates have had a distinctly theological quality. Partisans frequently defended their positions without recourse to relevant evidence. Some advocated strategic doctrines that were consistent with military postures that they supported. 'War-fighting' doctrines were invoked by the air force to justify silo-busting weapons like the MX missile.[1] Mutual Assured Destruction (MAD) was espoused by arms controllers to oppose the deployment of particular weapons systems.

More careful analysts have been alert to the difficulty of making definitive judgments about deterrence in the absence of valid and reliable information about Soviet and Chinese objectives and calculations. McGeorge Bundy, in

© The Author(s) 2018
R.N. Lebow, *Avoiding War, Making Peace*,
DOI 10.1007/978-3-319-56093-9_5

his masterful *Danger and Survival*, tells a cautionary tale of the impatience of leaders to acquire nuclear weapons, their largely futile attempts to exploit these weapons for political purposes and, finally, their efforts through arms control, to limit the dangers weapons pose to their owners as well as their targets. Bundy emphasizes the uncertainty of leaders about the dynamics of deterrence and their concerns about the risks of escalation in crisis.[2]

Richard K. Betts, in another exemplary study, illustrates how difficult it is to assess the efficacy of nuclear threats.[3] He found a great disparity between the memories of American leaders and the historical record. Some of the nuclear threats American presidents claim were successful were never made.[4] Other threats were so oblique that it is difficult to classify them as threats. Betts was understandably reluctant to credit any nuclear threat with success in the absence of information about the internal deliberations of the target states. When these states behaved in ways that were consistent with their adversary's demands, it was often unclear if the threat was successful or irrelevant. Leaders could have complied because they had been deterred or compelled, they could have been influenced by considerations unrelated to the threat, or they could have intended originally to behave as they did.

Newly declassified documents and extensive interviews with Soviet and American officials permitted us to reconstruct the deliberations of leaders of both superpowers before, during, and after the two most serious nuclear crises of the last 30 years. This evidence sheds new light on some of the controversies at the center of the nuclear debate. Needless to say, definitive judgments must await the opening of archives and more complete information about the calculations of Soviet and American leaders in other crises, as well as those of other nuclear powers.

THE FOUR QUESTIONS

Our analysis is organized around four questions. Each question addresses a major controversy about nuclear deterrence and its consequences. The first and most critical question is the contribution nuclear deterrence made to the prevention of World War III. The conventional wisdom regards deterrence as the principal pillar of the postwar peace between the superpowers. Critics charge that deterrence was beside the point or a threat to the peace. John Mueller, who makes the strongest argument for the irrelevance of nuclear weapons, maintains that the superpowers were restrained by their memories of World War II and their knowledge that even a conventional war would be many times more destructive.[5]

More outspoken critics of deterrence charge that it greatly exacerbated superpower tensions. The deployment of ever more sophisticated
weapons of destruction convinced each superpower of the other's hostile intentions and sometimes provoked the kind of aggressive behavior
deterrence was intended to prevent. The postwar peace endured despite
deterrence.[6]

The second question, of interest to those who believe that deterrence
worked, is why and how it works. Some advocates insist that it forestalled
Soviet aggression; in its absence, Moscow would have attacked Western
Europe and possibly have sent forces to the Middle East.[7] More reserved
supporters credit the reality of nuclear deterrence with moderating the
foreign policies of both superpowers. They maintain that the destructiveness of nuclear weapons encouraged caution and restraint and provided
a strong incentive for Moscow and Washington to make the concessions
necessary to resolve their periodic crises.[8]

The third question concerns the military requirements of deterrence. In
the 1960s, Defense Secretary Robert S. McNamara adopted MAD as the
official American strategic doctrine. McNamara contended that the Soviet
Union could be deterred by the American capability to destroy 50% of its
population and industry in a retaliatory strike. He welcomed the effort by
the Soviet Union to develop a similar capability in the expectation that
secure retaliatory capabilities on both sides would foster stability.[9]

Many military officers and civilian strategists reacted MAD on the
grounds that it was not credible to Moscow. To deter the Soviet Union,
the USA needed to be able to prevail at any level of conflict. This
required a much larger nuclear arsenal and highly accurate missiles necessary to dig out and destroy Soviet missiles in their silos and the under-
ground bunkers where the political and military elite would take refuge
in any conflict. 'War-fighting' supplanted MAD as the official strategic
doctrine during the presidency of Jimmy Carter. The Reagan administration spent vast sums of money to augment conventional forces and
to buy the strategic weapons and command and control networks that
Pentagon planners considered essential to war-fighting.[10]

An alternative approach to nuclear weapons, 'finite deterrence',
maintained that Soviet leaders were as cautious as their Western counterparts and just as frightened by the prospects of nuclear war. Nuclear
deterrence was far more robust than proponents of either MAD or war-
fighting acknowledged and required only limited capabilities—several-
hundred nuclear weapons would probably suffice. The doctrine of finite
deterrence never had visible support within the American government.[11]

Differences in the requirements of reflected deeper disagreements about the intentions of Soviet leaders. For war-fighters, the Soviet Union was an implacable foe. Its ruthless leaders would willingly sacrifice their people and industry in pursuit of world domination. They could only be restrained by superior capabilities and demonstrable resolve to use force in defense of vital interests. Partisans of MAD thought the Soviet Union aggressive but cautious. Soviet leaders sought to make gains but were even more anxious to preserve what they already had. The capability to destroy the Soviet Union as a modern industrial power was therefore sufficient to deter attack, but not necessarily to make its leaders behave in a restrained manner. Proponents of war-fighting and MAD stressed the overriding importance of resolve; Soviet leaders had to be convinced that the USA would retaliate if it or its allies were attacked and come to their assistance it they were challenged in other ways.

Finite deterrence was based on the premise that both superpowers had an overriding fear of nuclear war. Small and relatively unsophisticated nuclear arsenals were sufficient to reinforce this fear and the caution it engendered. Larger forces, especially those targeted against the other side's retaliatory capability, were counterproductive; they exacerbated the insecurity of its leaders, confirmed their belief in their adversary's hostility, and encouraged them to deploy similar weapons. Supporters of finite deterrence put much less emphasis on the need to demonstrate resolve. The possibility of retaliation, they believed, was enough to deter attack.

The fourth question concerns the broader political value of nuclear weapons. War fighters maintained that strategic superiority was politically useful and conferred bargaining leverage on a wide range of issues.[12] Most supporters of MAD contended that strategic advantages could only be translated into political influence in confrontations like the missile crisis, in which vital interests were at stake.[13] Other supporters of MAD, and all advocates of finite deterrence, denied that nuclear weapons could serve any purpose beyond deterrence.

RESTRAINING, PROVOCATIVE, OR IRRELEVANT?

Students of deterrence distinguish between general and immediate deterrence. General deterrence relies on the existing power balance to prevent an adversary from seriously considering a military challenge because of its expected adverse consequences.[14] It is often a country's first line of defense against attack. Leaders resort to the strategy of immediate deterrence only after general deterrence has failed, or when they believe that a more explicit expression of their intent to defend their interests is necessary to buttress general deterrence. If immediate deterrence fails, leaders will find themselves in a crisis, as Kennedy did when American intelligence discovered Soviet missiles in Cuba, or at war, as Israel's leaders did in 1973. General and immediate deterrence represent a progression from a diffuse if real concern about an adversary's intentions to the expectation that a specific interest or commitment is about to be challenged.

Both forms of deterrence assume that adversaries are most likely to resort to force or threatening military deployments when they judge the military balance favorable and question the defender's resolve. General deterrence pays particular importance to the military dimension; it tries to discourage challenges by developing the capability to defend national commitments or inflict unacceptable punishment on an adversary. General deterrence is a long-term strategy. Five-year lead times and longer are common between a decision to develop a weapon and its deployment.

Immediate deterrence is a short-term strategy. Its purpose is to discourage an imminent attack or challenge of a specific commitment. The military component of immediate deterrence must rely on forces in being. To buttress their defensive capability and display resolve, leaders may deploy forces when they anticipate an attack or challenge, as Kennedy did in the aftermath of the summit in June 1961. In response to Khrushchev's ultimatum on Berlin, he sent additional ground and air forces to Germany and strengthened the American garrison in Berlin. These reinforcements were designed to communicate the administration's will to resist any encroachment against West Berlin or Western access routes to the city.

General Deterrence

The origins of the missile crisis indicate that general deterrence, as practiced by both superpowers, was provocative rather than preventive. Soviet officials testified that the American strategic buildup, deployment of missiles in Turkey, and assertions of nuclear superiority, made them increasingly insecure. The president viewed all of these measures as prudent, defensive precautions. American actions had the unanticipated consequence of convincing Khrushchev of the need to protect the Soviet Union and Cuba from American military and political challenges.

Khrushchev was hardly the innocent victim of American paranoia. His nuclear threats and unfounded claims of nuclear superiority were the catalysts for Kennedy's decision to increase the scope and pace of the American strategic buildup. The new American programs and the Strategic Air Command's higher state of strategic readiness exacerbated Soviet perceptions of threat and contributed to Khrushchev's decision to send missiles to Cuba. In attempting to intimidate their adversaries, both leaders helped to bring about the kind of confrontation they were trying to avoid.

Kennedy later speculated, and Soviet officials have since confirmed, that his efforts to reinforce deterrence also encouraged Khrushchev to stiffen his position on Berlin.[15] The action and reaction that linked Berlin and Cuba were part of a larger cycle of insecurity and escalation that reached well back into the 1950s, if not to the beginning of the Cold War. The Soviet challenge to the Western position in Berlin in 1959–1961 was motivated by Soviet concern about the viability of East Germany and secondarily by Soviet vulnerability to American nuclear-tipped missiles stationed in Western Europe. The American missiles had been deployed to assuage NATO fears about the conventional military balance on the central front, made more acute by the creation of the Warsaw Pact in 1955. The Warsaw Pact, many Western authorities now believe, represented an attempt by Moscow to consolidate its control over an increasingly restive Eastern Europe.[16]

Once the crisis erupted, general deterrence played an important moderating role. Kennedy and Khrushchev moved away from confrontation and toward compromise because they both feared war. Kennedy worried that escalation would set in motion a chain of events that could lead to nuclear war. Khrushchev's decision to withdraw the missiles indicated that he too was prepared to make sacrifices to avoid war. His capitulation in the face of American military pressure was a humiliating defeat for the Soviet Union and its leader. Soviet officials confirm that it was one factor in his removal from power a year later.[17] For many years, Americans portrayed the crisis as an unalloyed American triumph. Kennedy's concession on the Jupiters and his willingness on Saturday night to consider making that concession public indicate that, when the superpower leaders were 'eyeball to eyeball', both sides blinked. One reason they did so was their fear of nuclear war and its consequences.

General deterrence also failed to prevent an Egyptian decision to use force in 1973. President Sadat and his military staff openly acknowledged Egyptian military inferiority. They had no doubt about Israel's resolve to defend itself if attacked. Sadat still chose to fight a limited war. He decided to attack Israel because of intense domestic political pressures to regain the Sinai. He had lost all hope in diplomacy after the failure of the Rogers missions, and although he recognized that the military balance was unfavorable, he expected it to get even worse in the future.

Israel's practice of general deterrence—it acquired a new generation of fighters and bombers—convinced Sadat to initiate military action sooner rather than later. Egyptian military planners devised a strategy intended to compensate for their military inferiority. Egyptian officers sought to capitalize on surprise, occupy the east bank of the Suez Canal, defend against Israeli counterattacks with a mobile missile screen, and press for an internationally imposed cease-fire before their limited gains could be reversed by a fully mobilized Israel. The parallels between 1962 and 1973 are striking. In both cases, attempts to reinforce general deterrence against vulnerable and hard-pressed opponents provoked rather than prevented unwanted challenges.

General deterrence had contradictory implications in the crisis that erupted between the USA and the Soviet Union at the end of the October War. Leaders of both superpowers were confident that the other feared war; general deterrence was robust. This confidence allowed the USA to alert its forces worldwide without fear of escalation. Brezhnev and some of his colleagues, on the other hand, worried about escalation if Soviet forces were deployed in positions in Egypt where they were likely to encounter advancing Israelis. The Politburo agreed that they did not want to be drawn into a military conflict that could escalate. Fear of war restrained the Soviet Union and contributed to the resolution of the crisis.

Immediate deterrence is intended to forestall a specific military deployment or use of force. For immediate deterrence to succeed, the defender's threats must convince adversaries that the likely costs of a challenge will more than offset any possible gains.[18] Immediate deterrence did not prevent the missile crisis. After Khrushchev had decided to send missiles to Cuba, Kennedy warned that he would not tolerate the introduction of Soviet missiles in Cuba. The president issued his threat in the belief that Khrushchev had no intention of establishing missile bases in Cuba. In the face of the president's warnings, Khrushchev proceeded with the secret deployment.

Students of the crisis disagree about why deterrence failed. Some contend that the strategy could not have worked, whereas others insist that Kennedy attempted deterrence too late.[19] Whatever the cause, the failure of deterrence exacerbated the most acute crisis of the Cold War. By making a public commitment to keep Soviet missiles out of Cuba, Kennedy dramatically increased the domestic political and foreign-policy costs of allowing the missiles to remain after they were discovered. A threat originally intended to deflect pressures on the administration to invade Cuba would have made that invasion very difficult to avoid if Soviet leaders had not agreed to withdraw their missiles.

Israel chose not to practice immediate deterrence in 1973. Its leaders were convinced that Egypt would only attack when it could neutralize Israel's air force. Confidence in general deterrence blinded Israel's leaders to the growing desperation of Sadat and his imperative to find a limited military strategy that would achieve his political objective. Israel's leaders worried instead that limited deterrent or defensive measures on their part might provoke Egypt to launch a miscalculated attack.

Even if Israel had practiced immediate deterrence, the evidence suggests that it would have made no difference. It is unlikely that public warnings and mobilization of the Israel Defense Forces would have deterred Egypt; Sadat had expected Israel to mobilize its reserves and reinforce the Bar-Lev Line in response to Egyptian military preparations. He was surprised and pleased that Israel did not take defensive measures and that Egyptian forces did not sustain the high casualties that he had anticipated and was prepared to accept.[20]

When the cease-fire negotiated jointly by Moscow and Washington failed to stop the fighting, Brezhnev threatened to consider unilateral intervention. The USA resorted to immediate deterrence to prevent a Soviet deployment. This was not the first time since the war began that Kissinger had attempted to deter Soviet military intervention. As early as 12 October, he told Dobrynin that any attempt by the Soviet Union to intervene with force would 'wreck the entire fabric of U.S.-Soviet relations'.[21] Later that day, he warned the Soviet ambassador that any Soviet intervention, regardless of pretext, would be met by American force.[22] On the evening of 24 October, when Brezhnev asked for joint intervention and threatened that he might act alone if necessary, the USA went to a DEFCON III alert.

Immediate deterrence was irrelevant since Brezhnev had no intention of sending Soviet forces to Egypt. Soviet leaders had difficulty understanding why President Nixon alerted American forces. Brezhnev and some of his colleagues were angered, dismayed, and humiliated. Immediate deterrence was at best irrelevant in resolving the crisis and, at worst, it damaged the long-term relationship between the superpowers.

Deterrence had diverse and contradictory consequences for superpower behavior. General and immediate deterrence were principal causes of the missile crisis, but general deterrence also facilitated its resolution. In 1973, general deterrence contributed to the outbreak of war between Egypt and Israel and provided an umbrella for competition between the USA and the Soviet Union in the Middle East. Immediate deterrence failed to prevent the superpower crisis that followed, but general deterrence constrained the Soviet leadership and helped to resolve the crisis. These differences can best be understood by distinguishing between the strategy and reality of nuclear deterrence.

The strategy of deterrence attempts to manipulate the risk of war for political ends. For much of the Cold War, Soviet and American policymakers doubted that their opposites were deterred by the prospect of nuclear war. They expended valuable resources trying to perfect the mix of strategic forces, nuclear doctrine, and targeting policy that would succeed in restraining their adversary. They also used military buildups, force deployments, and threats of war to try to coerce one another into making political concessions. In Berlin and Cuba, these attempts were unsuccessful but succeeded in greatly aggravating tensions.

The reality of deterrence derived from the inescapable fact that a superpower nuclear conflict would have been an unprecedented catastrophe for both sides. Superpower leaders understood this; by the late 1960s, if not earlier, they had come to believe that their countries could not survive a nuclear war. Fear of war, independent of the disparity in the strategic capabilities of the two sides, helped to keep both American and Soviet leaders from going over the brink and provided an important incentive for the mutual concessions that resolved the Cuban missile crisis. The moderation induced by the reality of deterrence helped to curtail the recklessness encouraged by the strategy of deterrence.

The contradictory consequences of deterrence are not fully captured by any of the competing interpretations. Proponents of deterrence have emphasized the positive contribution of the reality of deterrence but ignored the baneful consequences of the strategy. The critics of deterrence have identified some of the political and psychological mechanisms that made the strategy of deterrence provocative and dangerous.

But many ignored the ways in which the reality of deterrence was an important source of restraint.

WHEN AND WHY DOES DETERRENCE WORK?

Proponents of deterrence have advanced two contrasting reasons for its putative success. The conventional wisdom holds that deterrence restrained the Soviet Union by convincing its leaders that any military action against the USA or its allies would meet certain and effective opposition. Those who credit deterrence with preserving the peace assume that, in its absence, the Soviet Union would have been tempted to use force against its Western adversaries or their allies in the Middle East.

Throughout the years of Soviet-American rivalry, American leaders regarded their adversary as fundamentally aggressive and intent on expanding its influence by subversion, intimidation, or the use of force. Soviet leaders were frequently described as cold, rational calculators who were constantly probing for opportunities. They carefully weighed the costs and benefits and abstained from an aggressive action only if its costs were expected to outweigh the gains. In this context, the peace always looked precarious to American leaders and the remarkable success in avoiding war needed an extraordinary explanation. The strategy of nuclear deterrence provided the explanation.

The strategy of deterrence seemed ideal for coping with a fundamentally aggressive and opportunity-driven adversary. It sought to prevent Soviet aggression by denying its leaders opportunities to exploit. The USA consequently developed impressive military capabilities—general deterrence—and publicly committed itself to the defense of specific interests—immediate deterrence—when it appeared that these interests might be challenged. The conventional wisdom, eloquently expressed in many of the scholarly writings on deterrence, assumed that Soviet aggression would wax and wane as a function of Soviet perceptions of American military capability and resolve. Soviet leaders would be most restrained when they regarded the military balance as unfavorable and American resolve as unquestionable.[23]

Our analyses of the crises in 1962 and 1973 do not support this assessment of deterrence. In 1962, the strategy of deterrence provoked a war-threatening crisis, and, in 1973, nuclear deterrence provided the umbrella under which each sought to make or protect gains at the expense of the other until they found themselves in a tense confrontation.

The alternative interpretation holds that fear of nuclear war made both superpowers more cautious than they otherwise would have been in their competition for global influence and thereby kept the peace. Although far more convincing than the argument that credits the strategy of nuclear deterrence with preserving the peace, this explanation also is not fully persuasive. The reality of nuclear deterrence had a restraining effect on both Kennedy and Khrushchev in 1962 and on Brezhnev in 1973. When superpower leaders believed that they were approaching the brink of war, fear of war pulled them back.[24]

It is difficult to judge how much of the fear of war can be attributed to nuclear weapons. At the time of the Korean War, the USA had only a limited nuclear arsenal, but Stalin may have exaggerated American ability to launch extensive nuclear strikes against the Soviet Union.[25] Robert McNamara subsequently testified that President Kennedy worried primarily that the missile crisis would lead to a conventional war with the Soviet Union.[26] Other members of the Ex Comm disagree; they say it was the threat of nuclear war that was in the back of their minds and, probably, the president's.[27] McNamara also admits that he had little expectation that a conventional conflict could be contained. 'I didn't know how we would stop the chain of military escalation once it began.'[28]

Soviet leaders also worried about war in the missile crisis, but neither the written record nor the testimony of Soviet officials offers any evidence of the kind of war Khrushchev thought most likely. There is no evidence that Khrushchev or Kennedy speculated about war scenarios; they were desperately trying to resolve the crisis. They had no political or psychological incentive to investigate the consequences of failure—quite the reverse. Their fear of war remained strong but diffuse.

In 1973, the USA did not see war as a likely possibility, but Soviet leaders worried actively about war. They feared the consequences of a conventional Soviet-Israeli engagement somewhere between the canal and Cairo, or an accidental encounter at sea. However, there is no evidence that Soviet speculation progressed to more detailed consideration of how either could escalate to nuclear war. Again, the fear of war was strong but diffuse. Soviet leaders feared not only nuclear war but any kind of Soviet-American war. Their fear translated into self-deterrence;

Brezhnev ruled out the commitment of Soviet forces on Egypt's behalf before the USA practiced deterrence.

The absence of superpower war is puzzling only if at least one of the superpowers was expansionist and aggressive. On the basis of the evidence now available, the image that each superpower held of the other as opportunity-driven aggressors can be discredited as crude stereotypes. Khrushchev and Brezhnev felt threatened by what they considered the predatory policies of their adversary, as did American leaders by Soviet expansionist policies. For much of the Cold War, Soviet leaders were primarily concerned with preserving what they had; although like their American counterparts, they were not averse to making gains that appeared to entail little risk or cost. Serious confrontations between the superpowers arose only when one of them believed that its vital interests were threatened by the other.

With the benefit of hindsight, it is apparent that although both superpowers hoped to remake the world in their image, neither Moscow nor Washington was ever so dissatisfied with the status quo that it was tempted to go to war to force a change. It was not only the absence of *opportunity* that kept the peace, but also the absence of a strong motive for war. Without a compelling *motive*, leaders were unwilling to assume the burden and responsibility for war, even if they thought its outcome would be favorable. In the late 1950s and early 1960s, when the USA might have destroyed the Soviet Union in the first strike with relatively little damage to itself, American leaders never considered a preventive war. The Soviet Union never possessed such a strategic advantage, but there is no reason to suspect that Khrushchev or Brezhnev had any greater interest than Eisenhower and Kennedy in going to war. The reality of deterrence helped to restrain leaders on both sides, but their relative satisfaction with the status quo was an important cause of the long peace.

How Much Is Enough?

There was never a consensus in Washington about what was necessary to deter the Soviet Union. Proponents of MAD maintained that Soviet leaders would be deterred by the prospect of their country's destruction. Robert McNamara's 'whiz kids' at Defense calculated that MAD required the capability to destroy 50% of the Soviet Union's population and industry in a retaliatory strike.[29] McNamara recommended to

Premier Aleksei Kosygin in 1967 that the Soviet Union acquire roughly the same kind of second-strike capability so that deterrence would become more stable. Many military officers and conservative civilian strategists rejected MAD on the grounds that it was not a credible strategy. No American president, they argued, could ever convince his Soviet counterpart that he would accept certain destruction of the USA to punish the Soviet Union for invading Western Europe. To deter Soviet aggression, the USA needed clear-cut, across-the-board strategic superiority to decapitate the Soviet political and military leadership, destroy their command, control, and communications network, penetrate hardened targets, and outright Soviet forces at every level.[30] Proponents of finite deterrence, the smallest of the three communities, argued that nuclear deterrence was robust and required only limited capabilities. Strategic thinkers in France and Israel have, of necessity, voiced this kind of argument.

The outcome of the missile crisis supports the argument of finite deterrence. The American advantage was overwhelming. The CIA estimated that the Soviet Union, which had only a hundred missiles and a small fleet of obsolescent bombers, could attack the USA with at most three-hundred fifty nuclear weapons. The USA had a strategic nuclear strike force of thirty-five hundred weapons and far more accurate and reliable delivery systems. Because Soviet missiles were unreliable and Soviet bombers vulnerable to air defenses, it was possible that very few Soviet weapons would have reached their American targets. Had the missiles in Cuba been fully operational and armed with nuclear weapons, they would have augmented the Soviet arsenal by fewer than sixty warheads.[31]

Military superiority offered little comfort to the administration. It was not 'usable superiority', McGeorge Bundy explained, because 'if even one Soviet weapon landed on an American target, we would all be losers'.[32] Robert McNamara insists that 'The assumption that the strategic nuclear balance (or "imbalance") mattered was absolutely wrong'.[33] He recalled a CIA estimate that the Soviets might be able to deliver thirty warheads against the USA in a retaliatory attack. 'Does anyone believe that a president or a secretary of defense would be willing to permit thirty warheads to fall on the USA? No way! And for that reason, neither we nor the Soviets would have acted any differently before or after the Cuban deployment.'[34] In McNamara's judgment, no president would be willing 'to consciously sacrifice an important part of our population or our land and place it in great jeopardy to a strike by Soviet strategic forces, whether it be one city, or two cities, or three cities'. The Soviet Union had the capability to do this even before deploying any missiles in Cuba. 'And therefore, we felt deterred from using our nuclear superiority and that was not changed by the introduction of nuclear weapons into Cuba'.[35]

Proponents of war-fighting, MAD, and finite deterrence would all expect Khrushchev to be deterred by the one-sided American strategic advantage. Only proponents of finite deterrence would anticipate that Kennedy would be deterred by the small Soviet arsenal.

Ironically, Kennedy was not fully confident before or during the crisis that even overwhelming American strategic superiority would restrain the Soviet Union. Khrushchev, by contrast, was confident—before the crisis—that the small and inferior Soviet arsenal would deter Kennedy. He worried rather that the USA would exploit its strategic superiority for political purposes. His confidence in finite deterrence permitted him to deploy missiles in Cuba with the expectation that Kennedy would not go to war.

During the crisis, Khrushchev's confidence in deterrence wavered. He worried both that Kennedy would be unable to control the militants in the military and the CIA who did not share his sober recognition of the futility of war and that the crisis might spin out of control. These fears were partly responsible for the concessions that he made. Kennedy, too, worried that Khrushchev would be ousted by militants determined to go to war. Even when the USA had the overwhelming superiority that proponents of war-fighting recommend, Kennedy's confidence in deterrence was limited. He, too, then made the concessions necessary to resolve the crisis.

In making critical judgments about the robustness of deterrence during the crisis, Kennedy and Khrushchev paid little attention to the military balance. They concentrated instead on the political pressures that might push either side into using force. Their success in resolving the crisis increased their confidence that the other shared their horror of war.

Although deterrence was robust in 1962, not everybody drew the same positive lessons from the missile crisis as did Khrushchev and Kennedy. Influential members of the Soviet elite believed that the Kennedy administration had acted aggressively in Cuba because of its strategic advantage. Many Americans concluded that Khrushchev had retreated because of Soviet inferiority. The lesson of the missile crisis was clear: the USA needed to maintain its strategic advantage, or failing that, strategic parity. In Moscow, too, there was a renewed commitment to ending the strategic imbalance. The missile crisis did not trigger the Soviet strategic buildup of the 1960s—it had been authorized by Khrushchev before the missile crisis—but it mobilized additional support for that program and made it easier for Brezhnev to justify when resources grew scarce in the 1970s.[36]

The crisis in 1973, the most serious superpower confrontation since the missile crisis, occurred when the strategic balance was roughly equal and both sides had a secure second-strike capability. Proponents of finite deterrence would expect the reality of nuclear deterrence to be robust and the strategy of nuclear deterrence to fail unless the security of the homeland was threatened. Given the reality of nuclear deterrence when both sides had an assured capacity to retaliate, advocates of MAD would also expect the strategy of deterrence to fail unless vital interests were at stake. War-fighters would reason differently. Since neither side possessed 'escalation dominance', the side that estimated a lower risk of war would have the advantage.

The predictions of the three schools with respect to the American alert cannot be tested directly, since deterrence was irrelevant. The Soviet Union had no intention of sending forces to Egypt before the USA alerted its forces. We can nevertheless assess the Soviet interpretation of the American attempt at deterrence and examine its fit with the expectations of the three schools. Soviet leaders dismissed the American nuclear alert as incredible. They could do so in a context in which nuclear weapons were regarded as so unusable that nuclear threats to defend anything but the homeland or vital interests were incredible. There is no evidence, moreover, that political leaders in Moscow made any attempt to assess the relative strategic balance. The Soviet interpretation is consistent with the expectations of finite deterrence and MAD and inconsistent with those of war-fighters.

Analysis of these two crises reveals that it was not the balance or even perceptions of the balance but rather the judgments leaders made about its meaning that were critical. The understanding lenders had of their adversary's intentions was much more important than their estimates of its relative capabilities. Deterrence was as robust in 1962 as proponents of finite deterrence expected, and at least as robust in 1973 as proponents of MAD anticipated. Yet, worst-case analyses remained the conventional wisdom for many years among militants in both the USA and the Soviet Union. Many on both sides continued to assume that the strategic balance was and would continue to be the critical determinant of superpower behavior.

War-fighters drew a direct relationship between the strategic balance and Soviet behavior. The Soviet Union would be most restrained when the USA had a strategic advantage and would behave more aggressively when the military balance tilted in their favor.[37] Proponents of finite deterrence denied that any relationship existed between the strategic balance and aggression, whereas adherents of MAD could be found on both sides of the debate. The proposition that the aggressiveness of Soviet leaders intensified or diminished in accordance with their perception of the strategic balance became the fundamental assumption of strategic analysis and force planning in the USA. Deterrence was considered primarily a military problem, and many American officials and strategists worked on the assumption that Washington could never have too powerful a military or too great a strategic advantage.[38]

The link between Soviet foreign policy and the military balance is an empirical question. To test this relationship, we examined Soviet-American relations from the beginning of the Cold War in 1947 to 1985, when Mikhail Gorbachev came to power. Drawing on formerly classified estimates of the strategic balance and public studies of the balance prepared by prominent strategic institutes, we developed a composite measure of the relative strategic potency of the two superpowers. Our analysis suggests that the nuclear balance went through three distinct phases. The first, 1948–1960, was a period of mounting American advantage. The second, 1961–1968, was characterized by a pronounced but declining American advantage. The third, 1968–1985, was an era of strategic parity.[39]

There is no positive correlation between shifts in Soviet assertiveness and shifts in the strategic balance. Soviet challenges are most pronounced in the late 1940s and early 1950s in Central Europe and Korea and again in the late 1950s and early 1960s in Berlin and Cuba. A third, lesser period of assertiveness occurred from 1979 to 1982 in Africa and Afghanistan.[40] The first and second peaks occurred at a time when the USA had unquestioned nuclear superiority. The third peak coincides with the period of strategic parity, before the years of the putative American 'window of vulnerability'. During this period of alleged Soviet advantage, roughly 1982–1985, Soviet behavior was restrained.

The relationship between the military balance and Soviet assertiveness is largely the reverse of that predicted by proponents of war-fighting. The USA had unquestioned supremacy from 1948 to 1952 and again from 1959 to 1962, the principal years of Soviet assertiveness. Soviet challenges were most pronounced when the Soviet Union was weak and the USA was strong.

This pattern challenges the proposition that aggression is motivated primarily by adversaries who seek continuously to exploit opportunities. When leaders became desperate, they behaved aggressively even though the military balance was unfavorable and they had no grounds to doubt their adversary's resolve. In the absence of compelling need, leaders often did not challenge even when opportunities for an assertive foreign policy were present.[41] A definitive answer to the question, 'How much is enough?' must await detailed analyses of other nuclear crises with other leaders. Drawing on the analysis of leaders' thinking in these two cases and the broad pattern in their relationship during the Cold War, we can suggest a tentative answer: finite nuclear capabilities in the context of a shared fear of war. In this circumstance, a little deterrence goes a long way.

THE POLITICAL VALUE OF NUCLEAR WEAPONS

Just as there was no consensus during the Cold War on how much deterrence was enough, so there was no agreement on the political value of nuclear weapons. War-fighters contended that nuclear power was fungible; they insisted that strategic advantages could be successfully exploited for political purposes. Most proponents of MAD argued that nuclear threats were likely to be effective only in defense of a state's most vital interests. Proponents of finite deterrence took the most restrictive view of the political value of nuclear weapons. They argued that nuclear weapons could only deter attacks against one's own state and perhaps against one's closest allies.

War-fighters, who were dubious about the efficacy of deterrence and set the most demanding conditions, nevertheless expressed the greatest confidence in compellence. Advocates of finite deterrence, who maintained that nuclear deterrence was relatively easy to achieve, doubted that nuclear threats would succeed in compelling nuclear adversaries. Proponents of MAD thought deterrence was somewhat easier to achieve than compellence.

These seeming contradictions between the schools of war-fighting and finite deterrence can be reconciled by examining why each argued that deterrence and compellence would succeed or fail. For war-fighters, the critical factor was the military balance. When a state possessed a decisive strategic advantage, it could more convincingly demonstrate resolve and more readily deter and compel an adversary. Parity made deterrence possible but compellence extraordinarily difficult.

Advocates of finite deterrence reasoned that leaders had a pronounced fear of the consequences of nuclear war. This fear had a low threshold and was independent of the level of destruction leaders could inflict on their adversaries. The strategic balance was therefore irrelevant to deterrence, and strategic advantage did not make compellence any easier. So long as the target state had some nuclear retaliatory capability, nuclear threats for any purpose other than retaliation lacked credibility.

Proponents of MAD also denied the utility of strategic superiority. They placed the threshold of deterrence higher than did advocates of finite deterrence and argued that a state needed an unquestioned capability, after sustaining the first strike, to retaliate in sufficient force to destroy approximately 50% of its adversary's population and industry. Additional nuclear capabilities did not make deterrence any more secure. Some advocates of MAD believed that strategic advantages were critical for compellence but only in limited, well-specified circumstances. Like the advocates of finite deterrence, they argued that the unprecedented destructiveness of nuclear weapons made it very difficult to make credible nuclear threats against nuclear adversaries. Such threats would carry weight only when a state's most vital interests were unambiguously threatened.[42]

Proponents of war-fighting and MAD argued that the Cuban missile crisis was consistent with their expectations. They both maintained that Khrushchev sent missiles to Cuba because he doubted American resolve and withdrew them because he respected American military capability.[43] The crisis illustrated a general truth to war-fighters: strategic superiority confers important bargaining advantages in crisis. Advocates of MAD maintained that the missile crisis was a special case. Compellence succeeded not only because of the American military advantage, but because of the asymmetry of interests. The USA was defending a vital interest, the Soviet Union was not.[44]

Both arguments took as their starting point the apparently one-sided outcome of the crisis in favor of the USA. Khrushchev withdrew the

Soviet missiles in return for a face-saving pledge from Kennedy not to invade Cuba. Proponents of war-fighting and MAD treated this pledge as largely symbolic because the administration had no intention of invading the island other than to remove the missiles. Both believed that the missiles would have significantly affected the military or political balance and therefore treated their withdrawal as a major concession.

These interpretations that congealed in the 1960s are contradicted by newly available evidence. Although the administration had ruled out an invasion of Cuba, Khrushchev considered Kennedy's pledge not to invade an extremely important concession. With other Soviet leaders, he was convinced that the USA was preparing to overthrow the Castro government and was only prevented from doing so by the missile deployment. In the eyes of the president and his secretary of defense, the missiles in Cuba had much less military value than many students of the crisis have alleged. Their withdrawal was important for domestic and foreign political reasons.

We now know that Kennedy made a second, important concession to Khrushchev: he agreed to remove the American Jupiter missiles from Turkey at a decent interval after the crisis. The decision to withdraw the missiles was not made before the crisis, as some administration officials contended, but was offered to Khrushchev as a concession. However, Kennedy insisted that the Kremlin keep it secret. The removal of the Jupiters had little military value but was of enormous symbolic importance to Khrushchev.

The outcome of the missile crisis is best explained by finite deterrence. The terms of the settlement did not reflect the strategic balance, but mutual fears of war. Despite pronounced Soviet strategic inferiority, the crisis ended in a compromise, not in a one-sided American victory. American leaders judged it too risky to rely on their strategic advantage to compel withdrawal of the Soviet missiles without making compensating concessions.

The advocates of finite deterrence, MAD, and war-fighting would all expect compellence to be very difficult in the strategic context of 1973. War-fighters would predict that neither the Soviet Union nor the USA could compel the other side to achieve political benefit since neither had a decisive strategic advantage. Under conditions of parity and a secure capability to retaliate, proponents of MAD and finite deterrence would predict that compellence would be very difficult unless vital interests were demonstrably at stake.

The failure of Soviet compellence in 1973 is consistent with the shared expectation of all three schools. Brezhnev did not succeed in compelling the USA to restrain Israel, even though it was very much in Washington's interest to stop the fighting. On the contrary, Brezhnev's attempt to compel backfired and escalated the crisis. Although Kissinger recognized Soviet interests, particularly the heavy cost of its humiliating failure to stop the fighting, he nevertheless interpreted Brezhnev's threat that he might consider unilateral action as a direct challenge to the reputation and resolve of the USA.

All three approaches expect, although for quite different reasons, strategic parity to confer no political advantage. To distinguish among the three schools, we need detailed evidence of the calculations of American leaders about the strategic balance. Yet, when Kissinger and his colleagues chose to respond to Brezhnev's threat that he might consider unilateral military action, they made no reference at all to the strategic balance.[45] When they chose not to comply with Brezhnev's threat, the strategic balance was not salient in their minds.

Our analysis of these two cases is most consistent with the arguments of finite deterrence. The overwhelming strategic advantage of the USA in the missile crisis was negated by the fear of war. When the strategic balance was roughly equal, the Soviet Union could not compel even when the USA recognized the strong Soviet interest in protecting an endangered ally and their own interest in saving the Egyptian Third Army. Our evidence suggests that nuclear weapons are unusable for any political purpose but the defense of vital interests.

NUCLEAR THREATS AND NUCLEAR WEAPONS

The role of nuclear threats and nuclear weapons in Soviet-American relations during the Cold War runs counter to much of the conventional wisdom. Throughout the Cold War, superpower leaders expected their adversary to exploit any strategic advantage for political or military gain. Consequently, they devoted scarce resources to military spending to keep from being disadvantaged. For four decades, Soviet and American leaders worried about the political and military consequences of strategic inferiority. These fears, coupled with the worst-case analysis each side used to estimate the other's strategic capabilities, fueled an increasingly expensive arms race. In the late 1940s, the Soviet Union made an intensive effort to develop its own nuclear arsenal in the aftermath of Hiroshima and Nagasaki. In the early 1950s, both sides developed thermonuclear weapons. Following the success of Sputnik in 1957, the USA accelerated its commitment to develop and deploy ICBMs. President Kennedy's decision to expand the scope of the American strategic buildup in the spring of 1961 triggered a reciprocal Soviet decision. The Reagan buildup of the 1980s was a response to Brezhnev's intensive spending of the previous decade and widespread concern that it had bought the Soviet Union a strategic advantage.

This pervasive fear of strategic inferiority was greatly exaggerated. We offer a set of general observations about the impact of nuclear threats and nuclear weapons that summarize our arguments based on the new evidence. These observations must remain tentative until additional evidence becomes available about other critical confrontations during the Cold War and about the role of nuclear weapons in Sino-American and Sino-Soviet relations.

1. *Leaders who try to exploit real or imagined nuclear advantages for political gain are not likely to succeed.* Khrushchev and Kennedy tried and failed to intimidate one another with claims of strategic superiority in the late 1950s and early 1960s. Khrushchev's threats and boasts strengthened Western resolve not to yield in Berlin and provoked Kennedy to order a major strategic buildup. Kennedy's threats against Cuba, his administration's assertion of strategic superiority, and the deployment of Jupiter missiles in Turkey—all intended to dissuade Khrushchev from challenging the West in Berlin—led directly to the Soviet decision to send missiles to Cuba. Both leaders were willing to assume the risks of a serious confrontation to avoid creating the impression of weakness or irresolution.

2. *Credible nuclear threats are very difficult to make.* The destructiveness of nuclear weapons makes nuclear threats more frightening but less credible. It is especially difficult to make nuclear threats credible when they are directed against nuclear adversaries who have the capability to retaliate in kind. Many Soviets worried about nuclear war during the missile crisis, but Khrushchev judged correctly that Kennedy would not initiate a nuclear war in response to the deployment of Soviet missiles. Khrushchev's principal concern was that the president would be pushed into attacking Cuba and that armed clashes between the invading Americans and the Soviet forces on the island committed to Cuba's defense would escalate into a wider and perhaps uncontrollable war.

In 1973, the American alert had even less influence on the Soviet leadership. It was inconceivable to Brezhnev and his colleagues that the USA would attack the Soviet Union with nuclear weapons. They did not believe that the interests at stake for either the USA or the Soviet Union justified war. The American nuclear threat was therefore incomprehensible and incredible.

3. *Nuclear threats are fraught with risk.* In both 1962 and 1973, American leaders were uninformed about the consequences and implications of strategic alerts. In 1973, they did not fully understand the technical meaning or the operational consequences of the DEFCON III alert and chose the alert in full confidence that it entailed no risks. During the missile crisis, when conventional and nuclear forces were moved to an even higher level of alert, it was very difficult to control alerted forces. Military routines and insubordination posed a serious threat to the resolution of the crisis.

   Evidence from these two cases suggests that there are stark trade-offs between the political leverage that military preparations are expected to confer and the risks of inadvertent escalation they entail. American leaders had a poor understanding of these trade-offs: they significantly overvalued the political value of nuclear alerts and were relatively insensitive to their risks.[46]

4. *Strategic buildups are more likely to provoke than to restrain adversaries because of their impact on the domestic balance of political power in the target state.* Stalin, Khrushchev, and Brezhnev all believed that strategic advantage would restrain adversaries. Khrushchev believed that the West behaved cautiously in the 1950s because of a growing respect for the economic as well as the military power of the socialist camp. He was convinced that the visible demonstration of Soviet power, through nuclear threats and the deployment of missiles in Cuba, would strengthen the hands of the 'sober realists' in Washington who favored accommodation with the Soviet Union. Khrushchev's actions had the reverse impact: they strengthened anti-Soviet militants by intensifying American fears of Soviet intentions and capabilities. Kennedy's warnings to Khrushchev not to deploy missiles in Cuba and his subsequent blockade were in large part a response to the growing

domestic political pressures to act decisively against the Soviet Union and its Cuban ally.

Brezhnev's strategic buildup was a continuation of Khrushchev's program. American officials believed that the Soviet buildup continued after parity had been achieved. Soviet strategic spending appeared to confirm the predictions of militants in Washington that Moscow's goal was strategic superiority, even a first-strike capability. Brezhnev, on the other hand, expected Soviet nuclear capabilities to prevent the USA from engaging in 'nuclear blackmail'. Instead, it gave Republicans the ammunition to defeat President Carter and the SALT II agreement. The Soviet arms buildup and invasion of Afghanistan contributed to Ronald Reagan's landslide victory in 1980 and provided the justification for his administration's massive arms spending. American attempts to put pressure on the Soviet Union through arms buildups were equally counterproductive.

5. *Nuclear deterrence is robust when leaders on both sides fear war and are aware of each other's fears.* War-fighting, MAD, and finite deterrence all mistakenly equate stability with specific arms configurations. More important than the distribution of nuclear capabilities, or leaders' estimates of relative nuclear advantage, is their judgment of an adversary's intentions. The Cuban missile crisis was a critical turning point in Soviet-American relations because it convinced Kennedy and Khrushchev, and some of their most important advisors as well, that their adversary was as committed as they were to avoiding nuclear war. This mutually acknowledged fear of war made the other side's nuclear capabilities less threatening and paved the way for the first arms-control agreements.

By no means did all American and Soviet leaders share this interpretation. Large segments of the national security elites of both superpowers continued to regard their adversary as implacably hostile and willing to use nuclear weapons. Even when Brezhnev and Nixon acknowledged the other's fear of war, they used the umbrella of nuclear deterrence to compete vigorously for unilateral gain. Western militants did not begin to change their estimate of Soviet intentions until Gorbachev made clear his commitment to ending the arms race and the Cold War.

Deterrence in Hindsight

The Cold War began as a result of Soviet-American competition in Central Europe in the aftermath of Germany's defeat. Once recognized spheres of influence were established, confrontations between the superpowers in the heart of Europe diminished. Only Berlin continued to be a flash point until the superpowers reached an understanding about the two Germanies. The conventional and nuclear arms buildup that followed in the wake of the crises of the early Cold War was a reaction to the mutual insecurities they generated. By the 1970s, the growing arsenal and increasingly accurate weapons of mass destruction that each superpower aimed at the other had become the primary source of mutual insecurity and tension. Moscow and Washington no longer argued about the status quo in Europe but about the new weapons systems each deployed to threaten the other. Each thought that deterrence was far less robust than it was. Their search for deterrence reversed cause and effect and prolonged the Cold War.

The history of the Cold War provides compelling evidence of the pernicious effects of the open-ended quest for nuclear deterrence. But nuclear weapons also moderated superpower behavior, once leaders in Moscow and Washington recognized and acknowledged to the other that a nuclear war between them would almost certainly lead to their mutual destruction.

Since the late 1960s, when the Soviet Union developed an effective retaliatory capability, both superpowers had to live with nuclear vulnerability. There were always advocates of preemption, ballistic missile defense, or other illusory visions of security in a nuclear world. But nuclear vulnerability could not be eliminated. MAD was a reality from which there was no escape short of the most far-reaching arms control. Even after the dissolution of the Soviet Union and the proposed deep cuts in nuclear weapons, Russia and the USA will still possesses enough nuclear weapons to destroy each other many times over.[47]

Nuclear vulnerability distinguished the Soviet-American conflict from conventional conflicts of the past or present. In conventional conflicts, leaders could believe that war might benefit their country. Leaders have often gone to war with this expectation, although more often than not they have been proven wrong. The consequences of war turned out very differently than expected by leaders in Iraq in 1980, Argentina in 1982, and Israel in 1982.

Fear of the consequences of nuclear war not only made it exceedingly improbable that either superpower would deliberately seek a military confrontation with the other; it made their leaders extremely reluctant to take any action that they considered would seriously raise the risk of war. Over the years, they developed a much better appreciation of each other's interests. In the last years of the Soviet-American conflict, leaders on both sides acknowledged and refrained from any challenge of the other's vital interests.

The ultimate irony of nuclear deterrence may be the way in which the strategy of deterrence undercut much of the political stability the reality of deterrence should have created. The arms buildups, threatening military deployments, and the confrontational rhetoric that characterized the strategy of deterrence effectively obscured deep-seated, mutual fears of war. Fear of nuclear war made leaders inwardly cautious, but their public posturing convinced their adversaries that they were aggressive, risk-prone, and even irrational.

This kind of behavior was consistent with the strategy of deterrence. Leaders on both sides recognized that only a madman would use nuclear weapons against a nuclear adversary. To reinforce deterrence, they therefore tried, and to a disturbing degree, succeeded in convincing the other that they might be irrational enough or sufficiently out of control to implement their threats. Each consequently became less secure, more threatened, and less confident of the robust reality of deterrence. The strategy of deterrence was self-defeating; it provoked the kind of behavior it was designed to prevent.

The history of the Cold War suggests that nuclear deterrence should be viewed as a powerful but very dangerous medicine. Arsenic, formerly used to treat syphilis and schistosomiasis, and chemotherapy, routinely used to treat cancer, can kill or cure a patient. The outcome depends on the virulence of the disease, how early the disease is detected, the amount of drugs administered, and the resistance of the patient to both the disease and the cure. So it is with nuclear deterrence. Finite deterrence is stabilizing because it prompts mutual caution. Too much deterrence, or deterrence applied inappropriately to a frightened and vulnerable adversary, can fuel an arms race that makes both sides less rather than more secure and provoke the aggression that it is designed to prevent. As with any medicine, the key to successful deterrence is to administer correctly the proper dosage.

The superpowers 'overdosed' on deterrence. It poisoned their relation-ship, but their leaders remained blind to its consequences. Instead, they interpreted the tension and crises that followed as evidence of the need for even more deterrence. Despite the changed political climate that makes it almost inconceivable that either Russia or the USA would initiate nuclear war, there are still influential people in Washington, and possibly in Moscow, who believe that new weapons are necessary to reinforce deter-rence. Deeply embedded beliefs are extraordinarily resistant to change.

NOTES

1. In keeping with the theological quality of the debate, followers of the "war-fighting" sect of deterrence had a sacred text: *Voyenaya mysi'*, the Soviet Journal of *Military Thought*. Many of the professional Soviet mili-tary discussions of the contingent uses of military power were misused to infer and attribute offensive military intentions to the Soviet Union.
2. McGeorge Bundy, *Danger and Survival: Choices About the Bomb in the First Fifty Years* (New York: Random House, 1988).
3. Richard K. Betts, *Nuclear Blackmail and Nuclear Balance* (Washington, D.C.: The Brookings Institution, 1987).
4. Harry Truman claimed to have compelled the Soviet Union to with-draw from Iran in 1946, but no documentary record of a nuclear threat can be found. See Betts, *Nuclear Blackmail and Nuclear Balance*, pp. 7–8; Richard Ned Lebow and Janice Gross Stein, "Review of the Data Collections on Extended Deterrence by Paul Huth and Bruce Russett," in Kenneth A. Oye, ed., *Specifying and Testing Theories of Deterrence* (Ann Arbor: University of Michigan Press, in press); and Richard W. Cottam, *Iran and the United States: A Cold War Case Study* (Pittsburgh: University of Pittsburgh Press, 1988).
5. John E. Mueller, *Retreat from Doomsday: The Obsolescence of Modern War* (New York: Basic Books, 1989). Kenneth N. Waltz, *Theory of International Politics* (Reading, Mass.: Addison-Wesley, 1979), also dis-paraged the role of nuclear weap¬ons and argued that bipolarity was responsible for the long peace. Waltz, "The Emerging Structure of International Politics," paper prepared for the August 1990 Annual Meeting of the American Political Science Association, subsequently acknowledged nuclear weapons as one of "the twin pillars" of the peace. See Richard Ned Lebow, "Explaining Stability and Change: A Critique of Realism," in Richard Ned Lebow and Thomas Risse-Kappen, eds., *International Relations Theory and the End of the Cold War*, forthcoming, for a critical examination of the realist position on the long peace.

6. Richard Ned Lebow, "Conventional vs. Nuclear Deterrence: Are the Lessons Transferable?" *Journal of Social Issues* 43, 4 (1987), pp. 171–91.

7. McGeorge Bundy, "To Cap the Volcano," *Foreign Affairs*, 48, 1 (October 1969), pp. 1–20; Harvard Nuclear Study Group, *Living With Nuclear Weapons* (Cambridge, Mass.: Harvard University Press, 1983); Klaus Knorr, "Controlling Nuclear War," International Security 9, 4 (Spring 1985), pp. 79-98; Michael Mandelbaum, *The Nuclear Question: The United States and Nuclear Weapons, 1946-76* (New York: Cambridge University Press, 1979); Robert W. Tucker, *The Nuclear Debate: Deterrence and the Lapse of Faith* (New York: Holmes & Meier, 1985).

8. For example, Raymond Aron, *The Great Debate: Theories of Nuclear Strategy*, trans. Ernst Pawel (Garden City, N.Y.: Doubleday, 1965); Stanley Hoffmann, *The State of War: Essays on the Theory and Practice of International Politics* (New York: Praeger, 1965), p. 236; Betts, *Nuclear Blackmail*; Bundy, *Danger and Survival*; Robert Jervis, *The Meaning of the Nuclear Revolution: Statecraft and the Prospect of Armageddon* (Ithaca, N.Y.: Cornell University Press, 1989).

9. For the evolution of McNamara's strategic thinking, see Desmond Ball, *Politics and Force Levels: The Strategic Missile Program of the Kennedy Administration* (Berkeley: University of California Press, 1980), especially pp. 171–93; Lawrence Freedman, *The Evolution of Nuclear Strategy* (New York: St. Martin's Press, 1983), pp. 331–71.

10. For war-fighting critics of MAD, see Daniel Graham, *Shall America Be Defended?: SALT II and Beyond* (New Rochelle, N.Y.: Arlington House, 1979); Colin S. Gray, *Nuclear Strategy and National Style* (Lanham, Md.: Hamilton Press, 1986); Colin S. Gray and Keith B. Payne, "Victory is Possible," *Foreign Policy* 39 (Summer 1980), pp. 14–27; Albert Wohlstetter, "Between an Unfree World and None," *Foreign Affairs* 63, 5 (Summer 1985), pp. 962–94; Fred Hoffman, "The SDI in U.S. Nuclear Strategy," *International Security* 10, 1 (Summer 1985), pp. 13–24.

11. Morton H. Halperin, *Nuclear Fallacy: Dispelling the Myth of Nuclear Strategy* (Cambridge: Ballinger, 1987); Adm. Noel Gayler, "The Way Out: A General Nuclear Settlement," in Gwyn Prins, ed., *The Nuclear Crisis Reader* (New York: Vintage Books, 1984), pp. 234–43.

12. Graham, *Shall America Be Defended?*; Gray, *Nuclear Strategy and National Style*; Wohlstetter, "Between an Unfree World and None."

13. Robert S. McNamara, "The Military Role of Nuclear Weapons: Perceptions and Misperceptions," *Foreign Affairs* 62 (Fall 1983), pp. 59–80, at p. 68; Jervis, *The Meaning of the Nuclear Revolution*, pp. 34–38; Alexander L. George, David K. Hall, and William E. Simons, *The Limits of Coercive Diplomacy: Laos, Cuba, Vietnam* (Boston: Little, Brown, 1971); Betts, *Nuclear Blackmail*.

14. This distinction was introduced by Patrick M. Morgan, *Deterrence: A Conceptual Analysis* (Beverly Hills, Calif.: Sage, 1977).

15. Arthur Schlesinger, Jr., A Thousand Days: John F. Kennedy in the White House (Boston: Houghton, Mifflin, 1965), pp. 347–48. This point is also made by Alexander L. George and Richard Smoke, *Deterrence in American Foreign Policy: Theory and Practice* (New York: Columbia University Press, 1974), pp. 429, 579.

16. On the Warsaw Pact, see Robin Allison Remington, *The Changing Soviet Perception of the Warsaw Pact* (Cambridge, Mass.: MIT Center for International Studies, 1967); Christopher D. Jones, *Soviet Influence in Eastern Europe: Political Autonomy and the Warsaw Pact* (New York: Praeger, 1981); David Holloway, "The Warsaw Pact in Transition," in David Holloway and Jane M. 0. Sharp, eds., *The Warsaw Pact: Alliance in Transition?* (Ithaca, N.Y.: Cornell University Press, 1984), pp. 19–38.

17. Interview, Leonid Zamyatin, Moscow, 16 December 1991; Sergei Khrushchev, *Khrushchev on Khrushchev: An Inside Account of the Man and His Era,* trans. William Taubman (Boston: Little, Brown, 1990), pp. 156–57; Oleg Troyanovsky, "The Caribbean Crisis: A View from the Kremlin," *International Affairs* (Moscow) 4-5 (April/May 1992), pp. 147–57, at p. 149.

18. See Richard Ned Lebow, *Between Peace and War: The Nature of International Crisis* (Baltimore: Johns Hopkins University Press, 1981), pp. 82–97, for a discussion of the four traditional prerequisites of deterrence. For discussion of the conditions essential to deterrence success, see Richard Ned Lebow and Janice Gross Stein, *When Does Deterrence Succeed and How Do We Know?* (Ottawa: Canadian Institute for International Peace and Security, 1990), pp. 59–69.

19. Chapter 3 reviews this debate.

20. Janice Gross Stein, "Calculation, Miscalculation, and Conventional Deterrence I: The View from Cairo," in Robert Jervis, Richard Ned Lebow, and Janice Gross Stein, *Psychology and Deterrence* (Baltimore: Johns Hopkins University Press, 1985), pp. 31–59.

21. Henry Kissinger, *Years of Upheaval* (Boston: Little, Brown, 1982), p. 508.

22. Ibid., p. 510.

23. "United States Objectives and Programs for National Security," (NSC 68) (14 April 1950), *Foreign Relations of the United States,* 1950, vol. I (Washington, D.C.: Government Printing Office, 1977), p. 264; Vernon Aspaturian, "Soviet Global Power and the Correlation of Forces," *Problems of Communism* 20 (May-June 1980), pp. 1–18; John J. Dziak, *Soviet Perceptions of Military Power: The Interaction of Theory and Practice* (New York: Crane, Russak, 1981); Edward N. Luttwak, "After Afghanistan What?" *Commentary* 69 (April 1980), pp. 1–18; Richard

Pipes, "Why the Soviet Union Thinks It Could Fight and Win a Nuclear War," *Commentary* 64 (July 1977), pp. 21–34; Norman Podhoretz, "The Present Danger," *Commentary* 69 (April 1980), pp. 40–49.

24. There is also some evidence that the fear of war influenced Soviet behavior in Korea. Joseph Stalin authorized Kim II Sung to attack South Korea in June 1950 in the expectation that the United States would not intervene. When Washington did intervene, Stalin, afraid that the North Korean attack would provoke a Soviet-American war, quickly signaled interest in a cease-fire. N. Khrushchev, *Khrushchev Remembers: The Glasnost Tapes*, trans. and ed. Jerrold L. Schecter with Vyacheslav L. Luchkov (Boston: Little, Brown, 1990), pp. 144–47.

25. Oleg Grinevsky contends that Stalin feared that even a few atomic bombs dropped on Moscow would have destroyed the communist experiment. Interview, Oleg Grinevsky, Stockholm, 24 October 1992.

26. David A. Welch, ed., *Proceedings of the Hawk's Cay Conference on the Cuban Missile Crisis, 5-8 March 1987* (Cambridge, Mass.: Harvard University, Cen-ter for Science and International Affairs, Working Paper 89–1, 1989), mimeograph, pp. 81–83, hereafter cited as *Hawk's Cay Conference*.

27. Ibid., pp. 83ff.

28. Hawk's Cay Conference, author's record.

29. Ball, *Politics and Force Levels*, pp. 171–93; Freedman, *The Evolution of Nuclear Strategy*, pp. 331–71.

30. See Graham, *Shall America Be Defended?*; Gray, *Nuclear Strategy and National Style*; Gray and Payne, "Victory is Possible"; Wohlstetter, "Between an Unfree World and None."

31. Interview, Gen. Dimitri A. Volkogonov by Raymond L. Garthoff, Moscow, 1 February 1989; Anatoliy Gribkov, "Transcript of the Proceedings of the Havana Conference on the Cuban Missile Crisis, January 9–12 1992," mimeograph, in James G. Blight, Bruce J. Allyn, and David A. Welch, eds., *Cuba on the Brink: Castro, the Missile Crisis, and the Soviet Collapse* (New York: Pantheon Books, in press), pp. 18–21, hereafter cited as *Havana Conference*.

32. "Retrospective on the Cuban Missile Crisis," 22 January 1983, Atlanta, Ga. Participants: Dean Rusk, McGeorge Bundy, Edwin Martin, Donald Wilson, and Richard E. Neustadt (hereafter referred to as Retrospective), p. 6.

33. *Hawk's Cay Conference*, pp. 9–10.

34. Interview, Robert McNamara, Hawk's Cay, Fla., 6 March 1987.

35. Retrospective, p. 40.

36. Garthoff, Reflections on the Cuban Missile Crisis, 2d ed. rev. (Washington, D.C.: The Brookings Institution, 1989), pp. 158–86, on Soviet lessons from the crisis; Interviews, Leonid Zamyatin and Anatoliy F. Dobrynin, Moscow, 16–17 December, 1991.

37. The assertion that the Soviet Union could only be constrained by superior military power became something close to dogma in the United States government. It received its most forceful expression in National Security Council Memorandum (NSC) 68, written on the eve of the Korean War in 1950. NSC 68 is generally recognized as the most influential American policy document of the Cold War. See John L. Gaddis, *Strategies of Containment: A Critical Appraisal of Postwar American National Security Policy* (New York: Oxford University Press, 1982), chap. 4; Paul Y. Hammond, "NSC-68: Prologue to Rearmament," in Warner R. Schilling, Paul Y. Hammond, and Glenn H. Snyder, eds., *Strategy, Politics, and Defense Budgets* (New York: Columbia University Press, 1962), pp. 267–338; "United States Objectives and Programs for National Security," pp. 234–92.

38. Soviet leaders, with a mirror image of their adversary, made the same assumption about American foreign policy. Khrushchev put Missiles in Cuba in part to achieve psychological equality and constrain American foreign policy.

39. The accepted strategic wisdom, reflected in our analysis, holds that the United States had a decisive strategic advantage throughout the 1950s. It possessed an expanding capability to attack the Soviet Union with nuclear weapons without the prospect of direct retaliation. The Strategic Air Command had a large and growing fleet of strategic bombers based in the United States, Western Europe, and North Africa. This strike force was supplemented by carrier and land-based aircraft deployed along the Soviet periphery. The Soviet Union's bomber force was small, shorter range, and technologically primitive.

The relative military balance changed in the 1960s when both superpowers began to deploy ICBMs. In 1962, at the time of the Cuban missile crisis, the United States had some 3,500 warheads against approximately 300 for the Soviets. Only 20 of the Soviet warheads were on ICBMs. See Sagan, "STOP-62: The Nuclear War Plan Briefing to President Kennedy," *International Security* 12,1 (Summer 1987), pp. 22–51; David A. Welch, ed., *Proceedings of the Cambridge Conference on the Cuban Missile Crisis, 11–12 October 1987* (Cambridge, Mass.: Harvard University, Center for Science and International Affairs, April 1988), final version, mimeograph, pp. 52, 79, hereafter cited as *Cambridge Conference*. By the end of the 1960s, the Soviet Strategic Rocket Forces had deployed enough ICBMs to destroy about half of the population and industry of the United States. It had achieved the capability that McNamara considered essential for MAD.

Some time in the 1970s the Soviet Union achieved rough strategic parity. This balance prevailed until 1991, although some analysts have argued that one or the other possessed some margin of advantage. American missiles were more accurate throughout the 1970s. The United States was also the first to deploy multiple inde¬pendently targeted reentry vehicles (MIRVs). It put three warheads on Minuteman missiles, and fourteen on submarine-launched ballistic missiles (SLBMs). The Soviet Union began to deploy MIRVs in the late 1970s and, in the opinion of some analysts, gained a temporary strategic advantage because of the greater throw weight of their ICBMs. The SS-18 could carry thirty to forty MIRVs, but in practice was deployed with a maximum of ten.

40. Soviet aggressiveness is a subjective phenomenon. To measure it, we polled a sample of international relations scholars and former government officials. They were carefully chosen to ensure representation of diverse political points of view. These experts were given a list of events that could be interpreted as Soviet challenges to the United States, its allies, or nonaligned states. They were asked to rank them in order of ascending gravity. The survey revealed a surprising concurrence among experts. A description of the survey and its results appears in Richard Ned Lebow and John Garofano, "Soviet Aggressiveness: Need or Opportunity?" mimeograph.

41. This kind of need-based explanation of aggression provides a convincing explanation of both Soviet and American foreign policy in the Cold War since the Khrushchev and Kennedy years. See Richard Ned Lebow, "Windows of Opportunity: Do States Jump Through Them?" *International Security* 9 (Summer 1984), pp. 147–86.

42. McNamara, "The Military Role of Nuclear Weapons"; Jervis, *The Meaning of the Nuclear Revolution*; George, Hall, and Simons, *The Limits of Coercive Diplomacy*; Betts, *Nuclear Blackmail*.

43. Albert and Roberta Wohlstetter, "Controlling the Risks in Cuba," *Adelphi Paper* no. 17 (London: International Institute for Strategic Studies, 1965), p. 16. See also, Herman Kahn, *On Escalation* (New York: Praeger, 1965), pp. 74–82; Thomas Schelling, *Arms and Influence* (New Haven, Conn.: Yale University Press, 1966), pp. 80–83.

44. McNamara, "The Military Role of Nuclear Weapons"; Jervis, *The Meaning of the Nuclear Revolution*, pp. 34–38.

45. Years later, in an offhand comment, Kissinger claimed that he would not have felt secure enough to choose an alert if the Soviet Union had had a marked strategic advantage. Cited by Betts, Nuclear Blackmail, p. 125. This kind of indirect and fragmentary evidence fits best with the arguments of the war-fighters, largely because Kissinger thought very much as they did. It is of course debatable whether Kissinger would have acted differently had the United States been in a position of relative inferiority; the proposition has never been put to the test. Given Kissinger's heavy

emphasis on reputation and resolve, it seems unlikely that he would have complied even if the Soviet Union had had a relative strategic advantage. Proponents of finite deterrence and MAD would argue that Soviet compellence was unlikely to succeed even if the Soviet Union had had a marked advantage because the interests at stake were not sufficiently important.

46. This theme is developed at length in Richard Ned Lebow, *Nuclear Crisis Management: A Dangerous Illusion* (Ithaca, N.Y.: Cornell University Press, 1987).

47. By 2003, if the cuts proposed in the START II treaty are implemented, Russia will cut its missiles to 504 and its warheads to 3,000 and the United States will reduce its missiles to 500 and its warheads to 3,500.

CHAPTER 6

How are Conflicts Resolved?

The reconciliation of former enemies like France and Germany, Egypt and Israel, China and the USA, and the Soviet Union and the USA encourages cautious optimism about the ability of leaders and peoples to extricate themselves from deadly quarrels. This optimism must be tempered by the recognition that reconciliations are not always complete or irreversible. Egypt and Israel signed a peace treaty that has endured for many decades, but their relations remain cool and social contacts between their peoples are limited. The end of the Cold War was made possible by a reformist regime in the Soviet Union that was bitterly opposed by nationalists and more traditional communists. Nationalists have once again gained power in Russia and a new Cold War is possibly in the making. Sino–American relations, well on their way toward normalization in the early 1980s, have become more conflicted as a result of a series of incidents, disputes, and differences over Taiwan.

These caveats are intended to qualify, not to deny, the fundamental nature of the transformation that has occurred in these several relationships. In the past, ideological conflict, territorial disputes, and contested spheres of influence led to arms races, hostile alliances and wars, or the expectation of war. Today, the threat of war is remote and nonexistent in the case of Britain and France, and France and Germany. There is no sign of

This chapter draws from Richard Ned Lebow, 'Transitions and transformations: Building international cooperation', Security Studies, 2007, Vol. 6, No. 3, pp. 154-179, DOI: 10.1080/09636419708429317.

Egyptian–Israeli relations becoming more warlike, and they have weathered a series of Middle Eastern crises. Russian–American and Sino–American relations are more problematic but leaders on all sides seem intent on avoiding the kinds of provocations that could raise the threat of war.

The end of the Cold War inspired a spurt of optimism about conflict resolution and the prospect of a long-term peace. Hard-line realists questioned how lasting such reconciliations were likely to prove, and predicted that international relations would be as violent in the future as it was in the past. Other scholars were more optimistic about these relationships and about international relations in general, and offered a variety of justifications for their optimism. Writing in 2017, one cannot help be more jaundiced than the optimists, but more optimistic than the likes of John Mearsheimer and other realist pessimists.[1] It is interesting too that the principal threats to order largely arise from domestic politics and non-state actors, and less so from the kinds of threats foregrounded by realists. However, realists and advocates of power transition are doing their best to frame the foreign policies of China and Putin's Russia in these terms.

The burgeoning literature on accommodation distinguishes between conflicts that ended in the aftermath of a military victory that enabled one protagonist or its allies to remake the institutions of the other (e.g., France–Germany, Japan–USA), and those where political accommodation was reached without victory by regimes that had previously been committed to confrontation (e.g., Egypt–Israel, Soviet Union–USA). Research on the former has emphasized the positive role of democratic governments, transnational institutions, and norms. Research on the latter has given more importance to international and unit level structural constraints and the allegedly beneficial consequences of general deterrence.

This chapter addresses only accommodations that have been brought about by political compromise. I begin by examining the claims that can be explained by structural factors, in particular, by changes in the distribution of capabilities or general deterrence success. I find these claims unconvincing. Structural factors are undeniably important but only part of the story. Political considerations, independent of structure, appear to have played the decisive role in accommodation. I develop my argument with reference to the East–West and Israeli–Arab conflicts. They are recent and dramatic examples of accommodation, and they are also cases in which the most far-reaching claims have been made for structural explanations.

DECLINING CAPABILITIES

Until recently, there was very little political science literature devoted to the problem of change. Power transition theory, an important exception, seeks to explain the hegemonic war in terms of the rising capabilities of challengers and the declining capabilities of hegemons.[2] Since the end of the Cold War, change has attracted the attention of theorists, and realists have tried to explain the *volte face* in Soviet foreign policy under Mikhail Gorbachev in terms of that country's declining capabilities. They contend that the withdrawal from Afghanistan, the liberation of Eastern Europe, and the acceptance of one-sided arms treaties were all part of a rational attempt to manage decline.[3] There is little to no Soviet evidence in support of this account.[4]

Decline can sometimes lead to war, but not for the reasons that power transition theories predict. States in decline more generally attempt to manage their situation through diplomacy and disengagement.[5] Leaders of declining states often engage in denial; Russian, Austrian, and Ottoman leaders stuck their heads in the sand and behaved as if they were still healthy great powers. Soviet leaders Leonid Brezhnev and Mikhail Gorbachev recognized their relative decline sought to revitalize the Soviet economy and stem decline through, respectively, programs of pseudo- and real reform.[6]

Structural theories the invoke power transition, decline, or the balance of power invariably assume that actors make timely and accurate assessments of the relative power of their state and of others. If so, they need not be considered independently as agents; leaders are like electrons conveying or responding to forces and interchangeable. Behavior can be inferred directly from structure, allowing parsimonious theories of foreign policy. Realist theories that attribute the Soviet Union's accommodation with the West to its economic decline thus assume that Gorbachev understood the nature and implications of that decline and acted to cut his country's losses. But different leaders and their advisors often have diametrically opposed understandings of the balance of power and the direction of its likely change, and their understandings and favored responses cannot be separated from their ideologies and domestic politics.[7]

From the perspective of East–West relations, Gorbachev's most significant act was his willingness to allow Eastern Europe to break free of communism and Soviet control. Realist analyses treat Gorbachev's retreat from Eastern Europe as an attempt to strike the best deal possible with the West, or simply to shed an expensive and unmanageable sphere of influence.[8] Officials close to Gorbachev deny he was pursuing a policy of retrenchment. His public repudiation of the use of force to maintain existing governments in Eastern Europe was intended to undermine Warsaw Pact hardline leaders, all of whom bitterly condemned glasnost and *perestroika*, and to encourage their replacement by Gorbachev-like reformers. Reform-oriented communist leaders in Eastern Europe were expected to strengthen Gorbachev's position in the Politburo and to make Soviet bloc relations more equitable and manageable.[9]

Gorbachev's policies backfired because he failed to grasp the extent of popular and elite antagonism to communism in Poland, Hungary, Czechoslovakia, and East Germany.[10] His call for change triggered off popular revolutions that swept away communist governments and left him no choice but to accept this fait accompli and the once unthinkable absorption of East Germany by its Western nemesis.

Gorbachev's domestic assessments were equally inaccurate. The Soviet Union's precipitous economic decline was at least in part caused by his reforms. He unwittingly undermined communism in the Soviet Union, was blind to the growing threat of a conservative coup against him, and to the extent to which his domestic and foreign policies encouraged the centrifugal forces of nationalism that would lead to the breakup of the Soviet Union. Given Gorbachev's unquestioned commitment to socialism, it seems extremely unlikely that he would have behaved power are what matters.[11] It seems unlikely that he would have acted as he did, at home or abroad, if he and his advisers had understood the likely consequences of their policies. Domestic democratic reforms and the hands-off policy toward Eastern Europe were the results of—and probably could not have occurred without—strikingly unrealistic expectations about their likely consequences. Here, Gorbachev is hardly alone. Consider more recent decisions by President George W. Bush to invade Iraq and British Prime Minister David Cameron to hold a referendum on membership in the European Union.

Structural explanations for Mikhail Gorbachev's foreign policy are guilty of post hoc *ergo propter hoc* analysis. Knowing Gorbachev's policies and their outcomes, their proponents posit structures and assessments that must have led to these policies and outcomes. Those outcomes, however, were unwanted and unexpected, and the policies in question were carried out for other reasons. To explain Gorbachev's policies—and those of Sadat, Rabin, and Arafat—it is necessary to consider their goals, understand the foreign and domestic constraints and opportunities confronting them, and their assessments of the likely consequences of the various courses of action they saw open to them.

General Deterrence

The second general explanation for accommodation is successful general deterrence. It is a long-term strategy intended to discourage military challenge. The would-be deterrer strives to maintain a favorable military balance over time, or at least enough military capability to convince a would-be challenger that a resort to force would be too risky or costly. General deterrence differs from immediate deterrence in that the latter is a short-term strategy focused on specific challenges. The success of immediate deterrence is sometimes connected with that of general deterrence. The more general deterrence succeeds the less likely adversarial leaders are likely to consider a military challenge, and the less necessary immediate deterrence becomes.[12]

General deterrence success depends on adequate military capabilities, and in some conflicts may require a favorable balance of military power. Like its immediate counterpart, it also requires a demonstrable willingness to use those capabilities, if challenged, and that willingness must be credibly communicated to a would-be challenger. Deterrence accordingly has an important psychological–political component that is related to physical capabilities but by no means synonymous with them.

Some scholars, and many more journalists and politicians, have credited general deterrence with winding down the Cold War and Arab–Israeli conflicts. Three kinds of claims have been made:

1. *General deterrence success.* The military capability and resolve of a defender deter a challenger from using force. The challenger tries and fails to reverse the military balance and weaken the defender's resolve by building up its own military capability, perhaps making alliances with other dissatisfied states, and threatening the defender's allies. After some years of acute conflict, the challenger reluctantly concludes that deterrence is robust and that it is a waste of resources to continue the conflict. Gorbachev's efforts to end the Cold War have been described as the product of such a learning process.[13]

2. *Repeated defeat.* The same learning process leads to accommodation, but as a result of successive military defeats. The leaders of Egypt and Jordan turned to diplomacy only after five unsuccessful and costly wars (1948, 1956, 1967, 1969–1970, and 1973) convinced them that Israel could not be defeated, let alone destroyed. To achieve key foreign policy goals, they had to work with Israel.

3. *Lost competition.* In this variant, general deterrence not only restrains the challenger, but also convinces the challenger that military competition with the defender is impractical. The challenger hastens to make an accommodation before the military balance turns decisively against it with all the negative political consequences that this would entail. This is the logic of those who argue that the Carter-Reagan arms buildup and Strategic Defense Initiative compelled the Soviet Union to end the Cold War on terms favorable to the West.[14]

General deterrence may contribute to the resolution of certain kinds of conflicts, but the claims made for it to date in East–West and Arab-Israeli relations remain unsubstantiated.

Repeated Arab defeats may well have been a catalyst for rethinking the relationship with Israel. But such a process cannot be described as a general deterrence success. Deterrence succeeds when the military capability and resolve of a defender convince a challenger to refrain from using force. Four of the five Arab-Israeli interstate wars were the result of general and immediate deterrence *failures.* Whatever Arab learning occurred was the result of Israel's ability to defend itself, inflict costly defeats on its adversaries, and occupy their territory.

Deterrence failures are readily identifiable. They result in highly visible crises or wars. Deterrence successes are more elusive. Immediate deterrence is triggered by the belief that general deterrence is failing and that a military challenge is likely or probable. This expectation may be wrong but it is almost always a response to some kind of threatening adversarial behavior. These threats may be absent in general deterrence encounters. If general deterrence succeeds over time, a challenger may never consider military action or make explicit threats. The more successful general deterrence is, the fewer traces it leaves.

Assessments of general deterrence are also less reliable that those of immediate deterrence because they depend on the counterfactual argument. Immediate deterrence success can in theory be documented;

researchers need only to ascertain that a challenger intended to use force but decided against it because of the defender's display of capability and resolve. When there are no immediate preparations to use force, and possibly no considerations of such preparations, there is no behavioral evidence to indicate the success of general deterrence. Claims for its success rest assertions, generally impossible to document, that force would have been used in its absence.[15]

General deterrence further differs from immediate deterrence in its temporal dimension. General deterrence must be assessed over the course of an adversarial relationship. How well and how long does it have to work to be considered successful? We have no theoretical criteria for making such judgments. This gives considerable latitude to investigators and encourages arbitrary assessments.[16] In the Middle East, it is easy to offer the counterfactual claim that Israel would have been destroyed as a state and its Jewish inhabitants killed or expelled if they had lacked the means and will to defend themselves.

Arab states went to war in 1948 with the publicly proclaimed objective of destroying Israel and remained committed to it for many years afterward. The counterfactual argument is compelling because of the repeated failure of general and immediate deterrence and the evidence this provided of Arab intentions.

General deterrence in the Cold War is a different kettle of fish: the absence of war makes it difficult to assess the role of deterrence in keeping the peace. Lack of evidence about Soviet intentions and calculations did not prevent many scholars and journalists from hailing the success of deterrence in restraining the Soviet Union. They took as axiomatic that the Kremlin sought military conquests and was only kept in check by Western military capabilities and resolve. This is a political not a scientific argument. Evidence that has emerged since the end of the Cold War does not lend much support to these claims. The Soviet military prepared to invade Western Europe just as the Strategic Air Command prepared to annihilate the Soviet bloc with nuclear weapons. There is not a scintilla of evidence, however, that leaders on either side ever considered carrying out these plans or sought a decisive military advantage for the purpose of carrying out the first strike. Rather it suggests that Soviet and American leaders alike were terrified by the prospects of nuclear war.[17]

General deterrence cannot be discounted. The Soviet Union never possessed nuclear and conventional military superiority and we do not know how its leaders would have behaved in that circumstance. It is also impossible to substantiate or rule out other explanations for absence of war. In *We All Lost the Cold War*, Janice Gross Stein and I offer a political explanation for the long peace: we argue that neither superpower was ever so unhappy or threatened by the status quo that it was prepared to risk, let alone start, nuclear war to challenge or overturn it.[18] More recent research using formerly unavailable Soviet documents supports this interpretation.[19]

For the purposes of general deterrence, the Cold War and the Middle East must be regarded as fundamentally different kinds of conflicts. If neither superpower ever wanted or intended to initiate hostilities against the other, general deterrence was irrelevant, redundant, or provocative. In conflicts like the Middle East, where at least one of the protagonists would go to war if it thought it could win or otherwise gain from hostilities, general deterrence was relevant and may sometimes have succeeded in preventing war.

Even in the second kind of conflict, deterrence is at best a necessary but insufficient condition for accommodation. The fact that a challenger recognizes it cannot win a war does not mean its leaders are prepared to end that conflict and extend the olive branch to their adversary. Frustration does not ineluctably lead to enlightenment; there is ample evidence that it often does the reverse. Leaders can continue the struggle by other means (e.g., economic boycotts, terrorism, subversion) or wait for more favorable circumstances, as Egypt and Syria did between 1949 and 1967 and 1967 and 1973.

Soviet-American relations provide the most dramatic evidence against the proposition that accommodation follows upon the recognition that an adversary cannot be overcome by military means. Leaders of both superpowers recognized the impossibility of a meaningful military victory from the outset of the Cold War. That conflict nevertheless endured for almost a half-century. Investigators need to look elsewhere to explain its continuation and demise.

Resolution of most international conflict generally requires dramatic rethinking and corresponding policy shifts by both sides. This can be very difficult to accomplish. Important political and economic groups within protagonists are likely to have developed vested interests in conflict that make it difficult for conciliatory leaders to gain power or implement a conciliatory foreign policy agenda. Leaders who express interest in accommodation risk being rebuffed by public opinion, important allies or exploited by their adversary. The East–West and Middle East conflicts provide ample illustrations of all these problems. They indicate that a leader's commitment to reduce conflict is only the first, and by no means sufficient step, toward accommodation. Attempts to explain the transformation of the East–West and Middle East conflicts—or any enduring international conflict—need to explain shifts in goals of both sides and the emergence of the domestic and foreign conditions that encourage or enable accommodation.

PATHWAYS TO ACCOMMODATION

I hypothesize that leaders will consider conciliatory foreign policies when: they expect improved relations with adversaries to confer important domestic and international benefits, or prevent important domestic and international losses; have reason to believe that their adversaries will respond positively to their conciliatory overtures; and consider it feasible to mobilize enough domestic support to sustain and implement accommodation.

The first condition is the most important because it speaks to the incentives for accommodation. The second and third conditions pertain to feasibility. Leaders who expect to benefit from accommodation will nevertheless not attempt it unless they consider it to have a reasonable chance of success. Success will depend in the first instance on the response of the adversary; both sides must cooperate to ameliorate or resolve a conflict. Leaders must also have the authority or support at home to carry out and sustain a policy. The three conditions tell us nothing about the conditions in which leaders see accommodation as conducive to the attainment of their broader political objectives. Case studies of accommodation are helpful in this connection and suggest two distinct pathways to accommodation.

In the first pathway, the principal catalyst for accommodation is the commitment by leaders of one protagonists to domestic reforms and restructuring. Elsewhere I have demonstrated the links between domestic reform and conciliation in the Anglo–French, Egyptian–Israeli and East–West conflicts.[20] Here I provide a brief overview of the argument in the latter two cases.

In the early 1970s, Egypt's economy was in a shambles. President Anwar el-Sadat concluded that socialism from above had failed and that Egypt had to liberalize its economy. Sadat was also convinced that such a domestic transformation required some resolution to the Arab-Israeli conflict. When the 1973 war failed to achieve this end by military means, Sadat searched actively for a diplomatic solution that would create the stable climate necessary to attract foreign investment and aid from the West.[21]

Sadat expected that a peace agreement with Israel brokered by the USA would create the conditions for the successful liberalization of the Egyptian economy. The USA would provide extensive economic aid and technical assistance to jumpstart the Egyptian economy. In a more secure and stable environment, foreign investment from the capitalist countries would flow into Egypt, accelerating economic growth. Only if the Egyptian economy grew could Egypt begin to address the fundamental infrastructural and social problems that it faced. Peace with Israel was important not only because of the direct benefits that it would bring— the return of the Sinai oil fields and an end to humiliation—but because of the opportunity it provided to open Egypt to the West and particularly to the USA.[22]

Mikhail S. Gorbachev's efforts to transform East–West relations were also motivated in large part by his commitment to domestic restructuring. *Perestroika* required an accommodation with the West; this would permit resources to be shifted from military to civilian investment and production, and attract credits, investment, and technology from the West. According to Foreign Minister Shevardnadze, the chief objective of Soviet foreign policy became 'to create the maximum favorable external conditions needed in order to conduct internal reform'.[23]

For Gorbachev and his closest advisers, there was another important link between foreign and domestic policy. In the view of *perestroichiks*, the conflict with the West had been kept alive and exploited by the communist party to justify its monopoly on power and suppression of dissent.[24] 'New thinking' in foreign policy would break the hold of the party old guard and the influence of the military–industrial complex with which it was allied.[25]

For committed democrats like Shevardnadze, *perestroika* and *glasnost* also had an ideological component. For the Soviet Union to join the Western family of nations, it had to become a democratic society with a demonstrable respect for the individual and collective rights of its citizens and allies. Granting independence to the countries of Eastern Europe was the international analog to emptying the Gulags, ending censorship in the media, and choosing members of the Supreme Soviet through free elections. *Perestroika*, Shevardnadze explained, 'was understood to be universally applicable and could not be guided by a double standard. If you start democratizing your own country, you no longer have the right to thwart that same process in other countries'.[26]

The second mediating condition of a conciliatory response is the understanding leaders have of the consequences of confrontation. Leaders are more likely to pursue conciliatory foreign policies when they believe confrontation has failed. In all three conflicts, leaders recognized that confrontation had failed, had been extraordinarily costly, and was unlikely to succeed in the future.

Sadat's peace initiative took place in the aftermath of military failure, a costly war in which Egypt was frustrated in its battlefield goals. Egyptian officials recognized that military conditions in 1973 had been optimal—Egyptian and Syrian armies were armed with the latest weapons, mounted a joint attack, and achieved surprise—yet the war ended with Egyptian armies facing a catastrophic defeat. Sadat and his generals recognized that, even under the best possible conditions, Egypt could not hope to defeat Israel. Sadat thus began to search for a diplomatic solution that would return the Suez Canal to Egypt. He sought to involve the USA as a mediator, broker, and guarantor of a peace settlement.

Mikhail Gorbachev's search for accommodation was also a reaction to the failure and costs of confrontation. Under Leonid Brezhnev, the Soviet Union had steadily built up its conventional and nuclear arsenals in a bid for military superiority. Brezhnev and many of his colleagues, and the Soviet military establishment, were convinced that a shift in the correlation of forces in favor of the socialist camp would compel the West to treat the Soviet Union as a coequal superpower. Nixon and Kissinger's interest in détente, which came at a time when the Soviet Union was drawing abreast of the USA in strategic nuclear capability, confirmed their view of the political value of military forces.[27]

Soviet leaders reasoned that additional forces would further improve their position vis-à-vis the West and continued their buildup into die 1980s. Their policy had the opposite effect. Moscow's seeming pursuit of strategic superiority coupled with its more assertive policy in the Third World handed American militants a powerful weapon to use against détente. The Carter administration felt compelled to begin its own strategic buildup and withdraw the proposed SALT II Treaty from the Senate. The apparent upsurge in Soviet aggressiveness and Carter's seeming inability to confront it contributed to Reagan's electoral landslide and support for his more extensive military buildup and anti-Soviet foreign policy.

Soviet foreign policy analysts in the institutes were sensitive to the ways in which Brezhnev's crude military and foreign policy had provoked a strong American reaction. Their critiques of Soviet policy circulated widely among the Soviet elite. They were especially critical of the increasingly costly intervention in Afghanistan. Institute analysts also took Brezhnev and the military to task for their deployment of SS-20s in Eastern Europe and the western military districts of the Soviet Union. They maintained that the commitment of NATO to deploy Pershing II ballistic missiles and ground launched cruise missiles (GLCMS), which Moscow found so threatening, was a predictable response to Moscow's provocative and unnecessary deployment of highly accurate short- and intermediate-range nuclear systems.[28]

Analysts further contended that Brezhnev's buildup had provoked the same kind of pernicious overreaction in the USA that the Kennedy-McNamara buildup of the 1960s had in the Soviet Union. Soviet attempts to intimidate China with a massive military buildup along its border were said to have had the same effect. A different and more cooperative approach to security was necessary. Soviet failures in Afghanistan and in managing relations with the USA and Western Europe prompted a fundamental reassessment of foreign policy on the part of intellectuals and politicians not associated with these policies. Gorbachev and Shevardnadze maintain that their foreign policy views were formed in reaction to Brezhnev's failures and were significantly shaped by the analyses of Soviet critics in the foreign ministry and institutes. Both men had long conversations with analysts and foreign ministry critics of Brezhnev's policies before they decided to withdraw from Afghanistan. Such individuals were also instrumental in Gorbachev's and the Politburo's decision to accept on-site inspection, which helped to break the logjam in arms control.[29]

Soviet officials agree that economic stagnation and the running sore of Afghanistan paved the way to power for a reform-oriented leader. Once in the Kremlin, Gorbachev exploited Afghanistan and the deployment by NATO of Pershing Us and GLCMs in Western Europe to discredit the militants and gain the political freedom to pursue a more conciliatory policy toward the West.[30]

The third condition facilitating accommodation is the expectation of reciprocity. Leaders will be more likely to initiate conciliatory policies if they believe their adversary is receptive to them and will not to exploit their overtures to make unilateral gains. In many, if not most, adversarial relationships, leaders fear that any interest they express in accommodation, or any concessions they make, will communicate weakness to their adversary and prompt a more aggressive policy rather than reciprocal gestures or concessions. Given the serious foreign and domestic costs of failed efforts at accommodation, leaders are only likely to pursue conciliatory policies when they expect such policies to be reciprocated.

Anwar el-Sadat had reason to suppose that Israel might respond positively to an offer of a peace treaty. He made extensive private inquiries about Prime Minister Menachem Begin. He asked Nicolae Ceausescu of Rumania, who had met Begin several times, whether the prime minister was sincere in his interest in peace and if he could fulfill any commitment that he made. Reassured by the Romanian leader, Sadat sent his deputy premier, Hassan Tuhami, to meet secretly in Morocco with Israeli foreign minister Moshe Dayan to explore the outlines of an agreement. Dayan assured Tuhami that Israel would consider returning the Sinai to Egypt in exchange for a full peace. Only when his expectations of reciprocity were confirmed did Sadat undertake his public and dramatic visit to Jerusalem.[31]

For the Soviet Union, the importance of the expectation of reciprocity is best illustrated by the different policies of Nikita Khrushchev and Mikhail Gorbachev, the two Soviet leaders most interested in accommodation with the West. Gorbachev was able to persevere with his search for accommodation because of the positive evolution of superpower relations since the height of the Cold War in the early 1960s. He was much less fearful than Khrushchev that the USA and its allies would exploit any Soviet concession. Khrushchev's intense fear of the West had severely constrained his search for accommodation. He was unprepared to gamble, as Gorbachev did, that conciliatory words and deeds would generate sufficient public pressure on Western governments to reciprocate. Khrushchev did make some unilateral concessions; he reduced the size of the armed forces and proclaimed a short-lived moratorium on nuclear testing. When his actions were not reciprocated, he felt the need to demonstrate firmness to buttress his position at home and abroad. His inflammatory rhetoric strengthened the hand of militants in the West who all along opposed accommodation with the Soviet Union.[32]

Gorbachev succeeded in transforming East–West relations and ending the Cold War because the West became his willing partner. Unlike Khrushchev, whose quest for a German peace treaty frightened France and West Germany, Gorbachev's attempt to end the division of Europe met a receptive audience, especially in Germany and Western Europe. Disenchantment with the Cold War, opposition to the deployment of new weapons systems, and a widespread desire to end the division of Europe created a groundswell of support for exploring the possibilities of accommodation with the Soviet Union. Western public opinion, given voice by well-organized peace movements, was a critical factor in encouraging Gorbachev and his colleagues in their attempts at conciliation.

Gorbachev was intent on liberalizing the domestic political process at home and improving relations with the West. Within a month of assuming office, he made his first unilateral concession—a temporary freeze on the deployment of Soviet intermediate-range missiles in Europe. This was followed by a unilateral moratorium on nuclear tests and acceptance of the Western 'double zero' proposal for reducing intermediate-range nuclear forces (INF) in Europe. In subsequent speeches and proposals, he tried to demonstrate his support for sweeping arms control and a fundamental restructuring of superpower relations.[33]

President Ronald Reagan continued to speak of the Soviet Union as an 'evil empire' and remained committed to his quest for a near-perfect ballistic missile defense.

To break this impasse, Gorbachev pursued a two-pronged strategy. In successive summits, he tried and finally convinced Reagan of his genuine interest in ending the arms race and restructuring East–West relations on a collaborative basis. When Reagan changed his opinion of Gorbachev, he also modified his view of the Soviet Union and quickly became the leading dove of his administration. Gorbachev worked hard to convince Western publics that his policies represented a radical departure from past Soviet policies. The Soviet withdrawal from Afghanistan, freeing of political prisoners, and liberalization of the Soviet political system, evoked widespread sympathy and support in the West and generated strong public pressure on NATO governments to respond in kind to Gorbachev's initiatives.[34]

Gorbachev's political persistence succeeded in breaching Reagan's wall of mistrust. At their Reykjavik summit in October 1986, the two leaders talked seriously about eliminating all of their ballistic missiles within ten years and making deep cuts in their nuclear arsenals. No agreement was reached because Reagan was unwilling to accept any restraints on his Strategic Defense Initiative. The Reykjavik summit, as Gorbachev had hoped, nevertheless began a process of mutual reciprocation, reassurance, and accommodation between the superpowers.

That process continued after an initially hesitant George Bush became Gorbachev's full-fledged partner in ending the vestiges of forty years of Cold War.[35]

The second pathway to accommodation is the existence of domestic or foreign vulnerabilities that leaders believe can best, or perhaps only, be addressed through cooperation with their adversaries. This concern was a fundamental cause of the rapprochement in the Middle East between Israel and the Palestinians and Israel and Jordan.

Prime Minister Yitzhak Rabin, an experienced military officer, was convinced by Iraqi SCUD attacks during the Gulf War that Israel faced an increasing threat of biological and chemical attacks from its determined enemies. The civilian population would be increasingly at risk as there was no adequate defense against such weapons. Although Israel could retaliate, it could not adequately deter in Rabin's judgment. It was accordingly in Israel's interest to reach an accommodation with the Palestinians and Syria. The other driving factor was Rabin's preoccupation with the USA. The US–Israeli relationship had always been a preoccupation for Rabin. The Bush administration had put tremendous pressure on Israel over loan guarantees, tying them to a freezing of settlements on the West Bank. The two issues—the threat of unconventional attacks and the need to repair the rift in US–Israeli relations—combined to stimulate interest in accommodation.

The pressures on Yasir Arafat were greater. The PLO was at its lowest point in its history. Following the Gulf War, Arafat and the PLO had lost the financial support of the Gulf countries and Arafat was unable to pay the salaries of his large staff in the West Bank and Gaza. In both territories, the Intifada had been captured by indigenous Palestinian leaders who operated with growing autonomy. Hamas, vocally antagonistic to the PLO, was growing stronger. Arafat was also pushed toward accommodation by the disappearance of the Soviet Union and the loss of its support.

The two pathways have several features in common that have important implications for the study of accommodation.

Domestic politics Sadat and Gorbachev were intensely focused on their domestic agendas and adopted foreign policies they thought would advance those agendas. Domestic considerations were also critical for Rabin and Arafat. For at least three of the four leaders, the link between domestic and foreign policy was the reverse of that posited by most theories of foreign policy. By ignoring domestic politics, existing theories fail to capture some of the most important motives for foreign policy change.

Biased assessment: Risk assessments can be significantly influenced by what is at stake. Studies of immediate deterrence failures document numerous instances of leaders who committed themselves to aggressive challenges of adversarial commitments to cope with pressing strategic and domestic problems.[36] Because they believed that these problems could only be overcome through successful challenges, they convinced themselves, sometimes in the face of strong disconfirming evidence, that their challenges would succeed.

Gorbachev's behavior indicates that a commitment to accommodation can encourage the same kind of motivated bias in information processing. In the absence of any real evidence and against the advice of prominent advisers, he convinced himself that he could change Ronald Reagan's view of arms control and of the Soviet Union and achieve the kind of breakthrough essential for a wider political accommodation. Gorbachev's success suggests the corollary that expectations of reciprocity can sometimes be made self-fulfilling, just like expectations of conflict.

Miscalculation Gorbachev's public call for reform in Eastern Europe set in motion a chain of events that led to the overthrow of seven communist governments, demise of the Warsaw Pact and the reunification of Germany under Western auspices. Gorbachev's domestic economic and political reforms accelerated the decline of the Soviet economy and were the proximate causes of communism's collapse and the breakup of the Soviet Union.

Sadat made equally serious miscalculations. He misjudged the short-term consequences of accommodation with Israel. He expected the process to move quickly, so that Arab opposition to it would not have a chance to coalesce and organize. He further expected the Gulf states to support, at least tacitly, any accommodation that was backed by the USA. Finally, he expected that accommodation would result in a flood of foreign investment in Egypt. All these expectations were erroneous and put Sadat into a difficult political position. His political isolation at home and abroad and the failure of the peace process to address or assist the Palestinians were contributing causes to his assassination.

These miscalculations had many causes, but perhaps the most fundamental one was the contradictory nature of the goals these leaders sought. Gorbachev wanted to make the Soviet Union a freer, more productive country with more equitable relations with its Warsaw Pact allies and the West. He also wanted to preserve the core of political communism and its command economy. He deluded himself into believing that these objectives were not only compatible, but also reinforcing, when in reality the former could only be achieved at die expense of the latter.[37] Sadat was also caught in a fundamental contradiction between his desire for rapid economic growth and his commitment to autocratic and corrupt government. He also deluded himself into believing that he could have peace with Israel and continue to receive much-needed financial aid from the Gulf States.

These cases give rise to a disturbing thought. Would Sadat and Gorbachev have pursued their respective accommodations if they had had a better understanding of their consequences? Did accommodation depend on gross wishful thinking by the leaders responsible for initiating it? If so, would these leaders and countries have been better off eschewing accommodation? This is, of course, the contention of embittered Russian communists and uncompromising Arab nationalists.

Structural explanations assume that leaders are more or less interchangeable; rational leaders who confront the same combination of constraints and opportunities will respond in similar ways. My cases reveal enormous variation. Brezhnev and Gorbachev recognized the need to reinvigorate the Soviet economy, but implemented strikingly different reform programs and related foreign policies, just as Rabin and Shamir adopted different policies to safeguard Israel's security. These differences cannot be attributed to changing circumstances. Opponents of Sadat, Gorbachev, Rabin, and Arafat would not have pursued accommodation, and they were not powerless because of their opposition to accommodation; and the choice of leader in all these cases was determined by other issues and considerations.

Approaches that focus on the decisive and independent role of leaders confront a difficult challenge. They ultimately need to explain why different leaders adopt different policies. I have taken a step in this direction by identifying some of the political visions, pressures, and learning experiences that appear to promote accommodation. My propositions need to be tested in other cases and in other periods of the East–West and

Middle East conflicts. Were these conditions also present and were they associated with attempts at accommodation?

If my findings find additional support in other cases, they will be useful starting points for explanatory narratives and forward-looking forecasts. They take us only part way to our goal, however. They tell us nothing about the reasons why leaders develop the particular visions, goals, and lessons that prompt them to seek accommodation. The challenge posed by this question is most evident in the case of Sadat. He was almost unique among the Egyptian political elite in his belief that accommodation with Israel was advisable and feasible. His commitment to economic restructuring was controversial but more widely shared.

The beliefs and goals of leaders are often no less difficult to explain when they are more widely shared. An important segment of the Soviet elite also favored economic reform, liberalization of the political system, withdrawal from Afghanistan and improved relations with the West. Gorbachev was a relative latecomer to foreign policy and appears to have adopted many of his foreign policy goals from his most liberal advisers. Why did Gorbachev assimilate these views and not those of the more conservative officials with whom he worked? A number of explanations have been proposed (e.g., generational learning, domestic politics, coalition building), and they all encounter problems.[38]

Caveats

This chapter examined only two pathways to accommodation. They were critical in Anglo–French, Egyptian–Israeli, and East–West accommodation. There are undoubtedly other pathways, such as mutual fear of a third party. It played a role in Anglo–French relations in the years between 1905 and 1914, and was equally central to the Sino–American rapprochement of the 1970s. Economic incentives may have been important—but not fundamental—to the partial accommodations between the two Germanys in the era of *Ostpolitik* and the two Chinas during the People Republic's decades of industrialization.

There is also the important question of how leaders respond to conciliatory initiatives. Accommodation requires reciprocity. My first pathway describes how a leader adopts a more conciliatory foreign policy to facilitate domestic restructuring. The adversary must respond positively, reassure the initiator of its own interest in accommodation, and both sides must work together to resolve outstanding differences between them and institutionalize their new relationship.

Prior to 1986, there were four unsuccessful attempts to transform Soviet-American relations: by the post-Stalin troika in 1953–1955, Nikita Khrushchev in 1959–1960, Leonid Brezhnev and Richard Nixon from 1969 to 1973, and Jimmy Carter from 1976 to 1979. The Khrushchev and Carter experiences show the dangers of unsuccessful attempts at accommodation. Both leaders came under blistering criticism from hardliners at home and sought to protect themselves by intensifying confrontation with their adversary.[39]

Reciprocity is essential but by no means inevitable, as Soviet-American relations illustrate. We need to study successful and unsuccessful attempts at accommodation and develop propositions that explain divergent responses.

The explanations for reciprocity may prove quite different from those of initiation. This is not a problem in the second pathway that delineates how similar kinds of incentives move both sides simultaneously toward accommodation.

WHAT IS ACCOMMODATION?

Research on accommodation has focused almost entirely on its causes; researchers have advanced a series of competing propositions to explain accommodation in general and the East–West and Arab–Israeli accommodations in particular. We also need to address what we mean by accommodation. Is it a sharp decline in the probability of war (Israel–Egypt)? Or is it an improvement in relations to the point where war becomes almost unthinkable (UK–France, USA–UK, France–Germany)? Or is it perhaps something in between (Russia–USA, China–USA)?

A decline in the probability of war leads to, or reflects, an improved relationship.

Reconciliation, however, requires more than removal of the threat of war. If the Anglo–French and Franco–German experiences can be taken as guides, it requires resolution of important outstanding issues, the building of close economic and social ties, and a fundamental compatibility in political institutions and values.

There are different degrees of accommodation, and researchers need to specify just what they mean. Toward this end, it would be helpful to identify the stages relationships can pass through from outright hostility to full reconciliation. This would allow for more appropriate case comparisons. If, as we suspect, conflicts move—or fail to move—from one stage to another for different reasons, it would also break down the dependent variable into more analytically meaningful categories.[40]

For scholars interested in peace, the probability of war will initially remain the critical dependent variable. Peace, however, ultimately depends on the quality of the broader relationship. Conflicts in which the probability of war has been sharply reduced but otherwise remain frozen, like Israel and Egypt or Greece and Turkey, can readily heat up in response to regime changes or other threatening developments. This can also happen in relationships where accommodation has gone further.

Broader relationships are important in a second sense. Accommodation is not a stochastic process; it is more likely to occur under some circumstances than others. The pathways I have described require domestic or strategic incentives, the expectation of reciprocity and the ability to mobilize adequate domestic support behind the peace process, and any agreement and whatever implementation it requires. These conditions are more likely to develop after a conflict has been ongoing for some time. They may also reflect accumulated frustration and costs on both sides. The East–West conflict provides the best illustration of this proposition. As noted earlier, major improvements in East–West relations, however, took place long before Gorbachev came to power in 1985. By 1985, that conflict was characterized by a fundamental stability. Twenty-three years had elapsed since the last war-threatening crisis. The superpowers took each other's commitment to avoid war for granted and had signed a series of arms control and rules-of-the-road agreements to regulate their strategic competition and interaction. These accords weathered the shocks of the Soviet invasion of Afghanistan and Reagan's commitment to Star Wars. Gorbachev's initiatives were built on this preexisting foundation.[41]

Gorbachev's policies initiated the final phase of a reconciliation that had been proceeding fitfully since the death of Stalin. Gorbachev would never have contemplated, or have been allowed to carry out, his domestic reforms, asymmetrical arms control agreements, and encouragement of reform in Eastern Europe, if the majority of the Central Committee had expected a hostile West to respond aggressively to a visibly weaker Soviet Union. The willingness of Gorbachev and his key associates to make unilateral concessions without apparent fear of their foreign policy consequences indicates that for them the Cold War had already receded into the past. They were discarding its atavistic institutional remnants to facilitate cooperation with their former adversaries and reap its expected benefits.

These accommodations illustrate the importance of ideas. The fundamental cause of the resolution of the East–West conflict was a dramatic shift in the Soviet conception of security. Rejection of confrontation in favor of 'common security' paved the way for the series of unilateral gestures that broke the logjam of East–West conflict. This conceptual revolution was preceded by an earlier and equally important conceptual breakthrough: the recognition by superpower leaders that they both feared nuclear war and were committed to its prevention. This recognition was responsible for the stability that characterized East–West relations from the mid-1960s. Both conceptual changes were largely independent of military and economic capabilities, although not of foreign and defense policies. To understand these changes, analysts must look at how elite conceptions of security are shaped through personal and national political experiences, and contacts with one another, advisors, intellectuals and diplomats, and scientists and journalists who can function as conveyer-belts of ideas and information within elites and between adversaries.[42]

Arab-Israeli accommodation also involved learning, but of a different kind. Arab leaders recognized that they could not win a war. Once that recognition set in, the advantages of accommodation should have been obvious: territory regained, occupation ended, an improved relationship with the USA, and greater economic opportunities in the region and through the vehicle of American aid. Although defeat drove home these lessons to Sadat, it did not to most of his contemporaries. Palestinians and Israelis alike are deeply divided on the issue of peace. Proponents and opponents alike draw diametrically opposed policy lessons from the shared historical experiences.

My analysis indicates that structural explanations of accommodation are inadequate. At best, declining capabilities and deterrence success represent necessary but insufficient conditions for accommodation. The visions of leaders, the concrete goals, and their understanding of the constraints and opportunities they confront provide a more compelling explanation of accommodation. This is not to say that political visions are not themselves a reflection of underlying conditions. Ultimately, the explanation for accommodation must be sought in an understanding of the complex interplay of ideas, context, and politics.

Notes

1. John Mearsheimer, "Back to the Future: Instability in Europe After the Cold War," International Security 15 (Summer 1990), pp. 5–56; Kenneth N. Waltz, "The Emerging Structure of International Politics," International Security 18 (Fall 1993), pp. 44–79.

2. George Modelski, "The Long Cycle of Global Politics and the Nation-State," Comparative Studies of Society and History 20 (April 1978), pp. 214–235; Charles F. Doran and Wes Parsons, "War and the Cycle of Relative Power," American Political Science Review 74 (December 1960), pp. 947–965; William R. Thompson, ed., Contending Approaches to World System Analysis (Beverly Hills: Sage, 1983); A. F. K. Organski and Jacek Kugler, The War Ledger (Chicago: University of Chicago Press, 1980); Raimo Vayrynen, "Economic Cycles, Power Transitions, Political Management and Wars Between Major Powers," International Studies Quarterly 27 (December 1983), pp. 389–418; Robert Gilpin, War and Change in World Politics (New York: Cambridge University Press, 1981). For a review, Jack S. Levy, "Declining Power and the Preventive Motivation for War," World Politics 40 (October 1987), pp. 82–107.

3. Daniel Deudney and G. John Ikenberry, "The International Sources of Soviet Change," International Security 16 (Winter 1991/1992), pp. 74–118, and "Soviet Reform and the End of the Cold War. Explaining Large-Scale Historical Change," Review of International Studies 17 (summer 1991): 225–250; Kenneth A. Oye, "Explaining the End of the Cold War Morphological and Behavioral Adaptations to the Nuclear Peace," in International Relations Theory and the End of the Cold War, ed. Richard Ned Lebow and Thomas Risse-Kappen (New York: Columbia University Press, 1994), pp. 57–84; William C. Wohlforth, "Realism and the End of the Cold War," International Security 19 (Winter 1994/1995), pp. 91–129.

4. Steve Chan, China, the U.S., and the Power-Transition Theory: A Critique (New York: Routledge, 2008); Richard Ned Lebow and Benjamin A. Valentino, "Lost in Transition: A Critical Analysis of Power Transition Theory" International Relations 23, no. 3 (2009), pp. 389–410.

5. Gilpin, War and Change, pp. 192–197; Wohlforth, "Realism and the End of the Cold War"; Aaron L. Friedberg, The Weary Titan: Britain and the Experience of Relative Decline, 1895–1905 (Princeton: Princeton University Press, 1988).

6. Mark Sandle, "Brezhnev and Developed Socialism: The Ideology of Zastol," in Edward Bacon and Mark Sandle, eds, Brezhnev Reconsidered (London: Palgrave-Macmillan, 2002), pp. 165–187; Archie Brown, The Rise and Fall of Communism (London: Bodley Head, 2009), pp. 398–420.

7. On this point, Hans J. Morgenthau, *Politics Among Nations: The Struggle for Power and Peace* (New York: Knopf, 1948), Part 3.

8. William C. Wohlforth, *Cold War Endgame: Analysis, Oral History, Debates* (University Park, Pa.: Pennsylvania State University Press, 2002), for the most sophisticated analysis of this kind.

9. Jacques Levesque, *The Enigma of 1989: The USSR and the Liberalization of Eastern Europe* (Berkeley and Los Angeles: University of California Press, 1997); Robert D. English, *Russia and the Idea of the West: Gorbachev, Intellectuals, and the End of the Cold War* (New York: Columbia University Press, 2000) and "Power, Ideas, and New Evidence on the Cold War's End: A Reply to Brooks and Wohlforth," *International Security* 26:4 (2002), pp. 93–111.

10. Levesque, *The Enigma of 1989*; Valerie Bunce, "Soviet Decline as a Regional Hegemon: the Gorbachev Regime and Eastern Europe," Eastern European Politics and Societies 3 (Spring 1989): 235–267; "The Soviet Union Under Gorbachev: Ending Stalinism and Ending the Cold War," International Journal 46 (Spring 1991): 220–241.

11. Stephen F. Cohen and Katrina vanden Heuvel, *Voices of Glasnost: Interviews with Gorbachev's Reformers* (New York: Norton, 1989), passim; Jack F. Matlack, Jr., *Autopsy of an Empire: The American Ambassador's Account of the Collapse of the Soviet Union* (New York: Random House, 1995), 68–154; Archie Brown, *The Gorbachev Factor* (New York: Oxford University Press, 1996), chap. 7.

12. Patrick Morgan, *Deterrence, A Conceptual Analysis* (Beverly Hills: Sage, 1977), is generally credited with this distinction.

13. Daniel Deudney and G. John Ikenberry, "The International Sources of Soviet Domestic Change," *International Security* 13 (Winter 1991/1992): 74–118; For learning and adaptation, Michael W. Doyle, "Liberalism and the End of the Cold War," and Jack Snyder, "Myths, Modernization, and the Post-Gorbachev World," in Richard Ned Lebow and Thomas Risse-Kappen, eds., *International Relations Theory and the End of the Cold War* (New York: Columbia University Press, 1995), pp. 85–108, 109–126.

14. Elli Iieberman, "The Rational Deterrence Theory Debate: Is the Dependent Variable Elusive?, *Security Studies* 3, no. 3 (1994), pp. 384–427.

15. For a discussion of the methodological problems of studying general deterrence, Richard Ned Lebow and Janice Gross Stein, *When Does Deterrence Succeed and How Do We Know?* (Ottawa: Canadian Institute for International Peace and Security, 1990).

16. In his analysis of Israeli-Syrian relations, Yair Evron, *War and Intervention in Lebanon* (Baltimore: Johns Hopkins University Press, 1987), maintains that general deterrence succeeded between 1975 and 1985 because the two countries fought only one major war. Evron counts any year without

a war as a success, making deterrence 90% successful during the decade. He also begins his 10-year period in 1975, conveniently excluding the Israeli–Syrian conflicts of 1973 and 1974. Robert Jervis, "Rational Deterrence: Theory and Practice," World Politics 41 (January 1989): 183–207, also notes the arbitrary use of temporal indicators of success.

17. On Khrushchev and Brezhnev, see Richard Ned Lebow and Janice Gross Stein, We All Lost the Cold War (Princeton: Princeton University Press), 1994 esp. chap. 14.

18. Ibid, chap. 14; John Mueller, Retreat From Doomsday: The Obsolescence of Major War (New York: Basic Books, 1989). Lebow and Stein, We All Lost the Cold War.

19. Mihail M. Narinskii, "The Soviet Union and the Berlin Crisis, 1948–1949," in Francesca Gori and Silvio Pons, The Soviet Union in the Cold War, 1943–53 (New York: St. Martin's, 1996), pp. 57–75; Victor Gorbarev, "Soviet Military Plans and Actions During the First Berlin Crisis," Slavic Military Studies 10, no. 3 (1997), pp. 1–23. Vladislav Zubok and Constantine Pleshakov, Inside the Kremlin's Cold War (Cambridge: Harvard University Press, 1997), pp. 134–137, 194–197.

20. Richard Ned Lebow, "The Search for Accommodation: Gorbachev in Comparative Perspective," in Lebow and Risse-Kappen, International dilations Theory and the End of the Cold War, 167–186.

21. Janice Gross Stein, "The Political Economy of Strategic Agreement: The Linked Costs of Failure at Camp David," in Peter Evans, Harold Jacobson, and Robert Putnam, eds., Domestic Politics and International Negotiation: An Integrative Perspective, ed. (Berkeley: University of California Press, 1993), pp. 77–103.

22. Ibid.

23. Eduard Shevardnadze, The Future Belongs to Freedom, trans. Catherine A. Fitzpatrick (New York: Free Press, 1991), p. xi.

24. Author's interviews with Fedor Burlatsky, Cambridge, 12 October 1987; Vadim Zagladin, Moscow, 18 May 1989; Oleg Grinevsky, Vienna and New York, 11 October and 10 November 1991; Georgiy Arbatov, Ithaca, New York, 15 November 1991; Anatoliy Dobrynin, Moscow, 17 December 1991.

25. Ibid; David Holloway, "Gorbachev's New Thinking," Foreign Affairs 68 (Winter 1988/1989), pp. 66–81.

26. Shevardnadze, The Future Belongs to Freedom, pp. xii.

27. Lebow and Stein, We All Lost the Cold War, chap. 8.

28. Author's interviews with Oleg Grinevsky, Vienna, 11 October 1991, New York, 10 November 1991, Stockholm, 25 April 1992; Leonid Zamyatin, Moscow, 16 December 1991; Anatoliy Dobrynin, Moscow, 17 December 1991.

29. Ibid; Shevardnadze, *The Future Belongs to Freedom*, passim.

30. Ibid.; Interviews with Oleg Grinevsky, Vadim Zagladin and Anatoliy Dobrynin.

31. Janice Gross Stein, "The Political Economy of Strategic Agreement."

32. Lebow and Stein, *We All Lost the Cold War*, chap. 3, on Khrushchev's strategy.

33. Brown, *Gorbachev Factor*; Raymond L. Garthoff, *Great Transition: American Soviet Relations and the End of the Cold War* (Washington, D.C.: Brookings, 1994; **Hal Brands.** *Making the Unipolar Moment: U.S. Foreign Policy and the Rise of the Post-Cold War Order* (Ithaca: Cornell University Press, 2016); Robert Service, *The End of the Cold War 1985–1991* (London: Macmillan, 2016), pp. 143–148, 202, 329–338, 400–415.

34. Ibid; Jack Matlock, *Autopsy on an Empire: The American Ambassador's Account of the Collapse of the Soviet Union* (New York: Random House, 1995).

35. Garthoff, *Great Transition*, 252–259.

36. Richard Ned Lebow, *Between Peace and War: The Nature of International Crisis* (Baltimore: Johns Hopkins University Press, 1981); "Deterrence Failure Revisited: A Reply to the Critics," *International Security* 12 (Summer 1987), pp. 197–213; Janice Gross Stein, "Calculation, Miscalculation, and Conventional Deterrence I: The View from Cairo," and "Calculation, Miscalculation, and Conventional Deterrence II: The View from Jerusalem," in Robert Jervis, Richard Ned Lebow and Janice Gross Stein, *Psychology and Deterrence* (Baltimore: Johns Hopkins University Press, 1985), 34–59, 60–88; Lebow and Stein, *We All Lost the Cold War*, Richard Ned Lebow and Janice Gross Stein, "Deterrence: The Elusive Dependent Variable," *World Politics* 42 (April 1990): 336–369, on how not to study immediate deterrence.

37. Lebow and Stein, *We All Lost the Cold War*, chap. 3, argue that there was a similar contradiction in Khrushchev's goals and that it was a fundamental cause of many of his most important foreign and domestic policy miscalculations.

38. See, for example, Thomas Risse-Kappen, "Ideas Do Not Float Freely: Transnational Coalitions, Domestic Structures, and the End of the Cold War," in Lebow and Risse-Kappen, *International Relations Theory and the End of the Cold War*, pp. 187–222; Sarah E. Mendelsohn, "Internal Battles and External Wars: Politics, Learning and the Soviet withdrawal from Afghanistan," *World Politics* 45 (April 1993), pp. 327–360; George Breslauer, "Explaining Soviet Policy Change: The Interaction of Politics and Learning," in *Soviet Policy in Africa: From the Old to the New Thinking*, ed. George Breslauer (Berkeley: Berkeley-Stanford

Program in Soviet Studies, 1992); Jeff Checkel, "Ideas, Institutions, and the Gorbachev Foreign Policy Revolution," *World Politics* 45 (January 1993), pp. 271–300; Coit D. Blacker, Hostage to Revolution: Gorbachev and Soviet Security Policy, 1985–1991 (New York: Council on Foreign Relations, 1993). For a critical review of some of these explanations see Janice Gross Stein, "Political Learning by Doing: Gorbachev as Uncommitted Thinker and Motivated Learner," in Lebow and Risse-Kappen, *International Relations Theory and the End of the Cold War*, pp. 223–58.

39. Lebow and Stein, *We All Lost the Cold War*, chap. 3; Raymond L. Garthoff, *Detente and Confrontation: American-Soviet Relations from Nixon to Reagan* (Washington, D.C: Brookings, 1985), pp. 563–1009.

40. This is some good work on enduring rivalries. See, in particular, William R. Thompson, ed., *Great Power Rivalries* (Columbia, S.C.: University of South Carolina Press, 1993).

41. Richard K. Herrmann, "Conclusion: The End of the Cold War—What Have We Learned?" in Lebow and Risse-Kappen, *International Relations and the End of the Cold War*, pp. 259–284.

42. Risse-Kappen, "Ideas Do Not Float Freely"; Rey Koslowski and Friedrich V. Kratochwil, "Understanding Change in International Politics: The Soviet Empire's Demise and the International System," in Lebow and Risse-Kappen, *International Relations and the End of the Cold War*, pp. 127–66; John Mueller, "The Impact of Ideas on Grand Strategy," in Richard Rosecrance and Arthur A. Stein, eds, *The Domestic Bases of Grand Strategy*, (Ithaca: Cornell University Press, 1993), 48–62; Mary Kaldor, "Who Killed the Cold War?" and Metta Spencer, "Political Scientists," *Bulletin of the Atomic Scientists* 51 (July/August 1995), pp. 57–61 and 62–68; Matthew A. Evangelista, *Unarmed Forces: The Transnational Movement to End the Cold War* (Ithaca: Cornell University Press, 1999).

CHAPTER 7

Rethinking Conflict Management and Resolution

The essays in this volume offer a compelling conceptual and empirical critique of coercive strategies of conflict management. In this concluding chapter, I briefly review these findings, not to reiterate the Stein-Lebow critique, but to say something about the kinds of situations in which deterrence might be appropriate and the difficulties of applying it even then. This analysis is intended to alert readers to the need to practice deterrence in a more calibrated, cautious and restrained manner and, of equal importance, in conjunction with other strategies of conflict management. My plea is for a more holistic approach to conflict management that addresses the several causes and manifestations of international conflicts and embraces and coordinates deterrence, reassurance, and traditional diplomacy. These several strategies can be used sequentially or simultaneously depending on the character and history of the conflict in question. Effective conflict management requires a good understanding of the ways in which they can reinforce or undercut one another. This requires not only a good conceptual understanding but also intimate knowledge of the political context and skillful diplomacy. Conceptual understanding is helpful but context and agency are determining.

I begin as noted, with a succinct reprise of the critique of deterrence and compellence. I then examine reassurance, a strategy that might be described as their mirror image. All three strategies attempt to manipulate the cost calculus of adversaries: deterrence and compellence to raise the cost of non-compliance, and reassurance to reduce that of compliance. Their mechanisms differ: deterrence and compellence rely on

© The Author(s) 2018
R.N. Lebow, *Avoiding War, Making Peace*,
DOI 10.1007/978-3-319-56093-9_7

threats, and reassurance on clarification of intentions and rewards. They give rise to different psychological dynamics, which has important implications for their relative risks, side effects, and chances of success. Reassurance also has a downside, which I discuss. I then take up a third generic strategy: diplomacy aimed at finessing or resolving substantive conflicts of interest. Having discussed these three strategies in isolation, I make connections among them and suggest ways they can be productively combined or staged.

Several caveats are in order. Conflict management is no silver bullet. Even the most sophisticated and best-coordinated strategies can fail, and for multiple reasons. Target leaders can be obtuse to signals, miscalculate the costs and risks of cooperation or conflict, subordinate conflict avoidance or resolution to other foreign and domestic goals, or correctly conclude that continued conflict is in their national or political interest. Leaders attempting to reduce tensions can miscalculate the effects of their initiatives on key foreign or domestic constituencies. Many conflicts are simply not ready for serious amelioration, let alone resolution, because leaders do not have sufficient authority or control over their governments or armed forces, fear losing control if they appear weak or compromising, or believe the risks and costs of any move toward peace greater than those of enduring the status quo. As this book goes to press, the conflict in Syria displays several of these features, and in addition, the presence of multiple warring factions, at least some of whom are unwilling to accept a truce or interim political arrangements acceptable to other participants. For all of the reasons, the Syrian conflict remains intractable despite Herculean diplomatic efforts by many governments and diplomats.

Strategies of conflict management generally take time to produce positive effects. General deterrence aims to discourage an adversary in the long term from considering the use of force a viable option, and immediate deterrence to prevent a specific use of force when a challenge appears likely or imminent. Ideally, the two strategies work together not only to prevent challenges, but also to convince adversarial leaders that the military option is fruitless and that their national and political interests are best served by some kind of accommodation. When successful, deterrence can not only forestall armed conflict but also provide an incentive for adversaries to seek accommodation. Reassurance and diplomacy also take time, but have the potential to produce more rapid results—two to six years in the Anglo-British, Egyptian–Israeli, and Soviet–American conflicts—but only when preceded by dramatic domestic or foreign developments that pave the way for conflict resolution.

This empirical reality further highlights the importance of context. The most sophisticated and cleverly applied strategy of conflict management or resolution can fail when adversarial leaders are unreceptive or fearful of the consequences of grasping the olive branch. Less sophisticated and cleverly applied strategies can succeed when they are well disposed to accommodation. Ripeness is a concept used to describe the latter situation and often applied in a circular manner. Conflicts that are resolved are thought to have been ripe for resolution, and vice versa when not. I avoid this circularity by stipulating the conditions that facilitate or hinder conflict resolution. Most, but not all, are beyond the direct control of adversaries or third parties. Efforts at conflict resolution when there is little chance of success may make subsequent efforts more difficult, as may be true in several Middle Eastern conflicts.

We must distinguish conflict management from conflict resolution. Conflict management is a general term applied to the efforts to keep a conflict contained. This can mean preventing its military escalation (e.g., the use of armed force or development, the deployment of new weapons, or the forward deployment of existing weapons) or political escalation that extends a conflict to new regions or participants. Both kinds of escalation are, of course, related.

Conflict resolution aims to reduce tensions. As Chap. 6 indicates, it can take different forms. Minimal conflict resolution seeks only to reduce or remove the likelihood of war between adversaries. The 1978 agreement between Israel and Egypt, backed by the United States, achieved this goal. Relations between these countries have not significantly improved. By contrast, relations between the USA and China in the aftermath of the Kissinger visit, and post-Cold War relations between the USA and Soviet Union (subsequently Russia), became more or less normal; leaders cooperated in multiple problem areas, the barriers to trade, immigration, and tourism came down, and stereotypy in media about the other declined. Relations between Britain and France following the 1904 *Entente Cordiale* became positively warm and have remained this way. The same cannot be said of present day US–Russian or US–Chinese relations, where some analysts see new cold wars under way. Accommodation can be reversed.

We must be careful about the claims we make about the causes for successful conflict management and resolution because there is a pronounced tendency to confirm them by self-serving historical interpretations. The two Berlin crises were treated as immediate deterrence successes in the Cold War literature, and the Cuban missile crisis and 1973 Middle East crises were hailed as compellence successes. Access to Soviet and American archives and interviews with former leaders and their advisors indicate that neither Berlin crisis can be considered a deterrence success; Soviet leaders exercised restraint, but for reasons independent of American threats.[1] Compellence contributed to the resolution of Cuba, but reassurance played at least an equal role.[2] Compellence stood in the way of the resolution of the 1973 crisis.[3] Deterrence advocates make similar claims about the Israel-Egypt conflict and the end of the Cold War. I offered a different account of these accommodations, stressing the role of changing leadership and domestic goals, learning about adversaries, and reassurance. Deterrence undeniably played a contributing role in ending the Cold War, but its contribution was different from that envisaged by deterrence theorists. In the Middle East, general and immediate deterrence failed repeatedly giving rise to four wars between Israel and Egypt (i.e., 1956, 1967, 1969–1970, and 1973), some involving other Arab states. It was the failure of Egypt and Israel to achieve their objectives by force—and the costs involved in trying—that stimulated the search for alternatives.

Coercive Strategies

The critique of deterrence that Janice Stein and I developed has three interlocking components: political, psychological, and practical. Each exposes a different set of problems of deterrence in theory and practice.

The political component examines the motivations behind foreign policy challenges. Deterrence is unabashedly a theory of 'opportunity'. It asserts that adversaries seek opportunities to make gains, and that when they find these opportunities they pounce. It accordingly prescribes a credible capacity to inflict unacceptable costs as the best means to prevent challenges. Empirical investigations point to an alternative explanation for a resort to force, which I call a theory of 'need'. The evidence indicates that strategic vulnerabilities and domestic political constraints often constitute incentives to use force. When leaders become desperate, they may resort to force even when the military balance is unfavorable and there are no grounds to doubt adversarial resolve. Deterrence may be an inappropriate and even dangerous strategy in these circumstances.

If leaders are driven less by the prospect of gain than they are by the fear of loss, deterrent policies can provoke the very behavior they are designed to forestall by intensifying the pressures on an adversary to act. The psychological component is directly related to the motivations for deterrence challenges. To the extent that leaders believe in the necessity of challenging the commitments of their adversaries, they become predisposed to see their objectives as attainable. This encourages motivated errors in information process. Leaders can distort their assessments of threat and be insensitive to warnings that the policies to which they are committed are likely to end in disaster. They can convince themselves, despite evidence to the contrary, that they can challenge an important adversarial commitment without provoking war. Because they know the extent to which they are powerless to back down, they expect their adversaries to recognize this and be accommodating. Leaders may also seek comfort in the illusion that their country will emerge victorious at little cost if the crisis gets out of hand and leads to war. Deterrence can and has been defeated by wishful thinking.

The practical component describes some of the most important obstacles to the successful implementation of deterrence. They derive from the distorting effects of cognitive biases and heuristics, political and cultural barriers to empathy, and differing cognitive frames of reference that deterrer and would-be challengers use to frame and interpret signals. Problems of this kind are not unique to deterrence and compellence; they are embedded in the very structure of international relations. They nevertheless constitute particularly severe impediments to these strategies because of deterrer needs to understand the world as it appears to the leaders of a would-be challenger in order to manipulate effectively their cost-benefit calculus. Failure to do so correctly can result in deterrent policies that make the proscribed behavior more attractive to challengers, or the required restraint less attractive in the case of compellence.

The Lebow-Stein critique explains why deterrence is a risky and unreliable strategy. The problems associated with each component can independently confound deterrence. In practice, they are often reinforcing; political and practical factors interact with psychological processes to multiply the obstacles to success. In this section, I unpack this critique to offer some observations about the conditions in which deterrence is most applicable and the foundations for more sophisticated understandings of conflict management.

Political Failings

A good strategy of conflict management should build on a good theory of the nature and causes of aggression. Such a theory should describe the etiology of the malady it seeks to control or prevent. Theories of deterrence make no attempt to do this. They finesse the fundamental question of the causes of aggression by assuming both the existence of marked hostility between adversaries and a desire on the part of leaders of one of them to commit acts of aggression against the other. Deterrence further assumes that these leaders are under no political or strategic compunction to act aggressively, but will do so if they see an opportunity in the form of a vulnerable commitment of their adversary. It accordingly prescribes defensible, credible commitments as the most important means of discouraging aggression.

Case studies of international conflict contradict this depiction of aggression in important ways. They indicate that the existence of a vulnerable commitment is neither a necessary nor a sufficient condition for a challenge. At different times in history, 'vulnerable' commitments have not been challenged and commitments that most observers would consider credible have. The evidence suggests, then, that deterrence theory at best identifies only one cause of aggression: outright hostility. It reflects a Cold War mentality. Deterrence theorists took for granted, like the American national security elite more generally, that Hitler was motivated by hatred of his neighbors and intent on conquering the world. They assumed that Stalin, Khrushchev, and Mao Zedong were cut from the same mold. This homology was a matter of belief, not the product of careful analysis. They generalized from these cases to conflict in general, another unwarranted leap. The theory and practice of deterrence are accordingly rooted in and inseparable from a view of the Cold War subsequently refuted by evidence.

Deterrence theory takes for granted that when leaders undertake a cost calculus and conclude that they confront a credible commitment by a stronger adversary to defend its commitment, they will not initiate a challenge, at least not an irreversible one. However, there are many conflicts where the weaker side challenged the stronger one. Leaders convinced themselves that they could design around their adversary's advantage, as the Southern Confederacy did in 1861, the Japanese in 1941, or Egypt in 1973.[4] In *A Cultural Theory of International Relations* and in *Why Nations Fight?* I document how honor, anger, and national self-respect can push leaders into starting wars they do not expect to win.[5]

Deterrence mistakes the symptoms of aggression for its causes. It ignores the political and strategic vulnerabilities that can interact with cognitive and motivational processes to prompt leaders to choose force or challenge and adversarial commitment. This can be attributable to hubris, but is more often the result of their perceived need to carry out a challenge in response to pressing foreign and domestic threats. In contrast to the expectations of the theory and strategy of deterrence, there is considerable evidence that the leaders considering challenges or the use of force often fail to carry out any kind of serious risk assessment. In *Between Peace and War*, I documented the French failure to do in 1897–1898, the Austrian, German, and Russian failure in 1914, India's failure in 1962, and the Soviet Union's failure in 1962.[6] In *Psychology of Deterrence*, chapters by Janice Stein, Jack Snyder, and I do the same for Russia in 1914, Israel in 1973, and Argentina and Britain in 1981.[7] *A Cultural Theory of International Relations* offers more evidence on 1914 and the Anglo-American decision to attack Iraq in 2003.[8]

Why Nations Fight puts together an original data set of all wars since 1648 involving at least one rising or great power on each side. It reveals that initiators won slightly less than half the wars they began.[9] Benjamin Valentino and I found that in all wars since 1945, only 26% initiators achieved their goals in war, and if we relax the criteria of victory, only 32% defeated the other side's armed forces.[10] As most initiators go to war at a time of their choosing, a 50–50 win rate is not at all impressive. The drop to a third in the postwar era is compelling evidence that initiators fail to conduct a careful assessment of risk. Rationalists might counter than the low success rate is due to incomplete information, but in many, if not most, of these cases, evidence was available at the time that the initiators were heading for disaster, or at best, leaping into the unknown.[11]

When challengers are vulnerable or feel themselves vulnerable, a deterrer's efforts to make important commitments more defensible and credible will have uncertain and unpredictable effects. At best, they will not dissuade. They can also be malign by intensifying those pressures that are pushing leaders toward a choice of force. Great power interactions in the decade prior to World War I and the USA oil and scrap metals embargo against Japan in 1940–1941 illustrate this dynamic.[12]

Once committed to a challenge, leaders become predisposed to see their objective as attainable. Motivated error can result in flawed assessments and unrealistic expectations; leaders may believe an adversary will back down when challenged or, alternatively, that it will fight precisely the kind of war the challenger expects. Leaders are also likely to become insensitive to warnings that their chosen course of action is likely to provoke a serious crisis or war. In these circumstances, deterrence, no matter how well practiced, can be defeated by a challenger's wishful thinking. Motivated bias blocks receptivity to signals, reducing the impact of efforts by defenders to make their commitments credible. Even the most elaborate efforts to demonstrate prowess and resolve may prove insufficient for discouraging a challenger who is convinced that a challenge or use of force is necessary to preserve vital strategic and political interests.

Deterrence is beset by a host of practical problems. It is demonstrably difficult to communicate capability and resolve to would-be challengers. Theories of deterrence assume that everyone understands, so to speak, the meaning of barking guard dogs, barbed wire, and 'No Trespassing' signs. This assumption is unrealistic. Signals only acquire meaning in the context in which they are interpreted. When sender and recipient use quite different contexts to frame, communicate, or interpret signals, the opportunities for misjudgment multiply. Receivers may dismiss signals as noise, or misinterpret them when they recognize that they are signals. This problem is endemic to international relations and by no means limited to deterrence because of the different historical experiences and cultural backgrounds of policymaking elites. It is, however, more likely in tense relationships, where both sides use worst-case analysis, and are emotionally aroused.

If credible threats of punishment always increased the cost side of the ledger—something deterrence theory takes for granted—it would be unnecessary for would-be deterrers to replicate the value hierarchy and preferences of target leaders. This convenient assumption is belied by practice. As we have seen, leaders may be driven primarily by 'vulnerability', not by 'opportunity'. When they are, raising the costs of military action may have no effect on their unwillingness to tolerate what are perceived as the higher costs of inaction. Even when motivated by opportunity, leaders may reframe their cost-calculus in the opposite direction than intended in the face of threats. They may conclude that giving into them is more costly than resistance, especially if they believe that compliance will be interpreted by their adversary as a sign of weakness and give rise to new demands.

Deterrence in the Long Term

Case evidence of deterrence failures and successes indicates that deterrence is a risky and uncertain strategy. It suggests that deterrence has a chance of success in a narrow range of conflicts: those in which adversarial leaders are motivated largely by the prospect of gain rather than by the fear of loss, have the freedom to exercise restraint, are not misled by grossly distorted assessments of the political–military situation, and are vulnerable to the kinds of threats that a would-be deterrer is capable of making credibly. Deterrence must also be practiced early on, before an adversary commits itself to a challenge and becomes correspondingly insensitive to warnings that its action is likely to meet with retaliation. Unless these conditions are met, deterrence will at best be ineffective and at worst counterproductive.

These conditions apply only to deterrence in the short term—that is, to immediate deterrence. Proponents of deterrence generally concentrate on this kind of deterrence. However, our analysis of deterrence would be incomplete if we failed to examine its implications for the management of adversarial relationships in the longer term. Does deterrence facilitate or retard the resolution of international conflict?

Deterrence theorists maintain that it can play a positive role by convincing a challenger that its fundamental objectives cannot be met through a use of force. George and Smoke contend deterrence may give the parties to a dispute time to work out an accommodation and, in so doing, reduce tensions and the potential for overt conflict.[13] However, deterrence can also retard conflict resolution by exacerbating the causes of the conflict or by creating new incentives to use force. Three different processes can contribute to this kind of negative outcome.

As noted, deterrence can intensify the pressures on adversarial leaders to resort to challenges or the use of force. American deterrence did this for Khrushchev in the Cuban missile crisis and in the second Taiwan Straits crisis. In the wake of the 1954–1955 crisis, the United States reinforced deterrence in the Straits. President Eisenhower committed the United States to the defense of Taiwan and the offshore islands and, in 1957, authorized the deployment of nuclear-tipped surface-to-surface Matador missiles on Taiwan. To the president's annoyance, Chiang

Kai-shek began a major military buildup on the islands and by 1958 had stationed 100,000 troops there, one-third of his total ground forces. To leaders in Peking, the increased military preparedness and troop deployments indicated that Washington was preparing to 'unleash' Chiang. A series of provocative speeches by Secretary of State John Foster Dulles, suggesting that Chinese Nationalist forces might invade the mainland if significant domestic unrest provided the opportunity, fueled the Chinese perception of threat. This led the Chinese leadership to demonstrate resolve through a renewed artillery assault on Quemoy and Matsu.[14]

Deterrence can also intensify conflict by encouraging defenders to develop an exaggerated concern for their bargaining reputation. Deterrence does not attach great significance to the impact of the interests at stake in influencing an adversary's judgments of a commitment's credibility. It assumes—incorrectly—according to a growing number of empirical studies—that the most important component of credibility is the defender's record in honoring past commitments.[15] Thomas Schelling, author of one of the most influential studies of deterrence, emphasized the interdependent nature of commitments; failure to defend one, he argued, will make willingness to defend any commitment questionable in the eyes of an adversary. 'We tell the Soviets', Schelling wrote in 1966, 'that we have to react here because, if we did not, they would not believe us when we said that we will react there'.[16]

Schelling and other deterrence theorists ignored the possibility of escalation inherent in the connections among commitments. More importantly, they ignored the likelihood that deterrence pursued this way would make the state practicing deterrence look more aggressive than defensive. I described how this happened in the Taiwan Straits crises. It was more striking in the run-up to the Cuban missile crisis, where Soviet and American efforts at deterrence convinced the other of its aggressive intentions and prompted them to take a series of reciprocal actions that culminated in the Cuban missile deployment.[17]

Schelling's fears were in any case misplaced. Ted Hopf examined Soviet reactions to thirty-eight cases of American intervention over a 25 year period of the Cold War and could not discover a single Soviet document that drew negative inferences about American resolve in Europe or Northeast Asia. In *We All Lost the Cold War*, Stein and I demonstrated that neither Khrushchev and his advisors nor Brezhnev and his ever doubted American credibility but rather considered the Americans rash, unpredictable, and aggressive.[18]

Concern for credibility gives rise to symbolic commitments like that of John Foster Dulles to defend the Taiwanese occupied offshore islands of Quemoy and Matsu. Such commitments can easily become entangling because they tend to become at least as important to leaders as commitments made in defense of substantive interests. Their exaggerated importance is probably due in large part to the pernicious effect of post-decisional rationalization. Once a commitment is made, leaders, understandably uncomfortable about risking war for abstract, symbolic reasons, seek to justify the commitment to themselves and to others. This need motivates them to 'discover' important substantive reasons for these commitments—reasons absent in and irrelevant to their original calculations.

In the case of the Taiwan Straits, top-level administration officials, who previously had questioned the importance of the offshore islands, subsequently came to see them as the linchpin of security throughout Asia. Most senior policymakers subscribed in all solemnity to an astonishing version of the 'domino' theory. In a classified policy statement meant only for internal use, Eisenhower and Dulles both argued that loss of the islands would likely not only endanger the survival of the Nationalist regime on Taiwan, but also that of pro-American governments in Japan, Korea, the Philippines, Thailand, and Vietnam, and would bring Cambodia, Laos, Burma, Malaya, and Indonesia under the control of communist forces.[19] The most far-reaching expression of this 'logic' was Vietnam. American leaders had no substantive interests in the country but committed forces to its defense in large part because they were persuaded that failure to defend their commitment in Southeast Asia would encourage Moscow to doubt US resolve elsewhere in the world.[20]

Finally, deterrence can intensify conflict by encouraging leaders to interpret even ambiguous actions as challenges that require a response. This exaggerated sensitivity to challenge is very much a function of the heavy emphasis that deterrence places on a state's bargaining reputation. Its most paranoid formulation is Thomas Schelling famous dictum: 'If you are invited to play a game of 'chicken' and you refuse, you have just lost.'[21] Invitations to play chicken in the international arena, however, are rarely direct and unambiguous. Challenges must be inferred from the context of events, and given the inherent complexity of international affairs, policymakers have considerable leeway in determining their meaning. Challenges to play chicken are particularly difficult to substantiate because they are defined in terms of the intent of an action, not its expected effect. Leaders are much more likely to perceive a challenge—and often falsely so—when they believe damage to their state's interests and reputation is the principal goal of another's actions, not just its by-product.

These three processes are important contributing causes of tension, misunderstanding, and fear between adversaries. They point to the greatest long-term danger of deterrence: its propensity to make the worst expectations about an adversary self-fulfilling. Threats and military preparations—the currency of deterrence—inevitably arouse the fear and suspicion of those they are directed against. As noted, they tend to provoke the very behavior that they are designed to prevent. Over time, military preparations, initially a consequence of tensions between or among states, can become an important cause. This kind of dynamic has operated between the United States and the Soviet Union, Israel and the Arab states, China and the Soviet Union, and some fear is now operating between China and the USA. In all these cases, the misunderstanding and tension caused by deterrence, overlain on substantive issues that divide protagonists, made these conflicts more acute, more difficult to manage, and less amenable to resolution.

The outlines of the policy dilemma are clear. Protagonists may need deterrence to prevent their adversaries from resorting to force, but the use of deterrence can simultaneously make the conflict more acute and more likely to erupt into war. Because deterrence can be ineffective, uncertain, and risky, it must be supplemented by other strategies of conflict management.

REASSURANCE

Strategies of reassurance begin from a different set of assumptions than deterrence. They presume ongoing tensions but root them in feelings of acute vulnerability. Reassurance requires defenders to communicate to would-be challengers their benign intentions. They must attempt to reduce the fear, misunderstanding, and insecurity that can be responsible for escalation and war. Reassurance seeks to reduce the expected gains of challenges and increase those of cooperation. Even when leaders consider a conflict to be incapable of resolution, they can still practice reassurance with the goal of avoiding accidental or miscalculated war. In so doing, they may simultaneously help alleviate the underlying causes of conflict.

In the most ambitious applications of reassurance, leaders attempt to shift the trajectory of the conflict and induce cooperation through reciprocal acts of de-escalation and bargaining over substantive issues. They may begin with unilateral and irrevocable concessions. If they are pessimistic about the likely success of this approach, or politically constrained from attempting it, they can pursue more modest variants of reassurance. They can exercise self-restraint in the hope of not exacerbating the foreign or domestic pressures and constraints pushing an adversary to act aggressively. They can try to develop informal 'norms of competition' to regulate their conflict and reduce the likelihood of miscalculated escalation. They can attempt through diplomacy informal or formal regimes designed to build confidence, reduce uncertainty, and diminish the probability of miscalculated war. These strategies are neither mutually exclusive nor logically exhaustive.

Strategies of reassurance, like those of deterrence and compellence, are difficult to implement successfully. They too must overcome strategic, political, and psychological obstacles. Cognitive barriers to signaling, for example, can just as readily obstruct reassurance as they can deterrence.[22] Other obstacles are specific to reassurance and derive from the political and psychological constraints that leaders face when they seek to reassure an adversary. Nevertheless, reassurance can be used effectively and was a significant component of all long-standing rivalries that were resolved.

Reassurance Through Reciprocity: Reciprocity has long been a focus of sociologists, psychologists, game theorists, and analysts of the international political economy. In security, reciprocal behavior is understood to require contingent, sequential exchanges among adversaries. One variant of it has been described as reciprocal graduated reciprocation in tension reduction.[23]

Reciprocity assumes that adversaries are able to identify and distinguish effectively between policies intended to be cooperative and those that are competitive. This assumption is built into Robert Axelrod's famous tit-for-tat computer strategy, but is not necessarily warranted in the real world.[24] Students who play tit for tat have problems distinguishing 'tits' from 'tats', something more likely among adversaries. Policies—'moves' in the language of strategic bargaining—can be dismissed as noise, recognized as signals, and misinterpreted if thought to be signals. Leaders may differ in their perceptions of reciprocity and functional measures of equivalence. Such differences between the

United States and the Soviet Union were starkly evident as détente unraveled. Measures of equivalence in international security are defined subjectively by leaders' and are subject to cognitive and motivated bias. When opposing leaders use different measures, or different assessments of the same measures, they are likely to talk past one another. In the Cuban missile crisis, the USA and the Soviet Union both valued the status quo but defined it differently. For Washington, it was a Cuba without Soviet missiles, and for Moscow, a Cuba ruled by Castro. Each side accordingly saw itself on the defensive and took umbrage at the actions of the other.[25]

Policymakers and their advisors are also likely to dismiss, misunderstand, or interpret away conciliatory gestures by an adversary when it clashes with their beliefs about its leaders and their goals. They may attribute the cooperative actions of others to inescapable situational pressures, while believing that their cooperative behavior offers evidence of their benign disposition.[26] Israel's leaders in 1971 initially explained Sadat's cooperative overtures as a response to his political weakness at home, the growing economic crisis in Egypt, and the dearth of strategic options available to Egyptian leaders. Here, the fundamental attribution error interacted with prevailing cognitive images to defeat the possibility of reciprocation. Israel's failure to respond led Sadat to embrace war. Signals can also be missed or misread due to motivational biases, as they frequently are in deterrence encounters.

The difficulty in establishing common criteria of reciprocity can be mitigated in part if leaders share social norms. This is not often the case in international conflicts, many of which have arisen in part from a clash of values and their norms. If and when values and norms converge, conflict resolution becomes easier. Anglo-French accommodation reversed 600 years of hostility and was greatly facilitated by shared values and norms, political as well as cultural, because both countries had become democracies. The Cold War was more difficult to resolve. It began as a struggle for influence in Europe following the defeat of Germany, but it had a strong ideological component because leaders and elites on both sides believed their social systems to be incompatible. Arguably, the most fundamental cause of the resolution of the Cold War was a shift in key beliefs and goals by Soviet leaders that brought their values and norms closer to those of their Western European and American counterparts.[27] This shift made reassurance an attractive strategy to Soviet leaders and helped to make it viable.

Common criteria are essential conditions for far-reaching accommodations that bring about a normalization of relations. In their absence, any accommodation is difficult, and it may not be possible to go beyond the first step that reduces the likelihood of war. This may help explain why Egyptian-Israeli relations never progressed beyond this stage and why it was so difficult to reduce Cold War tensions before Gorbachev. It might also account for the failure of the brief era of détente. In the absence of shared norms, leaders must be explicit about their values and norms, come to recognize where they and their adversaries disagree and have divergent expectations, and find ways of working around or finessing these differences. By doing so, they might reduce some of the tensions between them. US-Soviet arms control agreements offer a successful example. Negotiations lead to several treaties that did not so much slow down the arms race as much as made it transparent and set limits to it. Success hinged on prior understandings of each other's strategic cultures and discourses, achieved through informal talks among scientists and the epistemic community they created.[28] This process offers a good example of how knowledge of different values, norms, and discourses can help find common ground on substantive interests.

Reassurance Through 'Irrevocable Commitment': When leaders recognize that misperception and stereotyping govern their adversary's judgments as well as their own, they can try to break through this wall of mistrust by making an irrevocable commitment.[29] In effect, they attempt to change the trajectory of the conflict through 'learning' and to make a cooperative reciprocal strategy more feasible. If successful, learning about adversarial intentions reduces the cost of moves toward peace because it decreases the likelihood in the estimate of leaders that they will be exploited or misinterpreted by them and prompt new demands. Reassurance of this kind seeks to rectify the political-psychological damage of deterrence.

President Anwar el-Sadat of Egypt turned to a strategy of irrevocable commitment to break through the prevailing images of Israel's leaders and public and to put an end to decades of Egyptian-Israeli conflict. He deliberately made a large, dramatic, and risky concession because of its cost and irreversibility. For both reasons, he hoped it would be seen as a valid indicator of Egyptian intentions rather than an ambiguous signal, or one whose meaning could be manipulated subsequently by the sender. It gained additional power by Sadat's ability to speak successfully over the heads of Israel's leadership to its public. By mobilizing support for peace among the Israeli people, he removed a constraint on the country's leaders and created a political inducement to reciprocate.

Gorbachev's policy was in part also one of irrevocable commitment. He publicly promised to withdraw Soviet forces from Afghanistan and began to do so without any prior promise from the West not to exploit this reversal. In October 1989, he made a speech in Finland, which in some ways was the equivalent of Sadat's in Jerusalem. He disavowed any right of the Soviet Union to intervene militarily in other countries, a promise that rapidly accelerated political change in Eastern Europe and the end of pro-Soviet communist regimes throughout the region. He also introduced political changes within the Soviet Union, associated with his programs of *glasnost* and *perestroika*, that further demonstrated his bona fides. These actions, together with arms control agreements, broke the logjam of the Cold War.[30]

We must be very careful in extrapolating from these two cases. As appeasement of Hitler indicates, it can be very risky to design a commitment that is high in cost and irreversible. Even if concessions are not exploited to further aggressive ends, they leave one exposed to key domestic and foreign constituencies. This is why Sadat secretly sounded out the Israelis prior to announcing his intention to come to Jerusalem. The Americans and Chinese also held clandestine talks before issuing an invitation to Henry Kissinger to come to Beijing. Success of that visit led to a subsequent invitation of President Nixon to visit China.[31] Before making any irrevocable commitments, leaders must assure themselves that their adversary is likely to respond positively and has equal incentives to reach some kind of meaningful accommodation.

Reassurance Through Self-Restraint: When leaders are pessimistic about the possibility of changing their adversary's long-term intentions, they are likely to focus on reducing the short-term likelihood of conflict. This is a valuable end in itself and also one that may help change long-term intentions. Immediate deterrence tries to do the former and general deterrence the later. Restraint through self-restraint is a counterpart to immediate deterrence.

Self-restraint has the potential to reduce some of the obvious risks of deterrence. Because it uses the language of reassurance rather than of threat, it can allay the fears of leaders caught in a process of escalation, as it did in India and Pakistan in 1987, and reduce the likelihood of miscalculation. However, it is both demanding and dangerous for those who use it. It is demanding because it requires leaders to monitor their adversary's political pressures, strategic dilemmas, leaders' estimates of the political and strategic costs of inaction, and assessment of the alternatives. A strategy of self-restraint encourages leaders to consider their adversary's calculus within the broadest possible political and strategic context. Like deterrence, it requires leaders to view the world through the eyes of their adversaries and, as we have seen, there are formidable cognitive and motivational impediments to reconstructing the calculus of another set of leaders. Perhaps because leaders pay attention to the vulnerabilities of their adversary as well as to its opportunities when they consider self-restraint, they may be able to overcome at least some of these impediments. At a minimum, they are more likely to do so than leaders who consider only deterrence.

A strategy of self-restraint can be dangerous if it culminates in miscalculated escalation. When would-be deterrers are attentive to the weaknesses of opponents, to the possibility that they may provoke adversaries who are as yet uncommitted to a use of force, they are more likely to exercise restraint. Would-be challengers may misinterpret restraint and caution as weakness and lack of resolve. The Argentine invasion of the Falklands-Malvinas Islands in 1982 is a case in point. Margaret Thatcher's diplomacy was a phony strategy of reassurance that encouraged the Argentine junta to believe that they could gain sovereignty over the Islas Malvinas-Falklands through diplomacy. When the Argentines realized that Thatcher was stringing them along, they became enraged and committed to using force. Failing to recognize this shift, the Thatcher government did not practice deterrence, all but guaranteeing an Argentine invasion.[32] The obvious lesson here is for leaders not to practice reassurance unless it is sincerely intended and they are prepared to accept its consequences.

Evidence of the use of restraint in the context of general deterrence is still fragmentary and episodic. Analysts have not yet examined the documentary record to identify the relevant universe of cases. The limited evidence that is available of the interactive use of restraint and demonstration of resolve suggests that each carries with it the risk of serious error. An exercise of restraint may avoid provocation of a beleaguered or frightened adversary, but it may also increase the likelihood of miscalculated escalation. The language of threat and demonstration of resolve, on the other hand, may reduce the probability that a challenger will underestimate a deterrer's response, but it may provoke a vulnerable and fearful opponent.

Reassurance Through 'Norms of Competition': Adversaries can attempt mutual reassurance by developing informal, even tacit, norms of competition in areas of disputed interest. Informal, shared norms among adversaries may prevents certain kinds of mutually unacceptable action and, consequently, reduce the need to manipulate the risk of war. Informal norms may also establish boundaries of behavior and reduce some of the uncertainty that can lead to miscalculated escalation.

The United States and the Soviet Union attempted to develop explicit understandings of the limits of competition when they signed the Basic Principles Agreement in 1972 and, a year later, a more specific agreement on consultation to deal with crises that threatened to escalate to nuclear war. These agreements were not a success, in part because the formal documents masked significant disagreements and differences in interpretation. If anything, the unrealistic expectations they aroused, the disputes over interpreting the agreements, the consequent allegations of cheating and defection, and the ensuing distrust and anger exacerbated the management of the conflict between the two nuclear adversaries.

The Middle East provides a better illustration of the ability of norms of competition to regulate conflict. The United States and the Soviet Union have tacitly acknowledged that each may come to the assistance of its ally if it is threatened with a catastrophic military defeat by the ally of the other. To avoid such an intervention, the superpower must compel the regional ally who threatens to inflict such an overwhelming defeat to cease its military action.[33] The Soviet Union invoked this tacit norm in 1967 and again in 1973, and although the United States attempted to deter Soviet intervention, it simultaneously moved to compel Israel to cease its military action and to reassure the Soviet Union immediately of its intention to do so. Deterrence and reassurance worked together and, indeed, it is difficult to disentangle the impact of one from the other on the effective management of that conflict.[34]

Alexander George argued that these tacit and informal norms of competition in and of themselves did not provide a sufficiently stable basis for the management of conflict between the two superpowers; they lacked both institutionalized arrangements and procedures for clarification of their ambiguities and extension to new situations. He further suggested that shared norms of competition are likely to vary in utility according to the resources and strategies the superpowers use, the domestic and international constraints they face, leaders' capacity to formulate and differentiate their own interests, evaluate the interests at stake for their adversary, the magnitude of each superpower's interest, and the symmetry of the distribution of interest.[35] Tacit norms and patterns of restraint are more likely to emerge, for example, in areas of high-interest asymmetry than in areas of disputed or uncertain symmetry.

Given these obstacles, it is surprising that, in an area of disputed symmetry like the Middle East, the United States and the Soviet Union were able to agree tacitly on a shared norm to limit the most dangerous kind of conflict. This strategy might have promising uses on the Indian subcontinent and in East Asia.

Reassurance Through Limited Security Regimes: In an effort to reduce the likelihood of an unintended and unwanted war, adversaries have agreed, informally at times, on procedures to reduce the likelihood of accident or miscalculated war. Technically, these arrangements are referred to as limited security regimes.

Adversaries may also consider participation in a limited security regime if it improves the accuracy of detection and reduces the likelihood of defection. Fear of a surprise attack can encourage leaders to try to build limited security regimes, but it can also make their attainment more difficult. Such regimes may permit adversaries to monitor each other's actions with increased confidence by providing more complete and reliable information, by increasing surveillance capabilities for all parties, or by invoking the assistance of outsiders as monitors. In the limited security regime in place between Egypt and Israel since 1974, the United States routinely circulates intelligence information about the military dispositions of one to the other. Such a regime can give leaders more leeway than they otherwise would have to meet a prospective defection by increasing available warning time. This makes estimation of capabilities and intentions less difficult and reduces the likelihood of miscalculation.

Reassurance through the creation of limited security regimes has not been restricted to Egypt and Israel. The United States and the Soviet Union agreed in 1967 to the demilitarization of outer space in an effort to limit the scope of their conflict. In 1970, they actively promoted the nonproliferation regime and, in 1972, negotiated a limited regime to reduce the likelihood of accident and miscalculated conflict at sea. They also regulated their conflict in Central Europe through the 1955 Austrian State Treaty, the 1971 Berlin accords, and the 1975 Final Act of the Conference on Security and Cooperation in Europe.

Reassurance through the creation of limited and focused security regimes can be of considerable help in the longer term in reducing fear, uncertainty, and misunderstanding between adversaries. At a minimum, adversaries gain access to more reliable and less expensive information about each other's activities, which can reduce uncertainty and the incidence of miscalculation. In a complex, information-poor international environment, valid information can be a considerable advantage in more effective management of conflict.

Reassurance by trade-offs: This form of reassurance seeks to defuse conflict and reassure at the same time by the means of quid pro quos. It has the short-term advantage of removing sources of conflict between adversaries and holds out the longer-term prospect of building trust and cooperation in other areas. It might be regarded as the international equivalent of David Mitrany's functionalism.[36]

The great example of reassurance by trade-offs is Anglo-French reconciliation. Anglo-French hostility had deep historical routes going back to the Hundred Years' War. In the eighteenth and nineteenth centuries, their colonial rivalry was acute and an extension of their conflict in Europe. The Fashoda crisis of 1898 was the culmination of their competition for influence in Africa and nearly led to war. The coalition that came to power in France after the crisis sought an accommodation with Britain because its members regarded Germany as their principal foe. The British prime minister, Lord Salisbury, held out the prospect of British support for a French protectorate in Morocco in return for France giving up any claims to the Sudan or Egypt. This colonial quid pro quo provided the basis for cooperation on European security issues where the two countries shared common interests.

Quid pro quos also played an important part in the Egyptian-Israeli and Sino-American accommodations. The initial accord between the two countries required Israel to withdraw from the Sinai Peninsula and Egypt to recognize the state of Israel. Implementation of these commitments built the modicum of trust necessary to move on to other issues and ultimately a peace treaty.[37] Taiwan had been a principal point of contention between Beijing and Washington since the founding of the People's Republic of China in 1949. China claimed Taiwan as a province, but the USA supported its de facto independence and provided arms and military protection to its nationalist regime. Kissinger and Nixon's visits to China led to an agreement whereby the USA recognized Taiwan as part of China and agreed to withdraw American troops from the island. China in turn promised to use peaceful means to resolve the Taiwan question and opened diplomatic relations with the USA. This arrangement provided the basis for subsequent economic, political, and strategic cooperation.[38]

Quid pro quos are an obvious first step because they have the potential to build trust and convey commitments to seek further agreement. They also have the advantage of addressing substantive or symbolic issues that have poisoned relations in the past. Sometimes there is the possibility of a trade-off here. Israel withdrew from the Sinai, a costly substantive concession, in return for a symbolic one—recognition—that might later be withdrawn. The USA made a substantive concession to China—the promise to withdraw troops—in return for two symbolic ones: the promise not to use force against Taiwan as long as it did not declare independence and establishment of diplomatic relations. As with unilateral steps toward accommodation, quid pro quos are more credible if they are public, irrevocable, and costly.

DIPLOMACY

Diplomacy is the third generic strategy of conflict management and resolution. It has long been recognized as critical in this regard, and there are many classical works extolling its positive role in eighteenth- and nineteenth-century Europe, and globally in the twentieth century.[39] In the last few years, international relations theory has become more interested in how diplomacy works.[40] The so-called diplomatic turn emphasizes the ways in which diplomacy constitutes states and others as actors, the independent role of diplomats, and how diplomatic arguments affect and are affected by shared understandings of what kinds of means and ends are legitimate.

For some time, there has been an extensive literature on mediation, Track Two diplomacy—talks among private individuals and groups—and other forms of unofficial, people-to-people diplomacy.[41] I am going to limit myself here to official diplomacy because I am concerned with how it can best be coordinated with other strategies, and this involves governments. They may, however, make use of non-governmental organizations or private individuals for informal soundings and discussions. They can offer the advantage of trust—as did the community of Soviet and American scientists involved in decades of Pugwash talks.[42] They also allow leaders to back away and disavow them or their recommendations if they prove politically difficult or inadvisable.

It is impossible to reduce and resolve international conflicts without diplomacy. Even unilateral actions require explanation and interpretation to achieve their desired effects. They are likely to be opening moves, as they often are in the strategy of reassurance. They require follow-up and diplomacy to move from successful ice breaking to substantive achievements.

All too often, theories of foreign policy and international relations that invoke structures (e.g., balance of power, changing nature of threats, technological developments) to explain conflict and its reduction ignore diplomacy or treat it as an unproblematic mechanism. If conditions demand a démarche or a détente, policymakers will respond as required and diplomats will carry out their instructions. Both are treated like non-reflexive electrons transmitting charges. Rationalist approaches are just as determinist. But agency matters, and not just that of leaders. They make choices, and so do diplomats. Even when diplomats follow their instructions to the letter, whom they speak to, when and where they do this, how they broach issues, and what arguments they make—and the tone they adopt—may have a determining effect on how target leaders respond to the message.

The resolution of the Cold War offers a telling example in a double sense. It illustrates the important and independent contribution of diplomacy, but also the propensity of diplomats, like many scholars, to see foreign policy outcomes as overdetermined. In conjunction with our edited book on the end of the Cold War, Rick Herrmann and I interviewed some twenty-five Soviet, American, and European policymakers, intelligence officials, advisors, and diplomats who were intimately involved in terminating this conflict. Independently of their country or ideology, they saw the end of the Cold War, the unification of Germany, and the collapse of the Soviet Union as more or less inevitable. At the same time, almost all of these officials confessed their surprise—even incredulity—as these events unfolded. The contradiction in their belief systems was made even starker by the insistence of almost every official we interviewed that the outcome of any decision or negotiation in which they participated was highly contingent. In conference discussions and conversations over drinks or coffee, they told amusing stories of how clever tactics, the nature of the personal relationship between themselves and their opposites, or just sheer coincidence, played decisive roles in shaping the outcome of negotiations.[43]

Some policymakers we interviewed maintained that the end of the Cold War, the unification of Germany, and the dissolution of the Soviet Union were all inevitable. They were nevertheless responsive to counterfactual suggestions that process and outcome might have been different. There was widespread agreement that there was nothing foreordained about the two plus four format for negotiations over the future of Germany. When pushed, former Soviet, American and German policymakers on the whole agreed that a different format, say one that involved more European countries as participants, might well have resulted in a different outcome given the widespread opposition to unification by Germany's neighbors. While there was general agreement that Gorbachev had little freedom to maneuver on the German question at the time of the two plus four talks, several Soviet officials suggested that he might have been able to negotiate a better deal if he broached the issue in 1987.

Some diplomats stress their importance of their profession, especially those writing memoirs about how central they were to benign outcomes.[44] It seems likely that policymakers and scholars are susceptible to what Baruch Fischoff has called the 'certainty of hindsight' bias. Experiments that he and others have conducted demonstrate that outcome knowledge affects our understanding of the past by making it difficult for us to recall that we were once unsure about what was going to happen. Events deemed improbable by experts (e.g., peace between Egypt and Israel, the end of the Cold War), are often considered overdetermined—indeed, all but inevitable—once they have occurred.[45]

My interest is less in the role of diplomats and more in that of diplomacy. When, how, and why is it effective in moving conflicts away from war and in resolving issues that divide adversaries? I noted in the introduction that there is a large literature on the diplomacy of peacemaking. It is more historical than conceptual, but valuable for insights it offers into particular situations. The conceptual literature in social science on conflict resolution is largely quantitative and ignores agency and diplomacy. It searches for correlations between independent and dependent variables. An important exception is the work of Bill Thompson and his collaborators on enduring rivalries and their resolution, who combine quantitative work with case studies and acknowledge the often-determining role of agency.[46]

The qualitative literature on conflict resolution is idiosyncratic and sometimes relies on poorly specified concepts. Consider the proposition of 'ripeness', as developed by Bill Zartman. It is the moment when parties in a mutually destructive stalemate recognize the destructive nature of the status quo and that they are in 'a mutually hurting stalemate'. Protagonists must also perceive a way out of this stalemate.[47] Zartman recognizes the entirely subjective nature of this double realization and further recognizes that it is a necessary but insufficient condition for peace. He and his acolytes offer few guidelines about the conditions, material, psychological, or political, responsible for these necessary adversarial beliefs and nothing about the other necessary conditions.

A useful analogy can be made between the causes of war and accommodation. Structural and regularity theories, and of course, rationalist accounts, assume that war—or accommodation—will occur, or is highly likely to, when stipulated conditions are present. If so, an appropriate catalyst will come along or be manufactured by leaders. This assumption is sometimes warranted. In February 1965, in the aftermath of a Vietcong attack on the American advisors' barracks at Pleiku, National Security Advisor McGeorge Bundy wrote a memorandum to President Lyndon Johnson urging the sustained bombing of North Vietnam. Bundy later acknowledged that Pleikus were like 'streetcars'. He could count on repeated Viet Cong attacks against South Vietnamese forces or their American advisors to provide him with the pretext he needed at the opportune moment to sell escalation to the president.[48]

Pretexts do not always resemble streetcars. They may be infrequent, inappropriate, or fail to materialize—as is, alas, true of many trams and buses—and without a catalyst, the predicted behavior may not occur. In a matter of months, or years, underlying conditions may evolve to make war less likely even if an otherwise appropriate catalyst ultimately comes along. The window of opportunity for war—or for peace—may be temporally narrow or broad depending on the nature and rate of changes in the underlying conditions. War may require a *conjunction* of underlying pressures and appropriate catalysts.[49]

Catalysts are often complex causes in their own right, as Sarajevo was in 1914. The twin assassinations caused the Austrian leadership to reframe the problem of Serbia. Risks that had been unacceptable in the past now became tolerable, even welcome. The independent role of catalysts creates another problem for theories and attempts to evaluate them.[50] All the relevant underlying causes for a war or accommodation may be present, but absent a catalyst, it will not occur. The uncertain and evolving relationship between underlying and immediate causes not only makes point prediction impossible. It renders problematic more general statements about the causes of war and system transformations— and many other international phenomena—because we have no way of knowing which of these events would have occurred in the presence of appropriate catalysts, and we cannot assume that their presence or absence can be treated as random. It is thus impossible to define the universe of such events or to construct a representative sample of them.[51]

Catalysts are equally important for accommodation, and theorizing about them is just as difficult because they are so often situation specific. In Chap. 6, I describe three conditions I found to be critical to at least one pathway to accommodation. They are the belief that war, or threatening military deployments, is counterproductive; that key domestic goals require a significant reduction in tensions with an adversary; and that overtures toward this end are likely to be reciprocated. The last two are unambiguously immediate causes as they very much depend on leaders' goals and visions of their countries and the world. All three beliefs are subjective and unlikely to be shared with other contenders for leadership. The French elite was deeply divided in 1904 as to whether Germany or Britain was the enemy. In the case of the Egyptian-Israeli and Soviet-American accommodations, it is difficult to imagine other leaders who would have pursued the conciliatory policies of Anwar el-Sadat or Mikhail Gorbachev.[52]

Catalysts mattered in each of these accommodations, and they were largely independent of underlying causes. The Anglo-French *Entente* required French soul-searching and hard choices, and that was encouraged by the disastrous Fashoda crisis of 1898. Along with the Dreyfus affair, it brought about a shift in power that made accommodation possible. In this instance, catalyst and confluence were critical in realigning French foreign policy. So too was agency. French and British leaders and diplomats established their credibility through repeated interactions and the Entente opened the door for further cooperation. What began as an effort to reduce the likelihood of war set in motion a full-fledged accommodation over the course of a decade. Agency was crucial at each step. Poorly considered and executed German foreign policies provided a strong incentive for Anglo-French cooperation, and clever French and British political, military leadership and diplomacy effectively capitalized on it.[53]

The Egyptian-Israeli peace treaty was equally dependent on a catalyst: the failure of Egyptian arms in a conflict where Soviet arms and new tactics had given them an initial advantage. Egyptian defeat, and subsequent American willingness to broker a peace, convinced Sadat that he had the need and opportunity to extend the olive branch. The war was equally mind changing for Israel. It emerged victorious, but only after initial and costly defeats. Sadat was not the only critical leader. Richard Nixon and Henry Kissinger were equally essential players, setting in motion the possibility of a peace in which Egypt regained the Sinai and Israel protected by US security guarantees. Once again, diplomacy proved critical, not only during and in the immediate aftermath of the war, but at the 1978 Camp David negotiations. Jimmy Carter was masterful in his handling of Sadat and Menachem Begin. And the latter was receptive to American overtures, opposed by right-wing nationalists in Israel.[54]

The end of the Cold War was also contingent and catalyst dependent. George Breslauer and I conducted a thought experiment in which we considered the likely interaction of other possible Soviet and American leaders.[55] None of the other combinations led to a resolution of the Cold War in the short term, and some led to its escalation. Gorbachev sought accommodation with the West to free resources and buy a political room for domestic change. Contrary to the claims of some realists, Soviet leaders were not compelled to seek accommodation, and certainly not by means of unilateral concessions, one-sided agreements, and abandonment of the communist governments of Eastern Europe. No other likely Soviet leader would have acted as Gorbachev did.[56] Equally important was the degree of trust Gorbachev established with Reagan, which allowed both leaders to move forward and for Gorbachev to take more risks.[57]

Most important for my argument is the independence of these several catalysts, or immediate causes of accommodation, from underlying ones. In the Anglo-French case, the Fashoda crisis and the *faux Henri* phase of the Dreyfus affair occurred all but simultaneously, having a multiplier effect on French opinion, leading to an electoral victory of the *Défense Républicaine* coalition that made accommodation possible and politically advantageous. The Dreyfus affair was entirely unconnected in cause—although not in effect—from Anglo-French colonial rivalry in Africa.

For Egypt and Israel, the catalyst was not so much a war as it was the cost and outcome of that war. Arab-Israeli wars were all expressions of the underlying causes of their conflict. As there had been four previous wars—1948, 1956, 1963, and 1970—it was not unlikely that there would be a fifth. However, it was the outcome, not the war, that mattered, and this war was unique in that the Arab side started with new weapons, an effective and coordinated two-front strategy, and the tactical advantage of surprise, and still lost. Defeat, and with it the encirclement and near destruction of their armies, convinced Sadat and his generals that they could never defeat Israel. Surprise, shock, early losses, and victory only by virtue of an American airlift bringing new weapons and ammunition, convinced Israelis of the need for peace with Egypt. This outcome was contingent entirely independent of the causes of this and previous wars.

The end of the Cold War had three principal catalysts. Gorbachev was willing to take risks in the hope of reforming and revitalizing the Soviet economy and political system. This was a response to underlying conditions, and conditions that may have been inseparable from an authoritarian regime and command economy. To bring about change Gorbachev had to overcome the opposition of much of the Communist Party, the military, and the even more conservative allied governments of Eastern Europe. The stalemated and costly war in Afghanistan, the forward American deployment of a new generation of missiles and cruise missiles in Western Europe—which Soviet generals said would never happen—the Chernobyl disaster, and the landing of Mathias Rust's Cessna in Red Square, all made this possible.[58] Most of these catalysts had independent and largely unrelated causes but a cumulative non-linear effect. Accommodation in all cases required committed leaders, catalysts, and good diplomacy.

What general lessons can we derive from these three cases? They suggest that neither realist nor 'ripeness' arguments are compelling. Realists invoke shifts in the balance of power to account for accommodations, just as they do for war, but there were no notable shifts prior to the Anglo-French, Egyptian-Israeli or Sino-American accommodations. To the extent there was a shift in the Egyptian-Israeli power balance, it was in favor of Israel, yet Begin was willing to enter into negotiations with Sadat and withdraw from the strategically important Sinai as part of a peace agreement. The end of the Cold War was a clear exception as the Soviet Union had been stagnating economically since the 1970s. Three Soviet leaders before Gorbachev were aware of this situation and did nothing dramatic to address it, so at best it was a contributing condition to Gorbachev's commitment to accommodation.

Ripeness is also indeterminate as the Arab-Israeli stalemate was a mutually hurting stalemate for at least two decades prior to the Camp David accords, and for four decades before the Oslo Accords. Nor did the latter accords lead to a peace. In contrast, the Anglo-French Entente was reached in the absence of any mutually hurting stalemate. France and Britain had not been at war since 1815, and the Fashoda crisis, while it brought the two countries to the brink of war, was resolved without bloodshed.

Accommodations are most likely to be sought when new leaders come to power with strong domestic or external incentives for winding down an existing conflict. Sadat was keen to reorganize the Egyptian economy and jumpstart it with Western aid, investment, and technology. For the French and Gorbachev, there were foreign as well as domestic incentives. French leaders wanted to make peace with Britain in proportion to the degree that they perceived Germany as a threat. They also wanted to do this to advance their domestic programme, which involved curtailing the power of the pro-German colonial ministry and the anti-Dreyfus Catholic Church. For Richard Nixon, Henry Kissinger, Mao Zedong, and Zhou Enlai, the incentives were primarily external; as China's conflict with the Soviet Union became more acute, it was strategically advantageous to draw closer to the USA.[59]

Additional evidence about the importance of new leadership can be drawn from divided nations and partitioned countries. The former are once unified countries that were divided due to the Cold War. They are—or were—the two Germanies, Koreas, Chinas, and Vietnams. Partitioned countries are products of the breakup of former colonial empires and the division of disputed territory between rival ethnic groups. They include the two Irelands, Greek and Turkish Cyprus, Israel–Palestine, and India–Pakistan. Movement toward normalization of relations in West and East Germany, the People's Republic of China and the Republic of China, the two Irelands, and in Cyprus could only begin when the generation of leaders and other important political and military associated with partition passed from the scene.[60]

Diplomacy also has the potential to be more fruitful when war, other forms of violence, or arms races and threatening deployments, have proven counterproductive—and are widely recognized as counterproductive. The Fashoda crisis drove this home to French leaders, the 1973 War to Egyptian and Israeli leaders, and NATO's forward deployment of Pershing II missiles and ground-launched cruise missiles in Western Europe to Soviet leaders. Ireland conforms to this pattern too, but in a more complicated way. The war of independence with Britain provoked an Irish civil war between moderates who were willing to settle for 26 of the 32 countries and hardliners who insisted on fighting on to gain control over the entire island. More recently, the failure of either Irish nationalists or Ulster Protestant paramilitaries to impose their will in

Northern Ireland, and their ultimate loss of support within their respective communities, split these groups to some degree and opened space for more moderate actors.[61]

Diplomacy is important in its own right. As noted, it played a critical role in all accommodations. Willingness of France to renounce any interest in Egypt and the Sudan, and British willingness to support France's colonial claims in Morocco paved the way for the Entente. This clever quid pro quo was not an obvious one; it required imagination and skill to implement. The Entente was solidified by bad diplomacy—on the part of Germany. Kaiser Wilhelm and Foreign Minister Bernhard von Bülow provoked a crisis over Morocco in 1904 that pushed France into Britain's arms, and the British backed the French, transforming their relationship from one of cautious accommodation to de facto alliance. Students of the Sino-American accommodation also credit leaders with careful, step-by-step, soundings, mostly in secret, that led to trips to China by Kissinger and Nixon, followed by rapid and effective diplomacy on both sides that clarified issues and led to an understanding that each side described its own way in separately issued communiqués.[62]

Leaders must be flexible in their thinking, as French Foreign Minister Théophile Delcassé and his British counterpart were in the aftermath of the Fashoda crisis. Delcassé did an about-face after Fashoda, and Salisbury, who had been on the verge of going to war with France, was remarkably open to his post-crisis overtures. Nixon and Kissinger overcame their enemy images of China; as early as the 1950s Nixon was willing to go beyond rigid Cold War thinking and explore other explanations than Communist ideology for Chinese hostility.[63] When he came to office, his view of China's leaders and their motivations was primed for positive change by his desire to find a so-called 'honorable' way out of the Indochina war with their assistance. Personal contacts led to large shifts in his and Kissinger's perceptions of Mao Zedong and Zhou Enlai.[64] I previously noted Reagan's receptiveness to Gorbachev in contrast to that of his vice president and many of his advisors. Had George Bush. been president, rather than Ronald Reagan, it seems unlikely that there would have been much progress toward accommodation.[65] The least flexible leader in these several accommodations was Menachem Begin, who was only brought around in the end by prodding and promises by President Jimmy Carter.[66] He was nevertheless more open to the prospect of peace with Egypt than other colleagues in Likud.

Finally, leaders must have the political room to extend the olive branch or grasp it when offered. Leaders may sometimes carve out room for maneuver for themselves by clever tactics such as sidetracking adversaries, positive coalition building, and masterful appeals to public opinion. Richard Nixon benefitted from being a Republican, but still had Cold War opinion and right-wing opposition with which to contend. In July 1971, 56% of Americans branded China the world's most dangerous state.[67] Nixon and Kissinger successfully used realist arguments to isolate opposition from pro-Taiwan, anti-communist, and certain business interests, and a pro-peace discourse to win over moderate Republicans and Democrats.[68] Following Nixon's highly televised trip to Beijing, a Gallup Poll revealed that 96% of the public had a favorable view of the Chinese people.[69] Gorbachev was less successful, as many elements of the Soviet military, industry, and the communist party remained hostile to his domestic reforms and foreign policy. He set in motion a process that ultimately undermined his support.[70] Sadat faced even greater obstacles; he failed to win over much of Egypt's political–military elite or public opinion and was assassinated.

Accommodation is a reciprocal process. Following their 1959 Camp David meeting, President Dwight Eisenhower and General Secretary Nikita Khrushchev seemed on the verge of achieving major tension reduction in the Cold War. Eisenhower's efforts came to naught because of his continued support of U-2 over flights of the Soviet Union and his need to placate a West German ally whose Christian Democratic leadership opposed accommodation. Khrushchev had gone out on a limb and Ike in effect sawed it off. By contrast, Lyndon Johnson, and Khrushchev's successor, Leonid Brezhnev, negotiated a détente because both leaders had strong domestic backing, and Johnson international support as well.[71]

The Eisenhower counterexample, the seeming Johnson-Brezhnev success, and the 1993 Oslo Accords between Israel and the Palestinian Liberation Organization, reveal the downside of stalled diplomatic progress. The U-2 affair led Khrushchev to torpedo the 1960 Paris Summit, in part to protect himself against Soviet hardliners.[72] Détente raised expectations that were not fulfilled and led to an intensified Cold War.[73] The Oslo Accords unraveled for a different reason: hardliners opposed to accommodation used violence to polarize public opinion and cut the ground out from underneath moderates. The key event was the assassination of Israeli Prime Minister Yitzhak Rabin in November 1995 by a Jewish ultranationalist. Hardliners on both sides in the Northern Irish conflict periodically tried and succeeded in sabotaging any move toward peace. Violence rose in proportion to the perceived likelihood of political cooperation across sectarian lines.[74]

These failed attempts at accommodation suggest several lessons for leaders and diplomats. First and most importantly is the need to make hard choices about accommodation versus other goals. Leaders who express willingness to wind down tensions, or respond to adversarial overtures to do so, make themselves vulnerable to political recrimination if they fail, and possibly also if they succeed. Extending or grasping an olive branch also raises the possibility of exploitation by the other side. Eisenhower was trying to protect himself and his country against the later threat when he authorized one final U-2 overflight because he sought reassurance that the Soviets had not deployed their first generation intercontinental ballistic missile [ICBM]. Eisenhower knew there was a risk because the Soviets had deployed a new surface-to-air missile, but he allowed the CIA to convince him that they could get away with it. Motivated bias can also work in favor of accommodation. In the mirror image of deterrence challenges, leaders who make peace overtures can convince themselves that they will succeed. Sadat and Gorbachev were confident beyond what the available evidence warranted and helped to make their optimism self-fulfilling.[75]

Efforts at accommodation should move both slowly and quickly. Caution and secrecy are necessary to assure leaders that they are on the firm ground at home and not likely to be exploited abroad. Once overtures become known, leaders must move as quickly as possible to limit the possibility of opposing coalitions forming and mobilizing public opinion through the media or violence. The Oslo Accords were intended to be a prelude to a peace treaty that would be reached by direct negotiations between Palestinians and Israelis. Each side knew that both wanted peace and would be politically exposed if they failed to reach an agreement. Each accordingly expected the other to make additional concessions and the negotiations dragged on long enough for Israeli hardliners to derail the peace process. President Bill Clinton played a central role in bringing about the famous 1993 Rabin-Arafat televised handshake and the Oslo Accords but the president and his diplomats failed to keep the pressure up on both sides to reach a quick agreement. The negotiations dragged on, Arafat got cold feet, and the assassination of Rabin changed the political calculus on the Israeli side. The failure of the Oslo process intensified conflict to the degree that subsequent diplomatic initiatives have had no positive effect.[76]

Peace overtures require careful assessment beforehand of their domestic and foreign risks. How will important foreign and domestic audiences respond? How much latitude will leaders have to pursue accommodation once their efforts become known? These assessments can be hit-and-miss because the goals and risk assessments of others are often opaque, and more so when based on different assumptions. As we have seen, this problem often confounds deterrence or compellence; it is an equal challenge for reassurance. Reassurance has a relative advantage in that it can often be practiced in small steps, which are reversible at low cost, and elicit some indication of how at least an adversary will respond. Cases in point are the secret consultations among diplomats prior to the Anglo-French Entente and Nixon's visit to China. However, irreversible, unilateral steps toward accommodation are more credible and may be necessary to break through solid walls of distrust. They arguably served this purpose for Sadat and Gorbachev. A major strand of contemporary Russian opinion regards Gorbachev as a traitor, or at least a naïf, who was exploited by the West.[77] Even successful accommodations are reversible, and for many reasons.

My analysis only addresses what I describe in Chap. 6 as the initial stage of accommodation: moving away from the likelihood of war. One of the major and under-researched topics in international relations is the process of moving from understandings that reduce the likelihood of war to more far-reaching accommodations that normalize relations. To date, very little research has been done on the follow-on stages of accommodation and the dynamics associated with them.

THINKING HOLISTICALLY

To this point, I have analyzed deterrence, reassurance, and diplomacy in isolation from one another. Any sophisticated strategy of conflict management must combine them because acute conflicts invariably have causes or manifestations to which they are all relevant. The key task of policymakers is to fathom the causes of the conflict they are addressing, which strategies of conflict management are relevant to them, and how they might be used in a synergistic manner.

A useful starting point is the recognition that most conflicts have primary and secondary causes, by which I mean original causes and follow-on ones. Consider the Cold War. Its principal and original cause, in my judgment, was the power vacuum that opened in Central Europe with the collapse of Germany. The Soviet Union and the USA reached an agreement beforehand on their respective zones of occupation, but a conflict arose as each sought to govern these territories in a manner consistent with its perceived interests. Conflict was most acute in what quickly became a divided Germany, which was the focus of three war-threatening crises between 1949 and 1962. Ideology might also be considered an underlying cause of conflict to the extent that it prompted different and incompatible occupation policies. What began as a European conflict quickly spread to other parts of the world: Korea became a divided country, so did China, and later, Vietnam.[78] The Soviet Union and the USA backed opposite sides in the Arab-Israeli conflict, and later, in South Asia and Africa. The Cold War gave rise to an arms race, which intensified after the Soviet Union exploded its first nuclear device in 1949 and both countries sought to develop thermonuclear weapons.

By the time Gorbachev came to power in 1986, nuclear arsenals and their delivery systems, which had the potential to decapitate both leaderships in a first strike, had become the principal bone of contention between the two sides. The 1975 Helsinki Accords resolved territorial European questions, and the manifestations of that conflict—arms racing and competition in the developing world—now become causes in their own right.[79] The Cold War indicates that conflicts accrue causes as they develop, and that resolution of their original causes may have no significant ameliorating effect on their secondary causes. It further reveals that primary and secondary causes can become connected in multiple ways.

In *A Cultural Theory of International Relations*, I argue that conflicts arise from two fundamental human drives—appetite, and *thumos*—and the powerful emotion of fear.[80] In international conflicts, appetite finds expression in the quest for material well-being. It can be achieved and protected by diverse means.

Thumos refers to the universal human quest for self-esteem, generally achieved by excelling in activities valued by our peer group or society. By winning their approbation, we in turn feel good about ourselves. In the modern era, many people associated closely with their states and a degree of transference occurs.[81] The struggle for national recognition and status becomes to some degree internalized by citizens whose self-esteem rises and falls with the success and setbacks of their country at home and abroad. Leaders can mobilize and exploit this transference for their own political ends, as indicated by Vladimir Putin's success in Russia and Donald Trump's electoral victory in the 2016. They or their successors may become prisoners of the transference and associated emotions they arouse. German foreign policy in the run-up to World War I and current Chinese foreign policy appear to illustrate the latter.[82]

Fear becomes a powerful motive to the extent that reason loses control over appetite and *thumos*. Actors fear for their ability to satisfy their appetites and gain or maintain self-esteem, and perhaps for their physical security too. Fear is endemic to international society because order is less robust than it is in most domestic societies. Leaders, their advisors, and public opinion have a tendency to rely on worst-case analyses to adversarial relationships. They convince themselves that the adversary is unremittingly hostile, constrained only by superior force, and intent on achieving a decisive military advantage.[83] As noted, deterrence theory operates on this assumption and may help to confirm it. Fear can readily become the central dynamic governing adversarial relations, as it did for much of the Cold War.

My three generic approaches to conflict management and resolution speak to these three sources of conflict (Fig. 7.1). They may ease the tensions they generate, but in the process possibly intensify others. I have already explored this dynamic with regard to deterrence and compellence. They rely on threats of military action to restrain or compel adversaries, and in the process, arouse fear and hostility among target leaders. Reassurance and diplomacy are less likely to intensify conflict, but still have the potential to do so. Failed diplomacy may heighten conflict by revealing just how far apart leaders and states are on questions of great political or strategic importance. Margaret Thatcher's efforts to use negotiations to buy time had this effect and were the catalyst for the Argentine junta's decision to invade the Falklands-Malvinas.[84] Failed efforts at reassurance can also backfire when they constitute appeasement of actors whose aggressive ambitions cannot be satisfied by concessions.

Leaders intent on managing conflicts or resolving them must accordingly fathom their likely causes, make some assessment of their relative importance, and decide the order in which they should be addressed. In some conflicts, overcoming fundamental causes successfully makes it easier to address knock-on causes or manifestations. The resolution of boundary disputes often has this positive effect, as it did in post-independence relations between Britain and the United States. In other conflicts, as in the Cold War, secondary manifestations remain intractable.

It is sometimes more productive to address secondary causes before primary ones. This was the case in the Anglo-French Entente, Egyptian-Israeli, and Sino-American accommodations. Taiwan was the principal bone of contention between China and the USA, and the two Taiwan Straits crises in the 1950s had threatened to provoke a war between them. Ping Pong diplomacy led to a quid pro quo concerning Taiwan that allowed China and the USA to normalize relations and reduce the fear and hostility. Unlike the territorial issue between Germany and its neighbors, the Taiwan question remains unresolved and periodically inflames Sino-American tensions, as it did after Donald Trump's pre-inaugural telephone conversation with Taiwan's president.[85]

These several conflicts suggest that there is no general rule about which cause to address first. Opportunity must dictate strategy. Leaders should be guided by their judgment of which cause of conflict is easiest to address. These judgments are never scientific but reflect, or should, politically informed understandings about the causes of conflict, their openness to resolution, and all the conditions, noted earlier, for setting a process of accommodation in motion. Analysis is useful, but leadership is critical.

Different strategies are more appropriate to different causes of conflict. We might frame these choices in terms of a conflict triangle with each vertex representing a generic source of conflict. I focus on *thumos*, and fear, because appetite, in the form of the quest for material well-being, has not been an acute source of conflict between the great powers since the late eighteenth century.[86] Hostility can be a source of conflict, as it was for Hitler's Germany vis a vis its neighbors, if not the world. More often, hostility is a follow-on effect of conflict. Leaders, and perhaps public opinion as well, become convinced that their adversary is unremittingly hostile and committed to their demise. We observed this phenomenon in the Cold War. Americans believed the Soviet Union and China sought to destroy their political system, a belief reciprocated by Soviet and Chinese leaders.

Deterrence is the appropriate strategy to use against a hostile adversary whom it is believed only superior force can restrain from attacking. But it is only likely to work when this perception is accurate, which, as we have seen, is often not the case. Deterrence is only likely to succeed when adversarial leaders are motivated largely by the prospect of gain

Hostility

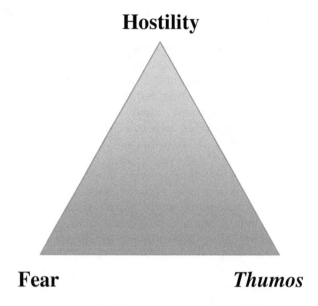

Fear   *Thumos*

Fig. 7.1   Conflict triangle

rather than by the fear of loss, free to exercise restraint, are not misled by rosy assessments of the political–military balance, and are vulnerable to the kinds of threats a deterrer is capable of credibly making. If challengers do not share these motivational, cognitive, and political attributes, the strategy of deterrence is more likely to intensify conflict. The timing of deterrence is also important. Its effectiveness is enhanced if it is used early, that is before an adversary becomes committed to a challenge or the use of force and becomes correspondingly insensitive to warnings and threats.

Fear and hostility are closely related. To the extent that leaders believe an adversary is hostile they become fearful. Reassurance seeks to reduce fear by changing this perception. It can be used duplicitously, as Hitler did to encourage French and British appeasement. More frequently, it is intended to reduce tensions by demonstrating benign or cooperative intentions. As noted, attempts at reassurance must overcome disbelief on the part of target leaders. They may believe, rightly or wrongly, that their adversary is unremittingly hostile, and interpret communications and behavior to the contrary as nefarious and designed to lull them or public opinion into letting down their guard. Key members of the Reagan administration felt this way about Gorbachev and tried to prevent and then to sabotage arms control negotiations.[87]

My several examples of successful reassurance achieved major breakthroughs that led to at least the first level of accommodation: a significant reduction in the likelihood of war. In the Anglo-French, Sino-American, and Cold War conflicts, it laid the foundations for more far-reaching forms of accommodation. I want to stress that reassurance is a useful strategy even when accommodation is not a feasible goal. When would-be challengers are motivated largely by need and are seriously constrained at home and abroad, variants of reassurance can supplement deterrence or compellence. They may reduce to some degree the distrust and fear that can propel a challenge.

The best historical example is the coupling of reassurance with compellence in the Cuban missile crisis. Building on *We All Lost the Cold War*, in Chap. 5 demonstrates how compellence in the form of the naval quarantine of Cuba and the threat of an invasion of Cuba and air strike against the Soviet missile bases on that island raised the risk of war, and reassurance, as practiced by President Kennedy reduced the cost of concession to Khrushchev. The Soviet premier came to believe that Kennedy was not a tool of the American military and Wall Street bankers but someone with a fair degree of independence and committed, as he was, to avoiding war. By withdrawing the missiles in Cuba, he would not invite new demands but rather resolve the crisis and reduce the likelihood of a future one. Khrushchev and Kennedy became partners as much as adversaries in the end game and aftermath of the crisis, paving the way for a subsequent détente.[88]

Consider the counterfactual that minimal deterrence had been practiced throughout the Cold War. Chapter 5 indicates that Soviet and American leaders were largely self-deterred; they were not dissatisfied with the status quo and their memories of World War II made them keen to avoid a military conflict. The advent of nuclear weapons made them that much more frightened of war but neither side knew the extent to which their adversary shared by their fear. They accordingly practiced deterrence, developed and deployed thermonuclear weapons, and later, sought a war-fighting capability. These policies made them more insecure, fearful, and convinced of each other's hostile intentions. Minimal deterrence, which held out the prospect of serious damage, if not mutual assured destruction, would have aroused the same fear of war but without provoking the same hostility based on worst-case analysis. Combined with reassurance, it might have provided the same incentive at an earlier date that mutual recognition of the horror of war ultimately did to find ways of managing the arms race and the fears it aroused.

Threat-based strategies and reassurance engage *thumos* in positive and negative ways. Deterrence, and even more compellence, threaten the self-esteem of actors because they demand that they give into threats, and sometimes suffer public humiliation for doing so. Visible subordination makes actors angry, if not defiant. Chapters 3 and 5 documented how they may reframe the conflict in ways that make it more acute. This happens when the goal of not giving into adversarial threats becomes more important than any substantive interests at stake. Threat-based strategies can also generate strong desires for revenge, as German threats in the Bosnian Annexation crisis of 1908–1909 did for the Russians, and the American deployment of Jupiter missiles in Turkey did for Khrushchev.[89]

Reassurance and diplomacy are the strategies relevant to the *thumos* vertex of the triangle. Thumos motivates competition for recognition, honor, and standing, and conflict arises to the extent that these goals are denied. There is a growing literature on recognition in international relations and its relevance to conflict reduction.[90] Recognition, honor, and standing are often described as 'symbolic' goals, implying that they are less important than 'substantive' ones. Nothing could be further from the truth. In *Why Nations Fight*, I constructed a data set of all interstate wars involving great and aspiring rising powers from 1648 to the present. The data set identifies initiators of war (often multiple); their motives (security, material advantage, standing, revenge and domestic politics); the outcome (win, lose or draw); the nature of the rules, if any, governing warfare; the duration and intensity of the war; and the character of the peace settlement. Contrary to realist expectations, I found security responsible for only 19 of 94 wars. Material interests were an even weaker motive for war, being responsible for only 8 wars, and most of them in the eighteenth century. Standing, by contrast, was responsible for 62 wars as a primary or secondary motive. Revenge, also a manifestation of the spirit, is implicated in another 11. There can be little doubt that *thumos* is the principal cause of war across the centuries, and that it and its consequences, until now, have been almost totally ignored in the international relations literature.[91]

Concern for recognition, honor, and standing can sometimes be addressed without making serious trade-offs in other goals. President Eisenhower's gracious reception of Khrushchev on his visit to the USA, where he was treated as a head of state, although only general secretary, is a case in point. Ike invited him to the presidential retreat at Camp David, which had a demonstrably positive effect on the insecure Soviet leader's estimate of his and his country's worth. It made him more receptive to cooperation.[92] In May 1972, Soviet Premier Leonid Brezhnev and President Richard Nixon met in Moscow, where they signed the first important strategic arms-limitation agreement and discussed ways of preventing war-threatening crises. Preventing war was obviously an overriding goal of both superpowers, and Soviet leaders hailed détente as a significant achievement.[93] They also emphasized the coequal superpower status they had gained by virtue of these agreements. Especially important to Moscow was the second article of the Basic Principles Agreement that referred to the 'recognition of the security interests of the parties based on the principle of equality and the renunciation of the use or threat of force', and recognition 'that efforts to obtain unilateral advantages at the expense of others, directly or indirectly, are inconsistent with these objectives'.[94] For Politburo members, these agreements symbolized their long-standing goal of American acceptance of their country as a co-equal global power. Speaking for Brezhnev, Leonid Zamyatin, chairman of the International Information Department of the Central Committee, explained that as America's recognized equal, the Soviet Union now expected to participate fully in the resolution of major international conflicts.[95] The clear implication was that the Soviet Union would act more like a satisfied power once its status claims were recognized and honored.

These examples are nevertheless sobering because the Eisenhower-Khrushchev thaw and the Johnson-Brezhnev détente were regrettably short-lived. They aroused false expectations, and détente allowed, perhaps encouraged, conflicting interpretations, that not only contributed to their demise but also to a sense of mutual betrayal, anger, and heightened tensions. There can be no doubt, however, that recognizing adversaries as equals—or with equal rights—and building a degree of personal trust with their leaders, is critical to meaningful accommodation. Diplomacy is central to these efforts. Diplomats and other emissaries must pave the way for the kinds of encounters and agreements that build positive relationships, and leaders in turn must develop them as far as possible. Good personal relationships between Lord Salisbury and French ambassador Paul Cambon, Richard Nixon and Henry Kissinger and Mao Zedong and Zhou Enlai, and Gorbachev with British Prime Minister Margaret Thatcher and Reagan, were arguably essential to the Anglo-French, Sino-American accommodations and the end of the Cold War. Such relationships are not absolutely necessary, as the Egyptian-Israeli peace treaty and Sino-American accommodation indicate. At Camp David, President Jimmy Carter met separately with Begin and Sadat and functioned as a critical go-between, as they were unable to reach an agreement on their own.[96]

I have addressed each vertex of my triangle but real world conflicts live somewhere within its boundaries as they usually involve fear, *thumos*, and hostility, albeit in varying degrees. Their respective importance is rarely self-evident. Different readings of context and the history of the conflict in question lead to different assessments and perhaps difference strategic preferences. Most importantly, they lead to different assessments about whether conflict can be reduced or resolved. People can be deeply committed to their perspectives for motivated and cognitive reasons. The former primes them to see the world in a manner consonant with the political and psychological needs. The more their worldview, career, status or wealth derives from or is associated with a particular view of a conflict and its causes, the less open they are to information that suggests another perspective. The latter leads people to see what they expect to see, and the more developed their schema, the more resistant they are to discrepant information.

Scholars are just as likely as policymakers, their advisors, and the media to succumb to motivated and cognitive biases. This may help explain why hardly anybody in the USA or the Soviet Union thought the end of the Cold War possible, or that Gorbachev and Reagan could do away with theater nuclear weapons, that Gorbachev would allow Eastern European states to reject communist government and agree to the reunification or Germany. It is exceedingly difficult to separate our analysis of politics from our political beliefs and expectations. To break through motivational and cognitive barriers to meaningful change and accommodation may take leaders who are not strongly committed to particular views of the conflict or strongly motivated for other reasons to seek accommodation.

This book makes apparent that designing strategies of conflict management that combine components of deterrence, reassurance, and diplomacy is a necessary but difficult task. There are formidable obstacles to the success of these strategies, individually and collectively. No single strategy is likely to work across cases under different strategic, political, and psychological conditions. Nevertheless, sensitivity to the limiting conditions of each strategy, to their relative strengths and weaknesses, and to their interactive effects is the first step in managing and resolving conflicts, and certain in preventing them from escalating to dangerous levels.

NOTES

1. Mihail M. Narinskii, "The Soviet Union and the Berlin Crisis, 1948–1949," in Francesca Gori and Silvio Pons, *The Soviet Union in the Cold War, 1943–1953* (New York: St. Martin's, 1996), pp. 57–75; Victor Gorbarev, "Soviet Military Plans and Actions During the First Berlin Crisis," *Slavic Military Studies* 10, no. 3 (1997), pp. 1–23. Vladislav Zubok and Constantine Pleshakov, *Inside the Kremlin's Cold War* (Cambridge: Harvard University Press, 1997), pp. 134–137, 194–197.
2. Richard Ned Lebow and Janice Gross Stein, *We All Lost the Cold War* (Princeton: Princeton University Press, 1994), Chap. 6.
3. Ibid, Chap. 11.
4. Michael A. Barnhart, *Japan Prepares for Total War: The Search for Economic Security, 1919–1941* (Ithaca, N.Y.: Cornell University Press, 1987); Gerhard L. Weinberg, *A World at Arms: A Global History of World War II* (Cambridge: Cambridge University Press 1994), pp. 260, 323, and 329–330; Janice Gross Stein, "Calculation, Miscalculation and Deterrence: The View from Cairo," in Robert Jervis, Richard Ned Lebow, and Janice Gross Stein, *Psychology and Deterrence* (Baltimore: Johns Hopkins University Press, 1984), pp. 34–59.
5. Richard Ned Lebow, *A Cultural Theory of International Relations* (Cambridge: Cambridge University Press, 2008) and *Why Nations Fight: The Past and Future of War* (Cambridge: Cambridge University Press, 2010).
6. Richard Ned Lebow, *Between Peace and War: The Nature of International Crisis* (Baltimore: Johns Hopkins Press, 1981), Chaps. 4–5.
7. Jervis, Lebow, and Stein, *Psychology and Deterrence*, Chap. 4–5, 7.
8. Lebow, *Cultural Theory of International Relations*, Chaps. 7–9.
9. Lebow, *Why Nations Fight*, Chap. 4.
10. Richard Ned Lebow and Benjamin Valentino, "Lost in Transition: A Critique of Power Transition Theories," *International Relations*, 23, no. 3 (2009), pp. 389–410.

11. Lebow, *Why Nations Fight*, Chap. 4, for elaboration.
12. Barnhart, *Japan Prepares for Total War*, Weinberg, *A World at Arms*, pp. 260, 323, and 329–330.
13. Alexander L. George, and Richard Smoke, *Deterrence in American Foreign Policy: Theory and Practice* (New York: Columbia University Press, 1974). p. 5.
14. Melvin Gurtov and Byung-Moo Hwang, *China under Threat: The Politics of Strategy and Diplomacy* (Baltimore: Johns Hopkins University Press, 1980), pp. 63–98; Jian Chen, *Mao's China and the Cold War: Beijing and the Taiwan Strait Crisis of 1958* (Chapel Hill, NC: University of North Carolina Press, 2001), Chap. 7.
15. Glenn H. Snyder and Paul Diesing, *Conflict Among Nations: Bargaining, Decision Making, and System Structure in International Crisis* (Princeton: Princeton University Press, 1977), pp. 183–184; George and Smoke, *Deterrence in American Foreign Policy*, pp. 550–561.
16. Thomas Schelling, *Arms and Influence* (New Haven: Yale University Press, 1966), p. 55.
17. Lebow and Stein, *We All Lost the Cold War*, Chap. 2
18. Ted Hopf, *Deterrence Theory and American Foreign Policy in the Third World, 1965–1990* (Ann Arbor: University of Michigan Press, 1994). Also, Daryl G. Press, *Calculating Credibility: How Leaders Assess Military Threats* (Ithaca: Cornell University Press, 2007). Lebow and Stein, *We All Lost the Cold War*, Chaps. 2, 10–11.
19. Morton H. Halperin and Tang Tsou, "The 1958 Quemoy Crisis," in Morton H. Halperin, ed., *Sino-Soviet Relations and Arms Control* (Cambridge: M.I.T. Press, 1967), pp. 265–304. George and Smoke, *Deterrence in American Foreign Policy*, pp. 386, 578, for quote.
20. Fredrik Logevall, *The Origins of the Vietnam War* (London: Routledge, 2001), Chap. 4; Brian VanDeMark, *Into the Quagmire: Lyndon Johnson and the Escalation of the Vietnam War*, (New York: Oxford University Press, 1995).
21. Schelling, *Arms and Influence*, p. 118.
22. Robert Jervis, *Perception and Misperception in International Relations* (Princeton: Princeton University Press, 1976), pp. 58–113; Lebow, *Between Peace and War*, Chaps. 4–5.
23. Louis Kreisberg, *Constructive Conflicts: From Escalation to Resolution* (Lanham, MD.: Rowman & Littlefield, 2011), Chap. 8.
24. Robert Axelrod, *The Evolution of Cooperation* (New York: Basic Books, 1984) and "An Evolutionary Approach to Norms," *American Political Science Review* (1986), 80, pp. 1095–1111; Robert Axelrod and Robert Keohane, "Achieving Cooperation Under Anarchy," *World Politics* (1985) 38, pp. 226–254.

25. Lebow and Stein, *We All Lost the Cold War*, Chap. 5.
26. Robert E. Nisbett and Lee Ross, *Human Inference: Strategies and Shortcomings of Social Judgment* (Englewood Cliffs, N.J.: Prentice-Hall, 1980); Lee Ross, "The Intuitive Psychologist and His Shortcomings: Distortions in the Attribution Process," in L. Berkowitz, ed, *Advances in Experimental Social Psychology*, vol. 10 (New York: Academic Press, 1977), pp. 174–241.
27. Brown, *Gorbachev Factor*; Jacques Levesque, *The Enigma of 1989: The USSR and the Liberalization of Eastern Europe* (Berkeley and Los Angeles: University of California Press, 1997); Robert D. English, *Russia and the Idea of the West: Gorbachev, Intellectuals, and the End of the Cold War* (New York: Columbia University Press, 2000) and "Power, Ideas, and New Evidence on the Cold War's End: A Reply to Brooks and Wohlforth," *International Security* 26:4 (2002), pp. 93–111.
28. Matthew A. Evangelista, *Unarmed Forces: The Transnational Movement to End the Cold War* (Ithaca: Cornell University Press, 1999).
29. Thomas A. Schelling, *The Strategy of Conflict* (Cambridge: Harvard University Press 1960), pp. 131–137.
30. Robert Service, *The End of the Cold War 1985–1991* (London: Macmillan, 2016), pp. 143–148, 202, 329–338, 400–415.
31. Goh, *Constructing the U.S. Rapprochement with China*, pp. 153–183; Margaret Macmillan, *Nixon and Mao: The Week That Changed the World* (New York: Random House, 2006).
32. Richard Ned Lebow, "Miscalculation in the South Atlantic: British and Argentine Intelligence Failures in the Falkland Crisis," *Journal of Strategic Studies* 6 (March 1983), pp. 1–29.
33. Bradford Dismukes, and James M. McConnell, eds., *Soviet Naval Diplomacy* (New York: Pergamon Press, 1979); Alexander L. George, "US-Soviet Global Rivalry: Norms of Competition," *Journal of Peace Research* (1986), 23, no. 3, pp. 247–262.
34. Janice Gross Stein, "Extended Deterrence in the Middle East: American Strategy Reconsidered. *World Politics* (1987) 39, pp. 326–352.
35. George, "US-Soviet Global Rivalry."
36. Jens Steffek, "The Cosmopolitanism of David Mitrany: Equality, Devolution and Functional Democracy Beyond the State," *International Relations*, (2015) 29, no. 1, pp. 23–44.
37. Shibley Telhami, *Power and Leadership in International Bargaining: The Path to the Camp David Accords* (New York: Columbia University Press, 1992); Yaacov Bar-Simon-Tov, *Israel and the Peace Process 1977–1982: In Search of Legitimacy* (Albany: State University of New York Press, 1994).
38. Raymond L. Garthoff, *Détente and Confrontation: American-Soviet Relations from Nixon to Reagan* (Washington, DC: Brookings, 1994),

Chaps. 6–8; Evelyn Goh, *Constructing the US Rapprochement with China, 1961–1974: From Red Menace to Tacit Ally* (Cambridge: Cambridge University Press, 2005).

39. Henry Kissinger, *Diplomacy* (New York: Simon & Schuster, 1994); G. R. Berridge, *Diplomacy: Theory and Practice* (London: Palgrave-Macmillan, 2015); Jean-Robert Leguey-Feilleux, *Dynamics of Diplomacy* (Boulder: Co.: Lynne Rienner, 2009); Andrew Cooper, Jorge Heine, and Ramesh Thakur, eds., *The Oxford Handbook of Modern Diplomacy* (Oxford: Oxford University Press, 2003).

40. For the so-called diplomatic turn, see Paul Sharp, ed., *Diplomacy Theory of International Relations* (Cambridge: Cambridge University Press, 2009); Ole Jacob Sending, Vincent Pouliot, and Iver B. Neumann, eds., *Diplomacy and the Making of World Politics* (New York: Cambridge University Press, 2015).

41. William D. Davidson, and Joseph V. Montville, "Foreign Policy According to Freud," *Foreign Policy*, 45 (1981–1982), pp. 145–157; Louise Diamond and John McDonald, *Multi-Track Diplomacy: A Systems Approach to Peace* (West Hartford, Conn.: Kumarian Press, 2006); Joseph Montville, "Track Two Diplomacy: The Arrow and the Olive Branch," in Vamik D. Volkan, Joseph Montville, and Demetriou A. Julius, eds., *The Psychodynamics of International Relations*. vol. 2. *Unofficial Diplomacy at Work* (Lanham, Md.: Lexington Books, 2003), pp. 161–175; Hussein Agha, Shai Feldman, Ahmad Khalidi, and Zeev Schiff, *Track II Diplomacy: Lessons from the Middle East* (Cambridge: MIT Press, 2003).

42. Evangelista, *Unarmed Forces*, pp. 144–146.

43. Richard K. Herrmann and Richard Ned Lebow, eds., *Ending the Cold War*, co-edited with Richard K. Herrmann (New York: Palgrave-Macmillan, 2003), Chap. 9.

44. A particularly egregious example is Jack Matlock, *Autopsy on an Empire: The American Ambassador's Account of the Collapse of the Soviet Union* (New York: Random House, 1995).

45. Baruch Fischoff, "Hindsight is not Equal to Foresight: The Effect of Outcome Knowledge on Judgment under Uncertainty," *Journal of Experimental Psychology: Human Perception and Performance*, 1, no. 2 (1975), pp. 288–299; S. A. Hawkins and R. Hastie, "Hindsight: Biased Judgments of Past Events after the Outcomes are Known," Psychological Bulletin 107, no. 3 (1990), pp. 311–327.

46. William R. Thompson, ed., *Great Power Rivalries* (Columbia, S.C.: University of South Carolina Press, 1999); Jack Levy and William R. Thompson, *Causes of War* (New York: Blackwell, 2010); Sumit Ganguly and William R. Thompson, *Asian Rivalries: Conflict, Escalations, and limitations on Two-Level Games* (Stanford: Stanford University Press, 2011).

47. I. William Zartman and Maureen Berman, *The Practical Negotiator* (New Haven: Yale University Press, 1982); I William Zartman, "The Strategy of Preventive Diplomacy in Third World Conflicts," in Alexander L. George, ed., *Managing US-Soviet Rivalry* (Boulder, Co: Westview, 1983), Saadia Touval and I. William Zartman, eds., *International Mediation in Theory and Practice* (Westview, 1985); I. William Zartman, *Ripe for Resolution* (New York: Oxford, 1989) and "Ripeness," in Guy Burgess and Heidi Burgess, eds., *Beyond Intractability*, Conflict Information Consortium, University of Colorado, Boulder, June 2013, http://www.beyondintractability.org/essay/ripeness (accessed 9 November 2016).

48. Senator Gravel Edition, *The Pentagon Papers: The Defense Department History of United States Decisionmaking in Vietnam* 4 vols. (Boston: Beacon Press, 1971), vol. 3, pp. 687–691; Townsend Hoopes, *The Limits of Intervention: An Inside Account of How the Johnson Policy of Escalation Was Reversed* (New York: David McKay, 1969), p. 30.

49. Richard Ned Lebow, *Forbidden Fruit: Counterfactuals and International Relations* (Princeton: Princeton University Press, 2010), Chaps. 1, 3–4.

50. Ibid, Chap. 3 for documentation.

51. Richard Ned Lebow, "Contingency, Catalysts and International System Change," *Political Science Quarterly* 115 (2000–2001), pp. 591–616; William R. Thompson, "A Streetcar Named Sarajevo: Catalysts, Multiple Causation Chains, and Rivalry Structures," *International Studies Quarterly* (2003), 47, no. 3, pp. 453–474; Richard Ned Lebow, "A Data Set Named Desire: A Reply to William P. Thompson," *International Studies Quarterly*, 47 (2003), pp. 475–458.

52. On the latter accommodation, see George W. Breslauer and Richard Ned Lebow, "Leadership and the End of the Cold War," in Lebow, *Forbidden Fruit*, pp. 103–136.

53. On the Anglo-French accommodation, see Richard Ned Lebow, "The Search for Accommodation: Gorbachev in Comparative Perspective," in Lebow and Risse-Kappen, *International dilations Theory and the End of the Cold War*, 167–186.

54. Telhami, *Power and Leadership in International Bargaining*, Bar-Simon-Tov, *Israel and the Peace Process*.

55. George Breslauer and Richard Ned Lebow, "Leadership and the End of the Cold War: A Counterfactual Thought Experiment," in Richard K. Herrmann and Richard Ned Lebow, eds., *Ending the Cold War* (New York: Palgrave-Macmillan, 2003), pp. 161–188. Brown, *Gorbachev Factor*, Raymond L. Garthoff, *Great Transition: American Soviet Relations and the End of the Cold War* (Washington, D.C.: Brookings, 1994; Service, *End of the Cold War*, Hal Brands. *Making the Unipolar Moment: U.S. Foreign Policy and the Rise of the Post-Cold War Order*

(Ithaca: Cornell University Press, 2016) also stress the importance of agency and of leaders in particular.

56. For the most intelligent statement of structural argument and critique, see William C. Wohlforth, *Cold War Endgame: Analysis, Oral History, Debates* (University Park, PA.: Pennsylvania State University Press, 2002).

57. Martin Klimke, Reinhild Kreis, and Christian F. Osterman, eds., *Trust, but Verify: The Politics of Uncertainty and the Transformation of the Cold War Order, 1969–1991* (Sanford: Stanford University Press, 2016); Brown, *Gorbachev Factor*; Service, *End of the Cold War*, p. 250.

58. Service, *End of the Cold War*, pp. 150–161, 185–186, 245.

59. John Garver, *China's Decision for Rapprochement with the United States, 1968–1971* (Boulder, Co.: Westview, 1982), Chap. 2; Robert S. Ross, *China, the United States, and the Soviet Union: Tripolarity and Policy Making in the Cold War* (London: M. E. Sharpe, 1993), pp. 1–2; Goh, *Constructing the US Rapprochement with China*, pp. 2–4, 171–175, 222–225.

60. Gregory Henderson, Richard Ned Lebow, and John G. Stoessinger, eds., *Divided Nations in a Divided World* (New York: David A. Mackay, 1974), Chap. 11.

61. Feargal Cochrane, *Northern Ireland: The Reluctant Peace* (New Haven: Yale University Press, 2012), pp. 254–281.

62. Robert Ross, *Negotiating Cooperation: The United States and China, 1969–1989* (Stanford: Stanford University Press, 1995), pp. 1–2; Goh, *Constructing the US Rapprochement with China*, pp. 4–5. 133–136, 143–147, 153–181, 192–204.

63. Goh, *Constructing the US Rapprochement with China*, pp. 121–122.

64. Ibid, pp. 4–5, 101–123.

65. Breslauer and Lebow, "Leadership and the End of the Cold War"; Service, *End of the Cold War*, pp. 364–366 on Bush's caution.

66. Telhami, *Power and Leadership in International Bargaining*; Yaacov Bar-Simon-Tov, *Israel and the Peace Process*.

67. Leonard A. Kusnitz, *Public Opinion and Foreign Policy: America's China Policy, 1949–1979* (Westport, Conn.: Greenwood, 1984), p. 138.

68. Goh, *Constructing the US Rapprochement with China*, pp. 6, 206–218.

69. Kusnitz, *Public Opinion and Foreign Policy*, pp. 138–139.

70. Archie Brown, *The Gorbachev Factor* (Oxford: Oxford University Press, 1996); Raymond L. Garthoff, *The Great Transition: American Soviet Relations and the End of the Cold War* (Washington, DC: Brookings, 1994), Chaps. 6–8; Service, *End of the Cold War*, pp. 482–495.

71. Richard Ned Lebow and Janice Gross Stein, *We All Lost the Cold War* (Princeton: Princeton University Press, 1994), Chaps. 3–5; Raymond L. Garthoff, *Détente and Confrontation: American-Soviet Relations from*

Nixon to Reagan, rev. ed. (Washington, DC: Brookings, 1994), Chaps. 2–4.

72. Lebow and Stein, *We All Lost the Cold War*, pp. 55–58; William Taubman, *Khrushchev: The Man and His Era* (New York: Norton, 2003), pp. 442–479.

73. Garthoff, *Détente and Confrontation*, pp. 1125–1146.

74. Cochrane, *Northern Ireland*, pp. 31–66; Richard English, *Armed Struggle: The History of the IRA* (Oxford: Oxford University Press, 2003), pp. 148–227.

75. On Gorbachev vs. other possible leaders, Richard Ned Lebow and Janice Gross Stein, "The End of the Cold War as a Non-Linear Confluence," in Herrmann and Lebow *Ending the Cold War*, pp. 189–218.

76. Ofira Seliktar, *Doomed to Failure: The Politics and Intelligence of the Oslo Peace Process* (Boulder, Co.: Praeger, 2009); Robert Rothstein and Moshe Ma'oz, eds., *Israeli-Palestinian Peace Process: Oslo and the Lessons of Failure, Perspectives, Predicaments, Prospects* (Eastbourne: Sussex Academic Press, 2004).

77. "Russians name Brezhnev best twentieth century leader, Gorbachev worse," RT Question more, 22 May 2013, https://www.rt.com/politics/brezhnev-stalin-gorbachev-soviet-638/ Quora, "What do Russian people think of Gorbachev?," 7 November 2015, https://www.quora.com/What-do-Russian-people-think-of-Gorbachev (both accessed 15 November 2016).

78. Henderson, Lebow, and Stoessinger, *Divided Nations in a Divided World*.

79. Garthoff, *Détente and Confrontation*, pp. 526–565.

80. Richard Ned Lebow, *A Cultural Theory of International Relations* (Cambridge: Cambridge University Press, 2008).

81. Harold Lasswell, *World Politics and Personal Insecurity* (New York: McGraw-Hill, 1935); Richard Ned Lebow, *The Politics and Ethics of Identity: In Search of Ourselves* (Cambridge: Cambridge University Press, 2012), and *National Identifications and International Relations* (Cambridge: Cambridge University Press, 2012).

82. Richard Ned Lebow, *Cultural Theory of International Relations*, Chap. 7; Peter H. Gries, *China's New Nationalism: Pride, Politics and Diplomacy* (Berkeley: University of California Press, 2004), "Chinese Nationalism: Challenging the State?" *Current History*, September 2005, pp. 251–256, "Identity and Conflict in Sino-American Relations," in Alastair Ian Johnston and Robert S. Ross, eds., *New Directions in the Study of China's Foreign Policy* (Stanford: Stanford University Press, 2006), pp. 309–339.

83. On the causes of innocent exaggerated assessments, John H. Herz, "The Security Dilemma in International Relations: Background and Present Problems," *International Relations* (2003), pp. 411–416. On deliberate

exaggeration, Anne H. Cahn, *Killing Detente: The Right Attacks the CIA* (University Park, Pa.: Pennsylvania State University Press, 1998); Richard Ned Lebow, "Misconceptions in American Strategic Assessment," *Political Science Quarterly* 97 (Summer 1982), pp. 187–206.

84. Richard Ned Lebow, "Miscalculation in the South Atlantic: British and Argentine Intelligence Failures in the Falkland Crisis," *Journal of Strategic Studies* 6 (March 1983), 1–29.

85. Mark Lander and David E. Sanger, "In Affront to China, Trump Speaks with Taiwan Leader," *International New York Times*, 2 December 2016, http://www.nytimes.com/2016/12/02/us/politics/trump-speaks-with-taiwans-leader-a-possible-affront-to-china.html?hp&action=click&pgtype=Homepage&clickSource=story-heading&module=a-lede-package-region&region=top-news&WT.nav=top-news (accessed 3 December 2016).

86. Richard Ned Lebow, *Why Nations Fight: The Past and Future of War* (Cambridge: Cambridge University Press, 2010), Chap. 4.

87. Service, *End of the Cold War*, pp. 169–220.

88. Lebow and Stein, *We All Lost the Cold War*, Chap. 6.

89. Lebow, *Between War and Peace*, Chap. 4; Lebow and Stein, *We All Lost the Cold War*, Chap. 2.

90. Axel Honneth, *The Struggle for Recognition* (Cambridge: MIT Press, 1996); Axel Honneth, and Nancy Fraser *Recognition or Redistribution? A Political-Philosophical Exchange* (New York: Verso Press, 2003); Thomas Lindemann and Erik, Ringmar, eds., *The International Politics of Recognition* (Boulder, Co.: Paradigm, 2012).

91. Lebow, *Cultural Theory of International Relations*, is an exception.

92. Nikita S. Khrushchev, *Khrushchev Remembers: The Last Testament*, trans. Strobe Talbot (New York: Bantam, 1975), pp. 420, 438, 471; Lebow and Stein, *We All Lost the Cold War*, pp. 54–56

93. Georgi Arbatov, "Soviet-American Relations at a New Stage," *Pravda*, 22 July 1973. Quoted in Garthoff, *Détente and Confrontation*, p. 333.

94. *Department of State Bulletin*, 26 June 1972, pp. 898–899.

95. Quoted by Murrey Marder, "Brezhnev Extols A-Pact," *Washington Post*, 24 June 1973; TASS, Radio Moscow, 25 June 1973, in Foreign Broadcast Information Service, Daily Report: Soviet Union, 25 June 1973. Garthoff, *Détente and Confrontation*, pp. 344–345; Lebow and Stein, *We All Lost the Cold War*, pp. 153–155.

96. Telhami, *Power and Leadership in International Bargaining*; Yaacov Bar-Simon-Tov, *Israel and the Peace Process*.

INDEX

© The Editor(s) (if applicable) and The Author(s) 2018
R.N. Lebow, *Avoiding War, Making Peace*,
DOI 10.1007/978-3-319-56093-9

CPSIA information can be obtained
at www.ICGtesting.com
Printed in the USA
LVHW081601050219
606472LV00020B/1128/P

9 783319 560922